Banana
Bending

To my parents Ban Siang and Audrey Swee-kuan Khoo,
for their constant love and encouragement,
and for what they don't say as much as what they do.

Banana Bending

ASIAN-AUSTRALIAN AND ASIAN-CANADIAN LITERATURES

TSEEN-LING KHOO

McGill-Queen's University Press
Montreal & Kingston · Ithaca

ISBN 0-7735-2551-3

First published by Hong Kong University Press 2003.
This edition available exclusively in Canada and the USA.

McGill-Queen's University Press acknowledges the financial support of the Government of Canada through the Book Publishing Development Program (BPIDP) for its activities.

National Library of Canada Cataloguing in Publication

Khoo, Tseen-Ling, 1970-
    Banana bending : Asian-Australian and Asian-Canadian literatures / Tseen-Ling Khoo.

Includes bibliographical references and index.
ISBN 0-7735-2551-3

    1. Canadian literature (English) — Asian-Canadian authors — History and criticism. 2. Asian Canadians in literature. 3. Australian literature — Asian Australian authors — History and criticism. 4. Asian Australians in literature. I. Title.

PR9080.5.K48 2003   C810.9'895   C2002-905691-8

Printed in Hong Kong, China.

Contents

Acknowledgements

I drafted the bulk of this book at the University of Queensland English Department, and completed the manuscript while with the School of Languages and Comparative Cultural Studies at the same university. During these years, I have been lucky to have the company of enthusiastic and motivating colleagues from a range of institutions who have encouraged and ushered me through key stages of my career, including David Carter, Helen Gilbert, Sneja Gunew, Alan Lawson, Jacqueline Lo, Kam Louie, Wenche Ommundsen, and Joanne Tompkins.

For their trans-Pacific generosity, intellect, and humour, I would like to thank Guy Beauregard, Lily Cho, Hiromi Goto, Karlyn Koh, Larissa Lai, Ashok Mathur, Roy Miki, Dorothy Wang, and Rita Wong. Much appreciation to Austin Cooke for resources and weather updates.

To my fellow travellers in 'Asian-Australian studies', thank you for the faith, hope, and charity. I am especially grateful to Dean Chan, Olivia Khoo, Miriam Lo, Robyn Morris, and Peta Stephenson; and to Natasha Cho and Jen Tsen Kwok for their energising perspectives.

Many thanks to the Association for Canadian Studies in Australia and New Zealand (ACSANZ) who funded travel to Canada for parts of this book's research.

Different versions of some sections in this book have been published elsewhere: "Angry Yellow Men: Asian-Australian and Asian-Canadian Masculinities," *Chinese and Japanese Masculinities,* edited by Kam Louie and Morris Low, London: Routledge Curzon Press, 2003; "Re-siting Australian Identity: Configuring the Chinese Citizen in Diana Giese's *Astronauts, Lost Souls, and Dragons* and William Yang's *Sadness*," *Bastard Moon: Essays on Chinese-Australian Writing,* edited by Wenche Ommundsen, Kingsbury, VIC:

Otherland, 2001, 95–109; and "The Ocker Ethnic: Hung Le and Australian Cultural Identity," *Interactions: Asian and Pacific Literatures*, edited by Dennis Haskell and Ron Shapiro, Perth: CSAL and University of Western Australia Press, 2000, 55–62.

This book would not have been completed without my patient, devoted, and compassionate network of friends and family. Thank you for helping me complete the job, and for your wisdom in interesting times.

Introduction

*B*anana Bending is concerned with mapping, interrogating, and creating critical pathways for diasporic Asian literary studies. The book argues that in order to examine the disciplines and production of Asian-Canadian and Asian-Australian literatures, work needs to be considered within layers of nation, community, and the gendered self. Examining these layers enables a rigorous interrogation of the politics of racialisation in existing national spheres of culture and forges new modes of research and analysis for these literatures. To this end, the chapters chart a progression of these concerns by, first, explicating the national contexts for Asians and racialised writing in Australia and Canada and then shifting to examine specifically the significance of these layers for Asian-Australian and Asian-Canadian texts and their construction.

The title, 'Banana Bending', is a playful reference to the physical site from which I write[1] as well as a reformation of an epithet that, in the main, functions as disapproval or dismissal. The judgement implicit in deeming someone 'yellow on the outside, white on the inside' indicates a reductionist attitude to issues of culture, community, and race. Contrarily, I welcome the complex, overlapping, and sometimes contradictory narratives of identity the term 'banana' conjures. It encapsulates the specific concerns of communities in diaspora and operates as both defiance and recuperation. To this extent, I am using the term to mean hybridised Asian identities in the West, rather than specific reference to mixed-race origins, which is sometimes how the term is used. Examples of claiming and flaunting the 'banana' tag can be found in a range of popular cultural sites and critical deliberations about identity, from the Chinese-Canadian 'Banana Bloggers' who take advantage of Web diaries to express their opinions[2] to Chinese-

Australian filmmaker Tony Ayres's use of the term in *China Dolls*, a film about queer Asian-Australians. Given that this book interrogates and examines new strategies of reading, identification, and politicisation, it should be considered as bending 'banana' literature, that is, transforming current understandings of diasporic Asian literatures and their attendant critical apparatus.

The Australian and Canadian styles of multiculturalism are relatively similar (Australia based its agenda on Canada's policy), and the criticism of the policy has engaged with comparable issues such as the forms and practices of liberal racism. Critics such as Jon Stratton and Ien Ang consider this 'top-down', policy-driven style of multiculturalism as robbing the concept of revolutionary potential. They compare it to the unofficial multiculturalism that exists in the United States: "in the United States multiculturalism can only be conceived as *subverting* the national, while the Australian [and Canadian] national can be represented as *constituted by* multiculturalism" (151).³ Of course, national structures are rarely homogeneous, and Stratton and Ang's point about the policy draining energy from radical change perhaps neglects to acknowledge the material advantages in official multiculturalism. Simplistic versions of multiculturalism and its consequences often circulate in right-wing discourse, and it usually reveals "a binary approach to power relations, where any questioning of positionality or power is translated into rule by the other . . . so that power structures are not redefined, merely inverted" (Gunew, "Multicultural" 451). A knowingly complex and adaptable multiculturalism is a valuable socio-cultural environment for Asian-Australian and Asian-Canadian authors. In contrast to Stratton and Ang's argument, Chinese-Canadian author Paul Yee believes that "multiculturalism gives a useful message: it's just one tool to fight racism. . . . But it's important that this come from the top, as government policy" (Interview 345). Indeed, the presence of official support for such issues as equality and anti-discrimination sets the tone for the type of society envisaged by its citizens. Moreover, Gordon Clark, Dean Forbes, and Roderick Francis argue that "[m]ulticulturalism involves a claim for recognition which goes beyond merely accepting the existence of difference" (xii), and it is on this point of fully recognising Other groups, particularly racial minorities, that official multiculturalism often fails. This book is predicated on the recognition of value in communities and individuals exercising confident cultural and social citizenships.

Many of the continuing debates on multiculturalism revolve around terminology and categorisation. It has even been claimed in Australia recently that the term 'multiculturalism' has "outlived its purpose" (Johnstone 29). In most discussions in Australia and Canada, multiculturalism has become synonymous with equity programmes, promoting diversity, and supporting those from identified ethnic communities. While some critics attempt to 'ethnicise' everyone in society to make the deployment of community or class membership more obvious, the term 'ethnic' still defines "one's sense of both belonging to a group and being 'exclu[ded] from the national definition of a country'" (Gunew, *Framing Marginality* 49). Among the major debates in multicultural studies is the erosion and destabilisation of the connection between ethnicity and marginal identities. In addition, this field regularly interrogates cultural and racial assumptions through diversifying sectors including politics, the arts, and social justice.

When Asian artists actively engage with discourses of how they and their creative works are represented, they work towards countering stereotypes and creating alternative, nuanced Asian-Canadian and Asian-Australian subjectivities. This necessary step of acknowledging the conditions of production and distribution for their work, and in other creative spheres, enables these groups to move towards fully exercising cultural citizenship. When I argue for these Asian authors to 'frame themselves' and their work, I am proposing an active, interrogative, and confidently political structure for Asian-Canadian and Asian-Australian writers and their attendant critical studies. Russell Leong has stated that "[a]s we imagine our lives, we invent ourselves" ("Home Bodies" 12). My deployment of 'framing' does not signify the limits of the fields in question but, in fact, sanctions what Vijayandran Devadas calls "the discursive densities" of "lived realities" (71). *Banana Bending* also incorporates considerations of class in discussions of racialisation and community. Class differences affect the practices available for individuals to negotiate issues of identity. Andrew Jamrozik, Cathy Boland, and Robert Urquhart assert that "[t]rue multiculturalism . . . would have to be concerned not only with life-styles but also with life chances" (105). The effect of social mobility and privileged class access on literary production leads to differing forms of discrimination. As Gillian Bottomley observes, "[w]hen ethnicity co-exists with class disadvantage, 'then powerful inducements exist for the members of such groups to assimilate into the mainstream culture, since this will improve their chances for a better life'" (*From Another Place* 24). Many of the works studied in this book reveal what these inducements are and how ambivalent personal and political negotiations address these lived conflicts. Discrimination is directed at lower socio-economic classes as much as those who are considered upper- or upper-middle class, as is evident in the controversy about the 'monster houses' of the affluent business classes who emigrated from Hong Kong to British Columbia in the 1980s.[4]

In constructing a frame of political activism and knowledge of coalitional powers for Asian literary production in Australia and Canada, this book produces unique comparisons between Australian and Canadian racial minority writers and their communities. Canadian author Larissa Lai describes her empowerment through writing as "a means of communication and discussion" and "a tool by which I find myself able to assert a presence" ("Stories" 3). These interventions into existing fields of national literature can transform writing and publishing conditions for Asian writers. Lai, and others, contend that 'asserting a presence' is a necessary step in validating cultural citizenship. Roy Miki takes this point further and states that "[w]hat is important for culture to thrive is a renewed belief in the viability of agency, so that writers from a diversity of subject-positions can develop the conditions in which social justice can be achieved through a language free from the tyranny of hegemonies of all kinds" (*Broken Entries* 123). Given Miki's exhortation, then, the existence of developing fields in Asian-Canadian and Asian-Australian studies disputes, re-creates, and gains control of defining notions of 'national literatures' while questioning their cultural efficacy.

The differing socio-cultural environments of Australia and Canada enable comparisons of how national multicultural agendas can influence, compromise, promote, or hinder fields of literary and artistic endeavour by Asian-Australians and Asian-Canadians. To explore the changing socio-cultural discourses in contemporary multicultural countries, I concentrate mainly on literary texts as forms of creative and political expression. These include works of fiction, autobiography, and some performances. The increasing numbers of publications, new writers, and academic researchers indicate a significant momentum in marking out and creating Asian-Australian and Asian-Canadian spaces.[5] In answer to the question of whether sheer numbers of works or presence of authors can alter racial and cultural perceptions or inequalities, or whether words can 'change things', Leo Bersani argues: "literature may not *have* much power, but it should certainly be read as a display of power . . ." (in Frow, *Marxism* 234). Gaining literary/authorial recognition, altering critical categories, and building cultural community remain important and ongoing objectives. While this urge to step over boundaries is necessary to develop areas further, the lack of an area against which to relate is the problem besetting both Asian-Canadian and Asian-Australian literary studies. The body of criticism and publication, although expanding, is still relatively small, and this means that the fields are only now achieving significant impetus. Don Goellnicht's recent overview of Asian-Canadian literature's "protracted birth" (1) points to the lack of ethnic studies programmes in Canada as one of the key reasons why Asian-Canadian literature seems to be always in the 'announcement' phase.

This book also addresses the issues involved when dominant codes recognise and incorporate certain kinds of diasporic Asian literature, allowing that this literature "may be contained within the particular understandings that the dominant grants it" and that it may lose "its latitude as a counterdiscourse and its ability to designate a shifting open space outside the hegemonic" (Palumbo-Liu, "Introduction" 17). These literatures have additional currency as components within the growing area of diasporic Asian literary studies — as contested as this discipline is — and 'travel' across contexts and reading strategies. Asian-Australian and Asian-Canadian literary studies also provide valuable comparative perspectives to the more well-established field of Asian-American 'lit-crit'.

The use of the term 'Asian' is strategically necessary to counter the plethora of ignorant, negative, or stereotypical images with in-depth and considered study. These studies oppose the configuration of the 'Asian' or 'Asian' communities as monolithic or hermetic categories and acknowledge the usefulness of tactical group naming in contemporary societies in which "complicated entanglement of togetherness in difference" is "a 'normal' state of affairs" (Ang, *On Not Speaking Chinese* 17). I focus particularly on writers and artists of 'East Asian' descent to oppose and question the collapsed category of 'Asian' while being aware that 'East Asian' is also a grouping that could iterate similar generalisations. I deploy 'East Asian' to refer mostly to groups of Chinese and Japanese descent. Occasionally in this book, this definition extends to include Korean, Vietnamese, and mixed-race groups. In contemporary Western societies, the figure of the 'Asian' is still evoked in all its generality, with xenophobic assumptions either intact or deliberately resurrected. Specifically in Canada, Australia, and the United States, this term tends to conjure images of peoples of Chinese or Japanese descent. This is due partly to the Pacific Rim positioning of these countries, facing each other across the ocean and juggling economic concerns alongside those of race and culture. While the book overall is concerned with Asian-Australian and Asian-Canadian authors, the analysis of their work does not categorise them as, say, the texts of an 'Asian-Canadian' writer but positions them with more specific sites of culture, community, and history. For instance, in examining Joy Kogawa's work, I situate her within versions of Japanese-Canadian community and locate her work inside distinctive Canadian literary and cultural histories.

The companion term to 'East Asian' is 'South Asian', which refers to writers of Indian, Pakistani, or Sri Lankan descent. It is not in common use in Australia but becoming more widely used in Canada. The demarcation between South and East Asian texts and communities is useful, because each of these groups comes from contrasting political and cultural sites. Generally speaking, South Asian literature and history engages more directly with post-colonial discourses and the socio-political legacies of colonialism. Similarly, East Asian literatures are often produced from histories of legislated exclusion and racist historical flashpoints (e.g., internment, riots). For South and East Asian authors in Western nations, however, experiences of racialisation or alienation are common tropes. The potential for coalitions between these groups to expose and interrogate inequalities and various forms of exclusion in Canada and Australia is significant. The increasing numbers of anti-racist groups and the implementation of their initiatives on a community level confirm the efficacy of group mobilisation for political ends. For the feasibility of this publication, however, discussion focuses particularly on East Asian diasporic texts. English-language texts are also emphasised, because an intrinsic part of the study is the circuits of production, circulation, and consumption for Asian-Australian and Asian-Canadian literature within each of their national contexts. In what ways do they tally with, alter, or reject, national literary bodies?

Chapter 1 provides an overview of race relations, racialisation in the arts, and multicultural politics in Australia, critically examining contemporary political and social formations for Asian-Australians within understandings of nation. It argues that the small population[6] of Asian communities in Australia, in addition to the enduring 'whiteness' and resistance to confronting racism in Australia, result in an environment that is not conducive to the growth or institutionalisation of Asian-Australian studies. Considering Australia's deliberate international position and the growing 'borderlessness' of world trade and economics, Stephen Castles observes that it is in these conditions that recycled racisms emerge and "it is only because global influences make national culture so precarious that immigrant minorities appear as a serious danger" (40). Australia's historical perception of itself as isolated is "an imperialist conceit" (Lake 90), and the waxing interests in the Asia-Pacific trade zones exposes this narrow idea. Adding to the Hansonite paranoia about a 'new world order' are the significant changes in the numbers and sizes of Australia's ethnic groups. Some of these groups have developed so that the local concentrations of ethnic communities (often referred to in right-wing rhetoric as 'ghettoisation') have become exotic aberrations in the Australian suburbs. Diane Powell notes that Cabramatta in New South Wales was declared "a tourist area in 1991, but it is essentially a tourist stop for Australians, not for travellers from abroad" (135). Even challenged by these significant communities, there is little momentum through federal or state governments to work towards equity and anti-racism in areas of Australian social and cultural life. In this conservative political climate, there is even more of a need for other organisations to be more politically vocal and to expose discriminatory practices. Prime examples of incidents that have galvanised Australian communities are those surrounding the SS *Tampa* and its 'cargo' of asylum-seekers, as well as ensuing government rhetoric about refugees and border-controls during the 2001 federal election.[7] For Asian-Australian groups, the government's lukewarm approach to anti-racism makes the process of lobbying for changes in policy or negotiating the restrictions of literary funding all the more difficult, and all the more necessary.

Chapter 2 addresses the other national focus of this book, the formations of Canadian multiculturalism. The chapter contends that Canada's recognition of racial minority citizens through official edicts and ensuing anti-racist initiatives combat, to some extent, the legacy of racism represented by its history of anti-Asian legislation and violence. As a government policy, multiculturalism draws censure from both right- and left-affiliated critics and authors. Franco-Canadians read multiculturalism's implementation as an attempt to dilute their influence on Canadian policy and politics. Multiculturalism allowed limited recognition of indigenous peoples and immigrants, and, in many respects, relegated Franco-Canadians to the position of 'one of the minorities'. The tensions between French-speaking Canadians and English-speaking Canadians manifest themselves in secessionist politics. When groups try to carve new nations out of existing ones, the manoeuvre speaks volumes about the level of frustration for these communities that do not exist happily in multicultural Canada. Janice Kulyk Keefer explains why French-Canadians so strongly favour secession: "[t]he Quebecois . . . have always objected to multiculturalism as a manoeuvre to displace them from their roles as one of the 'founding races' of the country, and as such, entitled to recognition as a distinct society rather than as one ethno-cultural minority among many" ("For or Against" 14). The implementation of multiculturalism in Canada has decreased the profile of Franco-Canadians as one of the 'original' founders of Canada. This, however, only lends power to the Bloc Quebecois' successive claims of Franco-Canadian marginalisation and exclusion with regard to conducting national affairs.

Chapter 2 proceeds to substantiate the important consequences of the Japanese-Canadian Redress movement, confirming its social, cultural, and political ramifications a decade later. In addition, it investigates the growth of racial minority community politicisation, especially in the arts, and the nurturing of Asian-Canadian literature as a discipline through community initiatives. Lynette Hunter suggests that the fraught category of what is colloquially known as 'CanLit' has many hurdles in its path of self-definition, and that there are factors that further complicate the circumstances for multicultural literature in Canada:

> [i]t was still the case in 1993 that people could take degrees in Canadian Literature, but study it only as a specialism [sic] within British Literature. Any English-language Canadian canon will necessarily be contesting the firmly-defined, dominant British or United States' ideologies that provide the larger virtual public sphere for reading and writing (25).

While Hunter may overstate the novelty of Canadian studies,[8] her observation of Canadian literature's squeezing between the major influences of Britain and the United States is valid. This squeezing results in a more aggressive assertion of 'Canadian literature', a set of circumstances that can often result in further marginalisation of minority literatures.

Chapter 3 concentrates on renditions of nationhood and citizenship in a range of Asian-Australian and Asian-Canadian texts. The chapter asserts the importance of actively reclaiming citizenship and positioning Asian communities and bodies within foundational narratives and the histories of Australia and Canada. The constructed nature of nation and nationalism informs both the status quo nationalism against which Asian authors are writing and the methods for challenging these nationalisms to become more inclusive, elastic ones.

Used initially in colonial situations to refer to countries that were considered 'not-nations', Benedict Anderson states that the purpose of adopting a single national identity is to fit "the short, tight, skin of nation over the gigantic body of empire" (*Imagined Communities* 13–4). To apply this apt analogy to the contemporary situation of Western countries like Canada, Australia, and the United States entails only a slight reinterpretation of terms. "The gigantic body of the empire" is not scattered across the globe but consists instead of culturally diverse communities existing in 'one' social space. The tensions are concentrated, then, on the processes of mediating cultural difference and societal (dys)functioning. The 'skin of nation' must now fit a wider range of cultural groups than ever before in Canada and

Australia, and the emphasis lies in recreating meanings for 'nation' rather than tailoring groups to represent any cohesive sense of the 'national'.

Chapter 4 shifts away from the structures of nationhood discussed in Chapter 3 to concentrate on issues of community and ethnicity for Asian-Australian and Asian-Canadian authors. It contends that the future strength of Asian-Australian and Asian-Canadian studies and their politics depend on negotiating contingent coalitions with other groups and more broadly defining community. The chapter discusses the term 'ethnicity' and its modulations when it is deliberated alongside multiculturalism in Australia and Canada. Ien Ang's article "On Not Speaking Chinese" clarifies the coalitions among Chinese groups (like the Hakka, Hokkien, and Cantonese) who formed "the greater imagined community of a unified pan-Chinese nation" (7) against the combined hostility of indigenous Indonesians and their discriminatory laws. Presenting a united front to convey a political message proves useful in such instances, but the danger of being engulfed by larger groups always remains. For the less politically established ethnic populations in particular, coalitions can be especially difficult.

While the chapter resists notions of any singular community identity or ethnicity, it does argue that the formation of contingent coalitions between certain groups remains valuable action for raising group profiles and cohering during political activities. Applying Rey Chow's observation that "part of the goal of 'writing diaspora' is . . . to *unlearn* that submission to one's ethnicity" (*Writing* 25), this chapter reads ethnic community negotiations through the events surrounding anti-racist initiatives in Canada such as the controversy surrounding the *Writing Thru Race* conference (Vancouver 1994) and, subsequently, critical analyses of Hiromi Goto's *Chorus of Mushrooms* and Simone Lazaroo's *The World Waiting To Be Made*. Addressing the issue of forging ethnic identities, Gillian Bottomley states that "[t]he central question of [her] research has continued to be: 'how do people maintain a positive sense of themselves in circumstances in which they are systematically devalued?' Rephrased in Foucauldian terms, this question could read: how is it possible to resist subjection?" ("Identification" 41). Goto and Lazaroo achieve precisely this form of resistance in their novels, overwriting the surrounding society's discriminatory ascriptions with their own versions of who an Asian woman can be. Their novels insist that the point of multiculturalism proper in Canada or Australia is not to "soften people's hearts — but to debunk the myths of difference that inform those attitudes" (Kay Anderson, "Otherness" 78). The abilities of the texts to render complex and engaging vignettes of growing up in Nanton, Alberta and Perth, Western

Australia, also integrate Other writings about childhood into Canadian and Australian fiction.

Chapters 5 and 6 focus more closely on gender issues and interrogate 'Asian' gender and sexuality as markers of critical cultural shifts in the emerging 'disciplines' of Asian-Canadian and Asian-Australian studies. Each chapter investigates distinct formations of gender in both nations, interrogating the binary of male and female within the twin contexts of Australia and Canada. These issues include literary reconstructions of sexuality for Asian individuals, as well as reassembling categories and ascriptions of masculinity or femininity. Given the deliberate simplicity of (white male) national representations, provocations and challenges for them are many, but these icons have the power to endure. Chapter 5 makes a return to the interrogation of nationalistic discourses, such as war, and contends that the range of Asian masculinities that can represent types of the 'national' are broad and more constructively concentrated in process than in resolution. It examines texts by Brian Castro (*Pomeroy*), Terry Watada (*Daruma Days*), and Wayson Choy (*The Jade Peony*). As well, the discussion of Asian-Australian masculinities draws attention to the photographic works of Hou Leong, who imposes himself on white Australian male bodies in "An Australian", and the performative work of Hung Le (*Yellow Peril from Sin City*), a Vietnamese-Australian comedian. Locating Asian masculinities within national discourses works in two ways: It erodes the whiteness and the 'rightness' of existing national representations while developing specific and alternative ways of representing Asian men.

Chapter 6, similarly, examines Asian women's fiction and versions of family and femininity in Asian women's texts. It focuses specifically on the politics of assimilation and tropes of border-crossing in Hsu-Ming Teo's *Love and Vertigo* and Larissa Lai's *When Fox Is a Thousand*. Asian-Australian and Asian-Canadian women's literature is evolving to speak to more and different audiences, developing into a field beyond the clichéd marketed categories of confessionals or other voyeuristic narratives.

These chapters examine the power of these gendered representations and their persistence in contemporary Canadian and Australian societies. In particular, the latter part of the book narrows the critical focus to Asian gender and sexuality in the context of the national environments detailed earlier in the book. While there is an emphasis on the textual contexts within discourses of nation and Australian or Canadian culture, the use of Asian-American texts and theory is unavoidable in discussing diasporic Asian gender and sexuality, as Asian-Australian and Asian-Canadian studies are in their early stages. In discussions of diasporic Asian homosexuality in particular, material from American sources provide the theoretical bases from which to recontextualise and specify gay and lesbian representations not yet significantly profiled in Australia or Canada. In the process of complicating and diversifying representations and ways of reading these dialogues, gender representations diverge from recognised tropes of Asian masculinity and femininity. In their lack of certainty about sexual preferences, or their confused gender identifications and roles, contemporary evocations of Asian gender and sexuality present new generations of multi-layered, ambiguous, and unclarified characters. Strategic group or community identifications can result in strong political or social statements, but it is the fractured nature of individual configurations of sexuality and gender that can often propel constructive reformations of masculinity and femininity.

Banana Bending concludes with a discussion of possible directions for both Asian–Canadian and Asian–Australian literary criticism. This document maps the situation as it can be assessed in the early part of the new millennium, but with the fields growing and diversifying so quickly, it indicates only the start of what are becoming dynamic areas of study. The beginnings of the activist impetus bode well for more direct challenges to, and revisions and recreations of, existing structures and canons. One of the most important differences between Australia and Canada with regard to their racial minority artists and the stimulus for further publications or initiatives is the availability of community support. This community support does not necessarily have to be culturally based but, ideally, it allows avenues for informed feedback, learning the restrictions and language of funding applications and for presenting works-in-progress. The success of several Asian–Canadian authors is due in no small part to their participation in the writers' circuits and community events (for example, Wayson Choy, Hiromi Goto, Larissa Lai, Shani Mootoo, and Terry Watada at various Asian Heritage and Writers' Festivals). Lillian Allen lists the combination of factors that can reverse racist practices and exclusionary literary canons as "meaningful change and critical mass" (in Monika Gagnon, "Building" 117). Although the situations in Australia and Canada appear positive for the growth of diasporic Asian criticism and writing, both of the aspects that Allen mentions are crucial if momentum is to continue in the future. The fields will not progress significantly to challenge existing conditions of literary production and consumption if the Asian communities that produce the texts are not participating in politicising themselves, their communities, and, ultimately, transforming their own constitution in configurations of Australian or Canadian culture and nationhood.

1

"A Chink in the Armour": Asian–Australian Space

Australia is not a transit lounge.

(Humphrey McQueen in Kalantzis 217)

Other cultures and languages reinforce and enrich us by powerfully affecting and destabilising our familial tongue. We gain by losing ourselves.

(Brian Castro, *Writing Asia* 9)

The 'visibility' of Asian–Australian communities has increased in the past two decades, with extended emphasis on Australia's potential trading relationships with Asia and controversies associated with various right-wing factions in the political environment. In 1996, an article in the *Australian Magazine* by former One Nation adviser John Pasquarelli details the 'chinks' in One Nation leader Pauline Hanson's armour. His catalogue of her weaknesses includes lack of knowledge about her supporters and neglecting the influence of ethnic voters. These could easily correspond to many of Australia's weaknesses as a nation, this analogy particularly ironic after twenty years of having a multicultural agenda. Australia is no longer a convincingly 'white' nation and is even marketing itself in some forums as an Asia-Pacific nation. Pasquarelli predicted the ways in which Hanson's party would fail at the 1997 federal election, but the 'chinks' in Australia's armour could be taken quite literally as the presence of its racial minority citizens. An unanswered question is whether Australia as a nation has the ability to include these citizens as a part of the multicultural present, in all its cultural and political structures. Australia's history of anti-Asian legislation, coupled with legacies of Aboriginal displacement and exploitation, continue to influence contemporary cultural politics. At the turn of the century, a persistent and highly volatile issue is the detention of asylum-seekers and the extreme measures implemented by the incumbent government (e.g., excising certain areas of Australia as illegitimate refugee landing zones).

This chapter argues that Asian-Australian studies is only now gaining momentum because Asian-Australian communities have been slow to politicise and this, combined with the resistance of Australian government and society against combating racism with active measures, results in a drawn-out and difficult process for those agitating for policy and other cultural changes.

The poor level of acknowledgement about, and dissemination of, race issues indicates a determination by government authorities and other institutions (such as schools) not to address them directly. The beginning of constructive, and possibly restorative, dialogue about past injustices between communities and national bodies is only initiated when there is official recognition of these acts.[1] Thus far, successive Australian governments appear unwilling to step beyond merely admitting inequity to offering reparation or amendments of any kind.

Australia's policy of Asian exclusion has been evident since the gold-rush period of the 1850s. When competition for claims became violent, the Australian government introduced restrictions on Chinese miners, including not being able to work a stake until they owned it, and owning a stake only after holding it for five years. This effectively meant that they could not work legally on the goldfields, and the legislation funnelled existing Chinese miners into jobs like market gardening, shopkeeping, or furniture construction to survive. After initially welcoming the extra labour of Chinese coolies in colonial Australia, authorities soon passed legislation to curtail the numbers and activities of these 'coloured' workers. Gradually, taxes and working conditions made passage to and living in Australia almost completely unfeasible for certain classes of Chinese. Morag Loh and Judith Winternitz interpret the raising of Australian immigration barriers as a response to the influx of early 'sojourners' who were perceived, in some ways, as part of "an unarmed invasion" (19). Australian historian Humphrey McQueen's epigraph at the beginning of this chapter draws attention to the fears of insecure cultural boundaries in Australia by implying that there are degrees of (dis)loyalty in certain citizens who treat Australia as a place on the way to somewhere else and not as a homeland. Given existing racist discourses of patriotism and embedded Western European and British mores, suspicions of disloyalty rest more heavily on racial minority citizens who are considered physically and culturally alien.[2]

While conceding that Australia and Asia are indeed important to each other economically, Australian philosopher John Passmore also notes in 1992 that, culturally, the divide is too pronounced. He emphasises in particular that "[t]he 'breasts that gave [Australia] sustenance' were and continue to be largely European" (in Hudson and Stokes 149). William Hall (Chairman of the Returned Services League), in an earlier rendition of Passmore's comment, spells out the troublesome presence of non-white, non-Anglo-Saxon or Anglo-Celtic citizens even more bluntly:

[t]here may be doubts about the loyalties of migrants from other countries . . . but it seems to me an insult to cast doubt on the loyalty of British people. They're our brothers and sisters — whereas European immigrants are like fourth cousins twice removed by marriage (in Jordens 161).

With perspectives like those of Hall and Passmore in mind, we might ask: What social and political spaces do Australians of Asian descent occupy, then, given the cultivated singularity of Anglo-Celtic (white) 'Australianness'? Asian-Australians remain somewhat problematically within the category of 'settler' in Australia, but they are also a group that is consistently 'Othered' by white Australian society. The increase in Asian-Australian populations from the 1970s onward disrupts and contradicts, to some degree, perceptions of the dominant Australian character. For the past two decades, many of the countries from which Australia's immigrants have come are non-Anglo-Celtic and non-European, consisting of families and individuals from places such as China, Malaysia, Hong Kong, and Taiwan. Significant for discriminating about who can be Australian is that, if citizenship is an indication of a commitment to the nation, Mike Steketee puts forward: "fewer than 50% of people from English-speaking countries, such as Britain, New Zealand, and the United States, become citizens, compared to 71% of other migrants" (4). Steketee implies that Asians and other non-English-speaking migrants are notably 'better' citizens than those who come from nations supposedly 'closer' culturally. Notable, also, during the same period, is the growing focus on Aboriginal issues and land rights rulings that continue to erode the persistent representation of Australia as an unproblematically 'white' nation.[3]

Most contemporary publications in the Asian-Australian field disseminate previously unacknowledged information about community establishment and history in Australia, detailing pertinent government policies, discussing layers of discrimination and the politics of representation. Aside from the taxes and property laws of the early 1900s, various methods were installed to curb immigration by non-white people, including the infamous language tests. These language tests were created specifically to be biased towards English-speaking and Anglo-European-educated immigrants and, therefore, against most non-white groups. What is commonly known as the 'White Australia' Policy was put in place officially in 1901 and applauded in 1919 by then Prime Minister William Morris Hughes as "the greatest thing we have achieved" (Department of Immigration and Multicultural Affairs 2). Ensuing governments gradually dismantled the policies over the next few decades, and the final vestiges were removed in 1972 by the Whitlam Labor government. Since then, the implementation of multiculturalism as a government agenda (modelled on Canada's multicultural policy) attracts regular research that attempts to assess its effectiveness or weakness. The body of multicultural criticism often fails to pay focused attention to issues of racialisation in Australia for Asian citizens. Although the volume of work about the tensions between black and white Australia, specifically addressing Aboriginal/settler-invader issues, is significant, there are few studies about other Others. Suvendrini Perera, Ien Ang, Jacqueline Lo, Ghassan Hage, and Joseph Pugliese are among those who investigate specific representations and racialisations for Australians of Asian descent.[4] More importantly, these researchers include studies of how globalisation and multiculturalism affect race politics in Australia and address particular Aboriginal, South-, and East-Asian issues. Alison Broinowski's *The Yellow Lady* focuses on Australian perceptions of 'Asianness' in a broad way, including newspaper and magazine representations, as well as those in art. For the study of racialisation in literary studies for Asian-Australians, only a small body of critical work exists thus far.

Many historical and social questions regarding Asian-Australians have not been adequately addressed, and one example worth detailing here is the internment of Japanese-Australians during the Second World War. The process of wartime internment required the incarceration of people who were perceived as threats to national security. Indeed, the resonance between the internees' situations and that of the current asylum-seeker detainees is manifest. Most often, internment meant groups of 'high-risk' communities were sequestered inland (away from potential escape or major cities). Conditions were spartan, and prisoners were used in various labouring projects. This matter of internment deserves some focus, as the whole process of creating internal boundaries between 'proper' and 'improper' citizens cogently demonstrates a nation's xenophobia and its policy of racially based removal when it came to the Japanese residents of Australia in the 1930s and 1940s. There was some consensus about this form of exclusion: This process occurred also in the United States and Canada. The major difference is that the situation for Japanese North Americans has reached closure, to some extent, through redress from the respective governments. In Australia, this part of history and its consequences are yet to be fully discussed and understood. While Australians of Italian and German descent were also interned by the Australian government during both World Wars, the process of Japanese-Australian removal was comprehensive and involved almost complete dislocation of the communities.

Yuriko Nagata's *Unwanted Aliens: Japanese Internment in Australia* (1996) is the only monograph thus far to address this topic specifically.[5] This historical study examines the Japanese communities in Australia, detailing their instrumental role in Australia's pearling industry and their subsequent imprisonment during the Second World War as 'enemy aliens'. Other books have focused on prisoners-of-war within Australia during the World Wars,[6] but Nagata's work is critically informed by the racial dynamics in the process of Japanese-Australian internment. *Unwanted Aliens* shows clearly that Australian authorities during the Second World War singled out Japanese residents of Australia purely on the basis of race. While 31% of Australians of Italian descent and 32% of German descent were interned after evaluations of their potential for sabotage were carried out, 97% of "registered aliens of Japanese descent were imprisoned" (60). These high figures of internment for Japanese-Australians could be explained by the proximity of Japan to Australia and the overt threat this was thought to carry. However, the internees included older residents, many of whom were over sixty-five (50). Women were not usually included in the internment process, as they were not considered "so involved in organizing activities inimical to the Empire as men of enemy nations" (50). Authorities applied this gender discretion to most female residents of Italian and German descent but summarily interned most Japanese women. Obviously, the issue of race mobilised bureaucratic and popular reaction against Japanese-Australians en masse. With regard to the size of these communities in Australia, the family reunion policies of the Australian government differed from those of Canada or the United States and contributed to the smaller populations of Japanese in Australia (271). The government decided to deport many of the internees at the close of the war, and the Japanese-Australian communities, scattered and small as they were, almost ceased to exist.

It was only in the late 1990s that groups of Japanese-Australians gathered to discuss their placement in Australian social spaces. These discussions, however, have not yet addressed the history of internship, forced repatriation, or the displacement of their communities.[7] For example, the one-day seminar "A Chrysanthemum By Any Other Name: Ethnicity and Identity of Japanese in Queensland" (organised by Nagata, who is based at The University of Queensland) was held in July 1998. The panels discussed diverse topics such as "Ethnic heritage and citizenship", "Ageing in another culture", and "Living in a second language." All of the speakers described experiences of discriminatory attitudes in their daily lives, some choosing to discount others' behaviour and focus on their own 'fault' for not knowing the language and not trying hard enough to fit in. From this compromised sense of belonging in Australia, an activist movement from which to confront issues of civil injustice seems unlikely. The number of Japanese-Australians is far smaller than in the United States or Canada, and the lack of information about these communities or their experiences (wartime or otherwise) reflects this.

Australian and Canadian resources diverge significantly in the number and breadth of these 'intranational' prisoner-of-war perspectives. The prime reason for this is the stimulus of a higher population in Canada compared to the significantly smaller groups in Australia. Canada has had a high-profile Japanese-Canadian Redress movement that was fed by the activist and enthusiastic momentum of the Japanese-American cause. Japanese-Canadians similarly sought, and were awarded, compensation for wartime discrimination in the form of confiscation of their homes and businesses and in the denial of freedom for these Canadian citizens.[8] The politics and implications of incarcerating residents for the interests of 'national safety' have yet to be sufficiently addressed in the Australian context, reflected though these concerns may be in the body of work that exists for Asian-American and Asian-Canadian situations. The wartime conditions exacerbated the desire for a homogeneous population with which hegemonic society could feel secure. The visual difference of race represented by Asian residents of Western nations ruptures this comfort zone. When there is competition for resources in Australia (usually economic) or when clashes outside Australia involving people marked by racial difference cause protests here (bringing violence 'back home'), exclusionary processes re-emerge to combat the perceived threat to White Australia.

Multicultural priorities have differed in effect and presentation but have stayed in political and cultural arenas as contentious issues with arguable consequences on the formation of 1990s Australian identities. Far from being inadequately defined, the strategy of Australian multiculturalism has been circumscribed studiously by scholars from many disciplines. Multicultural researcher James Jupp provides a re-vision of what the multicultural policy has *not* meant for Australia:

> [i]t has never been officially argued that all cultures introduced to Australia are equally valid in all respects. It has never been suggested that any language other than English should be officially adopted. What multiculturalism has been about is equality of treatment, acceptance, integration and the avoidance of structured disadvantage (12).

The disjunction between compulsory English in Australia and the "avoidance of structured disadvantage" that Jupp mentions is not clarified or further investigated. Especially since the Howard government's introduction of a two-year waiting period for new migrants' social security benefits and the increasing difficulty of undertaking subsidised language classes, this sought-after equality seems to recede even further.[9]

The move away from institutionalised multiculturalism in the 1990s brings the government little criticism from the nation, arguably because many people think that Australia is 'already multicultural' and, ostensibly, a strategic policy success. In certain ways, this is true. Australia has a complex and often effective set of anti-discrimination laws in place, as well as equal opportunity mechanisms. Donald Horne's comments in the Introduction to *Redefining Australians* (1995) clearly show a progression in the argument about who he feels an Australian is:

> To that end, we don't want an arbitrary *national* identity or *cultural* identity, even less, an artificially enforced *ethnic* identity. We need a *civic* identity, a sense of an Australian 'civic contract'. A statement of the basic rules, if you like, for the benefit of newcomers, and a basic affirmation for all of us (ix).

Horne's formulation, though, still seems to operate at a somewhat elementary level and does not supply details about who should dictate what that civic contract might be. More specifically though, while Australia's social changes are not merely superficial, "in effect, the manifest policy on multiculturalism means an acceptance of a culturally diverse society but one governed, administered and socialised by monocultural institutions" (Jamrozik, Boland, and Urquhart 92–3). In these circumstances, attempts to gain recognition of civic injustice against, say, Japanese-Australians, would be particularly fraught. This management and containment of diversity by a dominant group is the goal of most 'multicultural' nations in contemporary societies, a strategy that is seen as more realistic, and politically stable, than the previous one of assimilation. John Frow and Meaghan Morris, however, do not separate the two policies in Australia. Instead, they suggest that they are wholly implicated with each other:

> [the policy of multiculturalism] tends to reproduce imaginary identities at the level of the ethnic 'community' and thereby to screen differentiations and contradictions within the community [like class and gender]; it depends upon covering over an asymmetry between migrant and indigenous groups; and it depends, above all, on a final moment of absorption of difference back into unity at the level of language and national identity (ix).

This kind of pluralism has become a benchmark for 'enlightened' Western countries, and the successful acceptance and tolerance of diverse populations acts as a marker of national moral values. Castles points out, though, that pluralism functions quite unproblematically in a society that thinks of itself as inherently superior to those by whom it has been 'pluralised': "[t]he very idea of tolerance for minority cultures implies a belief in the superiority of the dominant one: immigrants and ethnic minorities can keep their own values and cultures, but they cannot complain if this leads to their marginalisation" (29). Precisely because of the problem Castles outlines, there is a general inability to conceive of non-white, non-Aboriginal groups in Australia as 'Australian'. Warning against overly optimistic views of postmodern cultural fractures, Geoffrey Brennan describes how social value is ascribed to the concept of multiculturalism. The implication of having a visible ethnicity and a visible, performable culture is that people come to "derive value from being culture-bearers rather than in their own right. Their ethical significance derives from being members of a multicultural society, a society . . . that needs representatives of the various cultures to secure that [sense of] betterness" (171–2). Brennan's argument implicitly critiques discourses of Australia's enrichment by immigrants and their cultures, a process of rejuvenation which does little to acknowledge or define forms of 'Anglo-Celtic' culture yet reifies all that differs from it. The epigraph from Brian Castro, which opened this chapter, argues that 'enriching' each other is what cultures are meant to do — with a very firm emphasis on the two-way nature of this relationship. He does not consider 'enrich' as merely a form of supplementation or absorption by a host society but as a process that promotes mutual exposure to cultural parts and pasts. In Castro's argument, the experience is not meant to be one of cosy and saccharine sharing but of challenge and confrontation for one's own values.

This process of enrichment for 'Australian values', however, often persists in ascribing value only to certain renditions of Otherness. In her analysis of a promotional multicultural poster with a picture of a smiling Asian woman as the main focus, Ien Ang asserts that the woman is a symbol of "particular national desires" ("Curse" 46). Aside from the more obvious material advancement that Australia hopes to gain from Asia, this smiling woman signals the additional craving for controlled examples of Australia's sophistication and cosmopolitanism, as a model of the highly developed postmodern nation. Cosmopolitanism through visible cultural pluralism fulfils the desire for Australia's entry into a "coveted cultural province" (Kay Anderson, "Otherness" 81) and, for both Canada and Australia after the Second World War, "[m]ulticulturalism signalled the possibility of a break with the culture of fear, borders and conformity that had been central to the post–war experience. The . . . middle–classes embraced multiculturalism because it was a culture of cosmopolitanism" (McDonald 19). Equal levels of cultural citizenship for members of racial minority groups are not readily achievable in countries that have majority populations of Anglo–Celtic and European descent. The use of an Asian woman to signify one 'extreme' of multicultural tolerance speaks volumes about who is considered the acceptable Other in Australian society. It implies that the woman is, symbolically, the beneficiary of Australia's multicultural policies, invoking the cliché of multiculturalism as existing for those who are not part of existing hegemonic processes.

Hunger for that cosmopolitan 'face' means that Australian civic acceptance is often conditional upon repeated and acceptable versions of that difference. In a contradictory way, the multiculturalism found in Australia can only continue to be 'useful' if cultural or national groups persevere in their difference. Once they are just like any other 'Australian', they are no longer suitable subjects upon whom hegemonic society can confer 'tolerance'. Ghassan Hage's influential article, "Locating Multiculturalism's Other", examines the processes of tolerance in Australian multicultural rhetoric and offers a scathing critique of liberal condescension. However, the positioning of racial minority citizens remains ambiguous within the rhetoric of multiculturalism, as the definitions of diversity and pluralism have not often extended to include specific considerations of racial difference. Ang argues that "Australia's desire to be seen as a tolerant, multicultural nation" is a tactic "to vindicate a redemptive national narrative" ("Curse" 37), considering its historic involvement in the excluding and vilifying of those of Aboriginal and Asian descent. It is precisely in this neglected area of criticism that this chapter (and the book as a whole) is situated.

Multiculturalism's existence has always posed a basic challenge to the way Australia configures nation and national identity. Its pluralist basis contravenes the ideal of the 'imagined community' at the core of nation-building and patriotism. For Australia in the early 2000s, the conduct of racial politics and examinations of racialisation have become primary markers in arguments about 'multicultural' matters. As a post-colonial settler/invader nation, Australia is continually grappling with issues of representational origins and ownership, the struggle focusing on the mythic figures of Native and Settler. The justification of, or criteria for, who belongs as Australian is broad and contradictory.[10] Alan Lawson contends that "[t]he need, then, is to displace the other rather than replace him; but the other must remain to signify the boundary of the self, to confirm the subjectivity of the invader-settler" ("Postcolonial Theory" 28). As the displaced other, Aboriginal Australians are kept at the boundaries of the white Australian self, allotted a restricted and utilitarian space in constructions of the national. Meanwhile, the potential 'integration' of non-white citizens into positions of power or influence is encouraged in small degrees and then defused by the managing strategy of multiculturalism.

Even with so much work devoted to the government agenda and its socio-political ramifications, some critics in Australian studies persist in using the terms 'multicultural' or 'multiculturalism' with obtuseness. They continue to set up trite racial binaries as the full parameters of the analysis carried out in this area, taking liberal shots at the "multicultural orthodoxy" (Docker, "Post Nationalism" 41) and its complicity in oppressing Aboriginal Australians, while disavowing the hegemonic power of 'white' Australia. While highlighting the insidiousness of community self-policing and the restrictiveness of insisting on a singular ethnic community voice, John Docker uses terms such as 'multicultural orthodoxy' and 'the multicultural discourse' without explication ("Post Nationalism"). Docker claims:

> … post-war migrants in Australia are migrants, empowered as part of a society that continues to be historically advantaged by the brutal dispossession of Aboriginal peoples and countries. Such a claim [to marginalisation] by the multicultural discourse can only hinder recognition of Aboriginal claims to sovereignty, to their difference rights and history as the indigenous people (41).

While not disputing the acquired privilege of living in an Australia without reconciliation or significant recognition of Aboriginal dispossession, I do take issue with Docker's lack of attention to issues of racialisation within the 'multicultural discourse' he is so keen to debunk. Acknowledging the work that still needs to be done in Australia for indigenous issues does not mean voiding 'multicultural' concerns about racism, inequity, and cultural marginalisation. Marian Boreland argues that Docker has "constructed the Aboriginal as the 'real' and sole victim here, and that the non-Anglo non-Aboriginal 'other' lacks authenticity as a victim" (180). This vying for "most favored victim status" (Barry Goldberg 207) is a consequence of a system in which ethnic and Aboriginal Australians are cast as directly in opposition for limited funding dollars, the 'divide and conquer' stream of governance. At the centre of this 'competition' is the double-edged nature of special consideration and encouragement through government grants, a situation faced by all artists in Australia but made more problematic for Aboriginal and (classified) ethnic artists because of the restrictive categorisation systems. The issue of 'excellence', which is a crucial part of grant criteria, is more fully investigated by Mary Kalantzis and Bill Cope. They come to the conclusion that "excellence is not just a matter of form, but a matter of cultural content — of social relevance, of being at the cutting edge, of asking the aesthetic questions of our time in new and invigorating ways" (32).[11] Whether the criteria upon which grant applications are assessed will change remains to be seen as the present government is moving away from officially endorsing a multicultural agenda (and, one assumes, its attendant 'benefits') to declaring rhetorically that Australia *is* multicultural and that the special focus on 'multiculturalism' has reached an end-point.

Whether contemporary multiculturalism means assimilation or 'ghettoisation' is a recurring debate that has moved, once again, into the popular and political spotlight with recent concerns over global capitalism, refugee intakes and border controls, and locating Australia in Asia. The number of current studies about whether Australia is (or should be) in Asia ignores something that is true at economic levels, and steadily becoming so for cultural ones as well: "[t]his is not a question of debate anymore: this is an inescapable reality. . . . The question is not *whether* but *how*" (Sheridan 13, emphasis added). Tensions in forming closer ties between Australia and Asian nations stem from a distinct and irrevocable shift in outlook for Australia: from casting its lot with a European-American base to one that is 'Other' (and historically, indeed hysterically, feared). Academics, journalists, and other critics alike, have engaged enthusiastically with the 'Asian question', arguing at length about the future of Australia should these changes occur. The urgency of assessing and establishing Australia's position in Asia is brought on by trade considerations and the realisation that, in Sheridan's words, it is no longer a question of deciding 'if' but working out 'how'. Since the economic downturn in many Asian countries, particularly in Southeast Asia since the late 1990s, the contingency of this acceptance has been made clear. Happily doing business with Asian nations is conflated with tolerating Asian individuals within Australia. The increasing Asian 'recession' coincided with the rise of the One Nation Party, and it is not by chance that 'Asians' once again became Australia's scapegoats, domestically and internationally.

This process of negotiating Australia in/and 'Asia' has been accelerated and imploded by recent public debates about racism and the future of national interest, many triggered by the rise of Hansonism. In the time since Hanson's maiden parliamentary speech in 1996, the 'race debate' in Australia became the focal point for national, and gradually international, commentary. Hansonism is a set of traditional discriminatory politics that works under the guise of wanting 'equality' for all Australians:

> Hanson's potency rests not only on racism but on a powerful sense of cultural loss — of displacement for [sic] the centre of things — which has been worked readily into a mythology of victimisation. Her Anglo constituency has not been excluded, but it has lost its exclusive claim on this society and its resources (Cochrane 11).

Her insistence on the divisive nature of multiculturalism and its emphasis on maintaining rather than breaking down barriers, and fostering rather than ending racism, ignores pre-multicultural Australia's record of xenophobia. As well, Hanson and her supporters want to 'end' multiculturalism. The faulty logic of trying, in effect, to turn back time indicates clearly the looking-backwardness of Hansonites as they yearn for a mythical monocultural society. Ellie Vasta argues that "[t]he position implies that the central problem is ethnic/racial categorisation, rather than the actual existence of racist practices. Refusing to name ethnic categories will not make them disappear, if they are constantly being reconstructed by exclusionary practices" (68). Although the One Nation Party participates in this discourse of blame, it does not refuse to name categories per se. Indeed, their speeches scapegoat Asians (among others) constantly in campaigns. This is done in the most contradictory and homogenising of ways when Hanson targets Asians as the ones lengthening the welfare queues and (paradoxically) buying up

Australian land and businesses. In the conservative government climate since 1996, Prime Minister John Howard has not equivocally confronted this racism, an action that enables what Leigh Dale calls "a euphemisation of racism that began with the demonisation of the so-called politically correct" (13). Further, Paul Newman contends that "Howard's refusal to undertake any meaningful engagement with Hanson's ideas, and preparedness to attribute the popularity of Hansonism to the silencing or neglect which white Australians have suffered, has significantly underwritten the legitimacy of her political status" (8). This stance indicated Howard's desire to ally himself with 'Hansonites' as a group, without necessarily having Hanson as a colleague. It emphasises the sympathy with which the Coalition government viewed some of One Nation's policies, especially with regard to aid for indigenous Australians and border-controls. Even though One Nation has ceased to be an influential political force under the weight of its own internal wrangling and general lack of organisation, the sentiments and simplistic fears that it articulated so well remain within the discourses and policies of the incumbent Coalition government.

It is precisely in Hansonism's climate that the forming of coalitions between Asian and other groups in Australia have taken place in unprecedented ways. The threatened nature of community and personal identities, and being turned into residents who suddenly did not 'belong', forced them to consider their position in Australia, their citizenship, and its attendant rights. This includes the formation of Unity, a political party whose platform consists of the encouragement of, and education about, multiculturalism and multiracialism in Australia: It was created specifically to combat the influence of Hansonism. These groups are made up of culturally, socially, and politically diverse individuals. In this way, the various fractured communities that are the 'Asian-Australians' have strategically emerged as 'visible' groups for political purposes, and some Chinese communities even thank Hanson for inciting their members to rally and protest against One Nation. By no means are the groups representative of all Asians in Australia[12] but, prior to the open racism of Hanson's comments and ensuing discussions, there was seemingly no politicised momentum in Asian-Australian communities. Black British cultural critic, Kobena Mercer, is careful to make the distinction that "solidarity does not mean that everyone thinks the same way, it begins when people have the confidence to disagree over issues because they 'care' about constructing a common ground" (in McLaren 57). For Asian-Australians, the 'confidence' involves affirming or discovering their enfranchisement as Australian citizens, while attempting to dissolve or combat the inherent racism of Hansonism and its supporters. On that point, Castles contends that "[r]acism is a form of white ethnic solidarity in the face of the apparent cultural strength of immigrant groups (41). This mythical 'cultural strength' is usually articulated as a tandem insult with 'political correctness'. Such diverse figures as Hanson, Les Murray, Robert Dessaix, and Robin Gerster have gestured to 'multicultural professionals' as having such power in 1990s Australia that minorities were now the ones 'in charge'. Needless to say, the gesture is never substantiated and works to deny the validity of 'ethnic' perspectives on public and general issues. Hearing the 'ethnic' voice as only speaking for (and not about) its own community or for him/herself exposes the narrow and intentionally ignorant way in which multicultural representation is addressed by conservative and liberal commentators alike. Further, the occasional Asian figure that agrees with conservative rhetoric about the undue influence of minority groups merely parrots the unfounded reasons behind the statement. Suvendrini Perera and Joseph Pugliese describe Australian Broadcasting Corporation reporter Helene Chung Martin as a "super-assimilated non-Anglo-Australian" who "claimed that as a multiculturalism maintained by 'ethnic warlords' had eroded the 'one nation' that had existed in the 1950s, Anglo-Australians had become the 'most disenfranchised' citizens of the country" (5). The extreme angle of Martin's perspective is only exceeded by the irony of her reiterating One Nation Party rhetoric.

The general lack of discernment between cultural or national groups of Asians in Australia intensifies their marginalisation. With the necessity for solidarity, for focused coalition politics, Asian-Australian groups could run the risk of underlining existing monolithic assumptions. To avoid political affiliations because of this, however, would detract significantly from the lobbying capacity of Asian-Australian communities. The representative institutions in which other cultural communities have found a political voice remain majority Anglo-European in administration and management. In a community and political organisation like the Federal Ethnic Communities Council of Australia (FECCA), the number of Asian-Australians involved is relatively low for several reasons, including lack of community confidence in participating in the public arena. In 1998, FECCA's national conference emphasised, once again, reconciliation with Aboriginal Australians and inclusiveness for all Australians. The latter theme was a direct call to address how a body like FECCA might strive to strengthen community cohesion and to create or maintain the coalitions which they deemed essential for the future lobbying power of ethnic communities around Australia. The 'inclusionary' aspect of the conference theme extended not only to Aboriginal groups but also to the less well-represented communities within FECCA, those with disabilities, and the improvement in rates of women's participation in FECCA administration and other community roles. The strategic importance placed on these 'ethnic' issues is borne out by the number of prominent politicians who addressed the convention delegates with their vision of an inclusive Australia.[13] Post-Hanson, the scramble to dissociate their own parties from One Nation Party policies continues to be a desire of almost all political groups, except for parts of the National Party.

Once the social and literary conditions in Australia are contextualised, the subsequent examinations of various texts can engage more constructively with particular Asian-Australian perspectives. It is not enough to only 'clear space' for Asian-Australian writers in literary arenas. Studies must also focus on the politics of those spaces and the processes for using, exploiting, and/ or expanding them. The way in which discursive threads used to describe and signify the 'Asian Other' in Australia has influenced the reading/writing of Asian-Australian literature. It is also timely to assess current multicultural literary practices in what some are calling "a post-multiculturalist stage" (Jamrozik, Boland, and Urquhart 222) in Australian society. Adam Jamrozik, Cathy Boland, and Robert Urquhart want to shepherd discussion of multiculturalism into the territory and terms used for 'democratic pluralist' contentions, bypassing discussion of whether a nation is, or should be, multicultural. Researchers can then concentrate more on other aspects of multiculturalism, particularly bringing attention to the existing state of negotiating multicultural nationhood.

Asian-Australian writers experience these socio-cultural conditions in various ways, from how they are read and received, to the market demand for certain genres of fiction or non-fiction. The history of criticism of multicultural literature in Australia exemplifies the heavy weighting of multicultural studies in historical and sociological streams. Cast according to what certain groups of ethnic Australians are 'really like', critics viewed their literature as documentary evidence of their opinions and ways of living. Through most of the 1970s to the mid-1980s, most multicultural texts were read as examples of personal narratives and incapable of irony, 'literariness', or entry to various Australian literary canons. Many anthologies attempted to break the narrow reading practices by bringing together work that editors thought were good literary examples (battling yet another stereotype of multicultural writing as 'bad literature') or to display the 'interestingness' of the diverse writers Australia now has.

Turning to the more specific cultural area of multicultural literary production in Australia necessitates a definition of multicultural or ethnic writer, as well as a discussion about whether these terms can be useful, or not, in critical work. Sneja Gunew is arguably the best-known academic in Australian multicultural literary studies, and she has published widely on the issues surrounding multiculturalism in Australia and the future implications for multicultural literature. She also helped create the Multicultural Advisory Board, with significant participation by Fazal Rizvi. The process of arguing for "informed advocates" (Gunew, "Ethnicity and Excellence" 6) to be present on funding bodies was one of the prime aims of the board and defined its relationship to larger structures of arts funding. In other words, the board existed to balance the hegemonic mediation of notions of 'excellence' which had previously gone unquestioned or which were only shallowly addressed. Of course, the nomination of only one or two figures to represent the entirety of multicultural arts or particular communities has its dangers as well. Helen Andreoni uses the analogy of the anode to describe the role of multicultural arts workers and the multicultural arts units themselves. She argues that their very existence serves to silence calls for representation while separating the multicultural arts from the 'normal' arts and not allowing the more 'noble' arts to be contaminated by them: "[a] sacrificial anode is a less noble metal which is used to attract impurities away from more noble metals that you do not wish to be eroded" (8). Rasheed Araeen observes that Others have a homeopathic effect on society because "a small (only small) amount of poison can act as a medicine for an ailing body" (5). Araeen knowingly invokes and twists the 'enrichment' of society by culturally Other groups that are often touted as a multicultural society's promise. The tokenistic presence of racial minority individuals on committees and in grants-recipient lists is even more achievable because of their racially marked bodies and the usually invisible status of whiteness in Western societies. Further, the term 'ethnic' has evolved from being only an (imposed) subject position to a component of larger identity politics, which include the categories of race and class. Some critics, like Gunew and Anne Brewster, prefer the move towards talking about 'ethnicity in literature' rather than 'ethnic literature'. This strategy succeeds in dismantling the automatic marginalisation of work by multicultural writers and interrogates the allocation of cultural traits and modes of literary consumption.

In the 1950s, 'new Australians' consisted mostly of the huge influx of postwar immigrants from southern Europe; for example, communities of Italian, Greek, Hungarian, and Yugoslavian immigrants who settled in the larger cities of Australia. These groups were subject to certain kinds of racialisation that were often effective but perfunctory.[14] It is only in recent decades that the term 'ethnic' has begun to encompass, and then somewhat awkwardly, the growing numbers of non-white Australians who were perceived as 'ethnic', including the Chinese, Malaysian, Indian, Vietnamese, Korean, Taiwanese, and other 'Asians'. The growing participation of Middle Eastern Australians establishes even broader terms of reference for the contemporary literature of multicultural Australia. A compilation edited by Peter Skryznecki, *Influence* (1997), demonstrates the new direction being taken by some authors and publishers. The book is an anthology of short stories, all grouped under the theme of 'influence'. Similar publications have peppered Australian bookstores in the past few years, including collections arranged around love, romance, drinking, and ghost stories. This one, however, is slightly more complex in the 'influence' that Skryznecki encourages his contributors to explore: "personal, geographical, sexual, cultural, religious, political, and so on" (x). Of particular interest to this project is the inclusion of seven 'Asian' authors in a collection of twenty-four stories,[15] approximately one-third of the representation. They include both South and East Asian writers and, within these broad categories, the authors claim cultural backgrounds ranging from Indian and Chinese to Vietnamese and Sri Lankan.

As well as broadening the possibilities for writing from culturally different authors in anthologies, contemporary literary politics shifts the ways in which this writing is received. The events surrounding, and issues invoked by, Helen Darville and her almost successful attempts to be Ukrainian in the mid-1990s cannot help but influence contemporary considerations of multicultural literature. Darville (who called herself Helen Demidenko at the time) won the Vogel Award for an unpublished manuscript and then was subsequently awarded the premier Australian literary prize, the Miles Franklin, in 1995. Controversy arose over the content of the book and the representations of various cultural groups. These debates amplified when Demidenko was 'unmasked' as not of Ukrainian descent. While I am not engaging in a close study of *The Hand that Signed the Paper* or the main issues within it of anti-Semitism, fascism, and 'justice', the exposing of Darville as 'non-ethnic' and the ensuing publicity around the book and author are timely for current formulations in multicultural literary research.[16] Vijay Mishra reads her as parodying "the seeming valorization of multiculturalism in Australia" ("Postmodern Racism" 350), and Gunew emphasises this in an article in which she calls the circling attacks and feeling of being duped the "Demidenko Show" ("Performing Ethnicity" 1). The events and ensuing commentary exposed two things about Australian literary critics and their new caution with 'multicultural' literature. The first came before the unmasking of Darville as non-Ukrainian: the furore over the contents and politics of the book, the demand for all levels of historical authenticity from a work of fiction. Gunew commented that "[native informants/multicultural writers] are constructed as sources for 'information-retrieval' rather than being deemed capable of postmodernist writing" ("Performing Ethnicity" 57). The subject of the Holocaust, or *shoah*, is very sensitive and emotionally loaded. Even so, there was a moral prescriptiveness in the response to Darville's book, which did not have much to do with the narrative as literature. The second situation is a result of exposing Darville and her very 'normal' English background, followed by months of anger from various literary establishments at having been duped into thinking and feeling for a person and work which were not 'truly' ethnic at all. There was an immediate transfer of focus from Darville's case to the larger group of 'multicultural writers' whom readers and critics now could not trust (an intriguing idea in itself). The change in opinion seemed "to delegitimize the demands of migrant groups, in the sense that attempts to explore or construct aspects of migrant groups in literary forms will now, to some, seem clichéd, less feasible or even desirable" (Levy 6). Gunew details this transformation as more to do with 'ethnics' proving that they merely hide "the parade of pathologies — anti-Semitism and those festering wounds (old rivalries) that all right-thinking Australians know lie behind the costumes and the cooking which continue to be the acceptable face of multiculturalism" ("Performing Ethnicity" 58). Within the scandals about literary and cultural authenticity that erupted in the wake of the Demidenko's cultural unmasking was certainly an element of fear about not being able to tell if one of 'them' might be one of 'us' (the white majority).[17]

Because of this apprehension about not being able to position certain people culturally, the racially marked body of Asians or Aboriginal Australians might seem more easily authentic because of the visual difference they represent. However, this racialised body is no more of an insurance against being accused of cultural duping. Recent instances of 'racial unmaskings', particularly accompanied by intracommunity tensions, reveal the complexities of ascriptions of authenticity for racial minority authors. One of Australia's most outspoken and radical 'Aboriginal' authors, Mudrooroo, was accused by his stepsister of not being Aboriginal Australian at all but the descendant of an African-American grandfather.[18] After revelations from his family about his non-Aboriginal background, Australian writer and critic Cassandra Pybus supported Mudrooroo's case by stating that his cultural 'shamming' was in the interests of bringing Aboriginal issues to light and to argue for their cause (2). While Pybus's barracking for certain writers to masquerade an ethnicity is problematic to say the least, perhaps the discussion is more constructively cast according to who allocates authenticity and whether the 'purposes' to which that authenticity is put justify its invocation. Especially with non-Anglo-European authors, the base of knowledge from which a mainstream reviewer writes might not cover the cultural specificities necessary to perform an "*informed* reading" (Gunew and Longley xvii). A certain wariness should exist towards the type of advocacy in which those who claim to make room for disenfranchised individuals do so by pushing others out of the discussion or blaming them for being the source of discrimination.

The momentum of Asian-Australian literary publication is relatively slow; most of the authors are first-generation Australians, and few novels have been published by Australian-born writers of Asian descent. Because of this general demographic, the ways in which the authors negotiate belonging in nation, community, and self are particularly important for further studies in the area. It is not so much a matter of wanting to become a part of the 'Oz Lit' canon, necessarily, that growth in Asian-Australian writing is desirable. In the same way that Greek-Australian writer Angelo Loukakis refuses a place in "the grand house of Australian Literature, the Oxford Manor of Kramer et al." (109), Asian-Australian literature emphasises the broadening, not contraction, of possibilities for different styles and histories of literature in Australia. In talking about the multicultural literature journal he edits, Manfred Jurgensen suggests that the whole purpose of 'naming' in multicultural literature is to aim for the stage when labels can be discarded: "[t]he ultimate aim of such a journal as *Outrider* ought really to be its self-destruction as a self-consciously multicultural publication" (in Loukakis 110). Currently, the field of Asian-Australian literary studies suffers from a lack of clarity about what it actually comprises, and part of the impediment while examining possible material is trying to move beyond the associations of 'Australians in Asia' or 'representations of Asia by Australians' type of work. While this is not to deny the validity of these areas for study, they have deflected energy from an analysis of the cultural production of Asian-Australians and the ensuing examination of diasporic experiences peculiar to East Asian writers living and writing in Western societies. That said, however, the increase in the number of events and publications addressing these specific topics, post-Hanson, is encouraging for the area. The basis for an Asian–Australian branch of Australian literary studies is already in place with significant and growing critical discussion about writers of East Asian (e.g., Brian Castro, Simone Lazaroo, Beth Yahp, Ouyang Yu) and South Asian (e.g., Yasmine Gooneratne, Chandani Lokuge, Adib Khan) descent.[19]

Alongside the national contextualisation of Asian–Australian groups is the study of Asian–Australian literary culture. These critiques examine the larger questions of Asian diaspora and community, as well as the significant, dynamic mediations and existing criticisms in Asian–American theory. For Vijay Mishra, multiculturalism and diasporic studies are not just complementary areas but ones that are integral to each other. Mishra edited and contributed to a special issue of *SPAN*, one of the earliest publications to focus on the critical issue of 'diaspora'. He states that "diasporic theory is what underpins multicultural theory" ("Diasporic" 3). I would argue, however, that much of the diasporic theory that exists at present engages with the contextualisation of texts in a desultory manner. The practice of working from established forms of national literary criticism, and only then drawing on aspects of diasporic scholarship, provides a stronger, more distinct base from which to discuss texts. Combining this with addressing specifically Australian historical questions allows explication of distinct national political and cultural formations for Asian–Australian writers. Choosing to address contemporary concerns for Asian–Australian authors and their literature means not only examining the current situation in Australia but also situating the book socio-historically. In doing so, I inflect the usual pattern of representing Asian migratory 'waves' by selectively examining the specificities of multiculturalism and Asian communities and individuals. The 'waves' analogy is suspect in view of the fact that it is most often a shorthand way of making simplistic, discreet packages out of what are very different, politically and socially influenced movements of people. This chapter does not purport to present the history of Asians in Australia (as this work has been, and is being, accomplished in other publications)[20] but draws on the main threads of that history which are pertinent to the study of Asian–Australian literary issues and current 'Asia-Pacific' Australian discourses.

The influence of Asian–American theory and politics on Asian–Australian discourses is undeniable. Unlike the history of Australia's multiculturalism that has a mainly ethnic European focus, however, the United States' situation of 'multiculturalism' is almost always cast in terms of interracial conflict (Siemerling 11). This perspective is gradually gaining currency in Australia, and multiculturalism, Aboriginal Land Rights, and Asian immigration are often discussed in conjunction with each other. In the United States, the failure of racial minorities to live in harmony, or what is known as "'minority-minority' conflict" (Gotanda 238), casts multiculturalism as an unsuccessful option precisely because the people for whom it was implemented do not appreciate it.[21] Angela Y. Davis stresses the importance of re-emphasising anti-racist perspectives and initiatives because of the cyclic nature of racist discourse. Her position on the anatomy of racism is cogent across nations and resonates within the majority white societies of Australia and Canada:

> the notion that if we simply correct those stereotypes with knowledge of the 'true' cultures, we will no longer be hated and will no longer hate each other, is extremely dangerous. I am certainly not opposed to enlightenment, but policies of enlightenment by themselves do not necessarily lead to radical transformations of power structures (47).

A significant amount of multicultural research makes visible the power structures alluded to in Davis's concerns about discrimination and inequality. The issue of which processes are needed to transform these unequal structures is what informs this book.

Arguably one of the most under-theorised and scarcely studied facets of multiculturalism in Australia is the significance of class and its ascription. In "Dialectics of Domination", Vasta takes some challenging steps towards making class structure as visible as gender or race (60–1), and this book builds on these. This is an issue that is often mentioned but hardly addressed, particularly in Asian-Australian work thus far. The complicity which Asian-Australian communities have with the 'Model Minority'[22] stereotype could explain the lack of engagement with these issues of class. As many parts of oral histories confirm, the communities prefer presenting themselves as successful Australians, and this often translates into less interest in those who are not prosperous or ostensibly 'successful'.

The sometimes grudgingly opened cultural borders of Australia — augmented by the globalisation of media, and the types of culture which gain global currency — influence the reading and reception of these Asian-Australian writers. Although not necessarily advocating a 'globalisation = homogenisation' argument, I would argue that the acceleration of information and social exchange certainly increases concern with regard to cultural diversity and autonomy. As Ulf Hannerz suggests, however, "[i]t is not . . . that diversity is disappearing. It is just not very neatly packaged" (3). It is in this Australian (post-)multicultural environment of postmodern fracturing of cultural and literary groups and ideas that Asian–Australian authors are writing. Looking outside Australia, to similar national formations and other histories of diasporic Asian literature, offers Asian–Australian studies the opportunity to re-site national arguments within global perspectives.

The scarcity of Asian–Australian critical work and publishing can be attributed to the early stage of Asian–Australian community politicisation as well as Australian resistance to including racial minority groups within governing and other social structures. Because of this, the field of Asian–Australian studies progresses slowly. Until there are significant changes in the perception of racial minorities and their literature in Australia, the work of Asian–Australian writers will always be offset from being part of national literatures. These changes require the constitution of Asian–Australians as full cultural citizens and the ability to conceive of their artistic or other contributions as transformative parts of Australian culture.

2

"Spitting in the Soup": Asian–Canadian Space

[A] Canadian is a hyphen and we're diplomats by birth.
(Joy Kogawa, "Interview with Magdelene Redekop" 96)

[The hyphen's] coalitional and mediating potentiality offers real engagement, not as a centre but as a provocateur of flux, floating, fleeting.
(Fred Wah, *Faking It* 103)

C anada's recognition of two official languages and the policy of multiculturalism seem to point to an already heightened government awareness of, and engagement with, the diversity of its national population that does not yet seem to prevail in Australia. Multiculturalism in Canada, as elsewhere, can be interpreted as a strategy of containment, the management of social relations in the interests of national, cultural, and political unity. Himani Bannerjee characterises this government strategy as "managing [the] seepage of persistent subjectivities of people that come from other parts of the world" (in Gunew, "Multicultural Multiplicities" 453). The normative or ethical strategy disseminated by government policy often clashes with another form of multiculturalism, one that is most aptly summarised as a utopian political system. This tension is particularly apparent in Canada where the significant populations of racial minority groups lend their politics more impetus and visibility, particularly in the larger, more culturally diverse cities of Vancouver and Toronto. Many of these groups engage with the utopian multicultural ideas on a level described by Sneja Gunew as seeking "full participatory cultural democracy" ("Multicultural Multiplicities" 452). This type of multiculturalism is often not supported by the management structures of the governmental multicultural policies described above. The coexistence of these versions of multiculturalism — one a general set of values and the other an optimistic end-point for diverse societies — creates constructive friction in the development of an Asian-Canadian movement that alternates between establishing itself with government aid and maintaining itself with community participation and motivation.

Canada is more amenable than Australia to the development of Asian-Canadian literature as an area of study because of the ways in which its successive governments have implemented social and literary policies, as well as the major factor of community momentum. These policies recognise the importance of equity in society through practical (funded) means, and this 'top-down' approach is crucial for some aspects of creative pursuits, particularly in establishment phases. That is, while the Canadian government could certainly be more responsive to and thorough at following through on anti-racist rhetoric, it is a valuable starting point. As the Canadian examples discussed in this chapter demonstrate, the creative possibilities for racial minority artists are heightened by their validation as cultural citizens and political entities.

The increases in contemporary Asian-Canadian publication and critical work are due in part to successive Canadian governments' promotion of diversity initiatives and the somewhat uneven embrace of anti-racist responses. These include the awarding of redress to Japanese-Canadians in 1988, the subsequent establishment of the Race Relations Foundation, and the establishment of other initiatives to promote multiculturalism and to combat racism. Other prime factors which affect the current socio-cultural environment of Asian-Canadians include the ambivalent nature of Canadian-United States coalitions and the cultural ties of artists within and between Asian-Canadian communities.

Kogawa's quotation in my epigraph gestures to the 'nation of migrants' model that is applicable to many nations in the world. However, it has particular inflections for Asian-Canadians and the assumptions made about visibly different groups and individuals. The 'ambassadorial' role for certain classes of Asian-Canadians is explicit in the issues around the Hong Kong 'monster house' stories in Vancouver as well as the emphasis on Asia-Pacific trade and the abilities of certain 'Canadians' (that is, of Asian descent) to contribute to the gross national product. Critics agree that the differences in implementation of Canada's and Australia's multiculturalism are most apparent when levels of language and community recognition are considered.

While Australia has ongoing black–white tensions, the situation in Canada is further complicated by three parties: Anglo-, Franco-, and Native Canadians. John Frow and Meaghan Morris point to the already doubled vision of Canadian cultural discourses in its "profound linguistic split" (ix), suggesting that Canada is a country without a unified national discourse. Janice Kulyk Keefer stresses this when she states that the nation of Canada was formed while Others were already there — meaning Franco-Canadians, however, not Native Canadians ("Multiculturalism" 3). Somewhat ironically, the official 1988 Multiculturalism Act in Canada owes its establishment to the Bilingualism and Biculturalism ('Bi and Bi') Commission in the 1970s, when multiculturalism "effectively supplanted that dual identity" (Keefer, "Multiculturalism" 4). Despite the gesturing to the 'Anglo-Franco' doubled nature of Canadianness, the relationship has never been equal, and neither has the bicultural model worked successfully to unify the nation. Mark Williams's summary of the similarly uneven form of biculturalism found in New Zealand is also applicable to Canada:

> If biculturalism means tinkering with existing institutions to include a Maori perspective and settle outstanding grievances, as many Pakeha believe it does, then New Zealand is a bicultural country. If it means sharing resources and creating new institutional systems that reflect the interests and outlooks of both groups, as many Maori believe, then New Zealand is not truly bicultural (2).

In many ways, the lack of equality in bicultural models is repeated in multicultural systems in which difference ends up being accommodated and the structures of discrimination — of Anglophone domination — are left intact. The tension between the official languages demonstrates the impossibility of linguistic or cultural equality and reveals the ways in which the "technology of ethnicity" (Kamboureli, "Technology" 211) shifts in function according to the priorities of the government in power.

In Canada, there is an undeniable bias towards English as the dominant language and Anglophone Canadians as the controllers of the nation's culture. The title of this chapter is taken from an article describing another secessionist moment in Quebecois politics: this one referring to the late 1995 referendum to decide whether or not Quebec would function as an independent nation. The original use of the phrase 'spitting in the soup' referred to then Premier Jacques Perizeau's opinion of what those voting *Non* were doing to their province and potential country, but it also applies to the agitation that disrupts the united front of Canada's multicultural mosaic. This uneven consideration of a 'founding tongue' in Canada, along with other perceived biases against Francophone Canadians, gives rise to recurring bouts of secessionist politics. To demonstrate the foreignness of Franco-Canadians to those not of Quebec, poet and critic Fred Wah recounts his adoption of the name "Fredois" because "French *is* exotic in Western Canada" ("Half-Bred" 4). Far from being a straightforward case of fighting for Francophone representation, Quebec's politics are diffused by different priorities:

> Quebecois nationalism, like more other nationalisms, has two souls. There is the old cultural nationalism with its slogan of *la pure laine* (the pure wool) — an ethnocentric calling to the original French Quebecois (about 82 per cent of the population) who settled there more than two centuries ago. The other soul is a more progressive anti-imperialist nationalism rooted in the trade unions, community groups and women's organizations. These groups see independence as a chance to break with the more predatory forms of North American capitalism in a socially-oriented Quebec (Swift 21).

Even though the vitality of the 'pure' Quebecois movement vacillates according to certain political exigencies, the dominance of Anglophone Canadians in determining what constitutes Canadian culture is not unquestioned. It is this Anglophone dominance that racial minority artists and communities contest through their creative work and coalitions. While multiculturalism encourages a circumscribed form of participation, the growth of racial minority arts and activism sharply challenge status quo renditions of Canadian culture. In late 2001, the Canadian Senate passed a bill recognising May as 'Asian Heritage Month'. Although these events have not effected radical change and could be accused of diverting Asian-Canadian cultural concerns along designated paths, it is a significant recognition of community and cultural presence.

Similar to most post-colonial nations in the Western world, the historical dominance of white groups underwrites the contemporary marginalisation of non-white concerns. Newer immigrant communities have not reached a level of cultural and political confidence necessary to challenge the status quo on political issues. This is possibly not as true for those of Asian descent who are born in Canada itself, because the relatively recent history of Asian citizenship and activism is now gaining significant profile and momentum.

Canada's anti-Asian history parallels those of the United States and Australia where fears of, and barriers to, the 'yellow peril' are concerned.

Canada had similar immigration exclusions, such as head taxes, internment of Japanese-Canadian citizens during the Second World War, and vilification of Asian communities as threats of 'uncivilisation' to the majority European society that existed in the New World. As early as 1907, the Asiatic Exclusion League was formed in Vancouver (Ujimoto, "Racism" 130), and violence against those who lived and worked in Chinatowns was common. The exploitation and subsequent abandonment of Chinese workers during the building of the Canadian Pacific Railway is an outright rejection of Chinese labourers as potential 'Canadians', a notorious example of the always conditional acceptance of migrant labour. For the period of the Chinese Exclusion Act (1923–47), Charles Ungerleider notes that "fewer than 50 Chinese immigrated to Canada" (9), leaving existing Chinese communities in debilitated and ageing states. Often, discriminatory workplaces and restricted opportunities for employment exacerbated these circumstances. These histories of displacement and alienation are now being written by Chinese-Canadians themselves and, with their publication, the texts disturb significant layers of existing versions of Canadian history and literature. Histories of Chinatowns and Chinese groups in smaller towns sketch a more inclusive and representative picture of contemporary Canada's roots. For Japanese-Canadians, the turn of the century meant less severe restrictions than those visited upon the Chinese communities. Victor K. Ujimoto argues that "[t]he Anglo-Japanese alliance of 1902 and 1905 strengthened the political ties between Britain and Japan and this meant that domestic political matters were subordinated for the sake of the unity within the British Empire" ("Racism" 133). This preferential treatment for the Japanese, however, was wholly dependent on the relationship between the British Empire and the Japanese government. The internment of Japanese-Canadians during the Second World War further reflects this tenuous and inconsistent alliance.

Many Australian cultural debates have difficulty combining discussion about multiculturalism with the consequences of racist attitudes, but grappling with issues of racism is not something for which Canadian multiculturalism is known either. Criticisms of Canada and its "polite veneer of racism" (Carpenter C1) focus on the insidious ways in which people and institutions can discriminate against racial minority groups. A character from Rohinton Mistry's *Tales from Firozsha Baag*, Nariman, declares:

> The Multicultural Department is a Canadian invention. It is supposed to ensure that ethnic cultures are able to flourish, so that Canadian society

will consist of a mosaic of cultures — that's their favourite word, mosaic — instead of one uniform mix, like the American melting pot. If you ask me, mosaic and melting pot are both nonsense, and ethnic is a polite way of saying bloody foreigner (in Malak 160).

Nariman captures beautifully the dilemma of living in a country interested in limited levels of 'multi-colour' more than true 'multi-cultures'. Considering Canada's cultural emphasis on differentiating itself from the United States' 'melting pot' where possible, the question of comparative race relations lends the discussion an interesting angle. In terms of racial awareness and efficacy, multiculturalism developed in Canada in marked contrast to the way in which the United States embraced the bundle of ideologies. As historian Alexander Woodside stresses, the United States' form of 'multiculturalism' grew out of the civil rights movement and a direct confrontation by the nation's citizens with racial conflict within and without its borders (for instance, the Black Panthers and the United States' involvement in the Vietnam war respectively). Canada's 'multiculturalism' "focussed on communities such as the Jewish, German, Ukrainian, and Mennonite" (in Cook i), probably reflecting the "Wonder-Bread days before the civil rights movement" in North America (Kim, "Beyond Railroads" 14). The oft-noted disparities in levels of racial violence and unrest between Canada and the United States lead some to conclude that Canada is a more tolerant and well-blended nation and, therefore, more peaceful. However, it is the amount of disturbance present which often dictates how confident and free people feel to protest:

> The absence of open conflict in such systems, therefore, does not necessarily imply a harmonious integration of racial elements to permit interracial cooperation and reciprocal participation. It may simply mean that different units of society are compelled to accept the activities and objectives of the dominant group and, in this sense, different units arrive at a new level of integration that is fundamentally antagonistic. If this is the case, then the absence of open conflict may well suggest maximal rather than minimal racial oppression (Bolaria and Li 25).

B. Singh Bolaria and Peter Li's argument is supported by the post-redress history of Japanese-Canadians and the level of validation they feel as citizens, as well as the lack of momentum in Australia about these same issues. For Canadian multiculturalism, then, the past few decades of activism and cultural community growth for non-Anglo-European groups offers a significant challenge to the management of multicultural policies and their principles of equity. The appearance of anti-racist groups such as the now-defunct Minquon Panchayat and the Anti-Racist Action groups in several cities around Canada offers opportunities for further sustained contestations. The recovery project of acknowledging Asian-Canadian roles in Canada's history, as well as in its literary canons, encourages a change in perception about who can hold the power to control national interests.

A danger that accompanies this steady historical salvaging is the assumption that these past events are disconnected from contemporary manifestations of community, immigration, or discrimination. A signal that this displacement has occurred is the 1995 changing of the title of 'Ministry of Multiculturalism' to the 'Ministry of Canadian Heritage'. Scott McFarlane argues that "this shift devalues issues of race" ("Haunt" 31) and, I would add, deflects current tensions ensnaring immigration and the future directions of Canadian society. This action is taken possibly in response to the backlash against diversity politics that is taking place in most Western nations, placating those who feel that the status quo and their dominance is threatened. In the recent past, the popularity of Preston Manning's Reform Party[1] among WASP voters, and its anti-immigration, conservative politics, mirrors this trend, as does British Columbia's incumbent Premier Gordon Campbell and his Liberal Party, elected in 2001. Campbell appears to deliver the same flavour of social rhetoric as Reform, his first year in office generating much criticism of the Liberal Party's policies on social reform and economic 'rationalism'.

The main difference between the Australian (One Nation) and Canadian (Reform) situations in this respect, however, is that the Asian population of many Canadian cities is significant enough for Reform to acknowledge the electoral power of Asian citizens and to attempt fielding a handful of South Asian candidates in certain areas. In Australia, One Nation continually attacked Asian immigration, Asian crime and violence, and lamented the forgotten Anglo (especially fringe rural) population. In this show of demographic voting power, it is apparent that the difference in size between Australian and Canadian Asian populations is a significant factor in the national interpolation of Asian citizens.

In contemporary social politics, established fears include those of Canadian incorporation into an 'Asian' future, Canada being taken over by 'them', economically and, as always, demographically. The anxiety over the economic issue manifested itself in one way with the negative community and media reaction to the so-called 'monster houses' of Vancouver. This particular wariness was not born of fear of being overrun by the 'traditional' hordes of refugees, but by the new middle- to upper-middle class immigrants, or "Yacht People" (Katharyne Mitchell, "Hong Kong" 306) from Hong Kong. Usually, the resentment manifested in targeting Asian immigrants encompasses all classes, and the situation of Japanese-Canadians in the Second World War demonstrates this multi-layered scapegoating well (Stasiulis and Jhappan 116). Repeated historical vilification leads to Asian groups in Canada with high levels of internalised racism and first-hand knowledge of the processes of racialisation. During the coverage of community tensions between new Asian immigrants and 'older' Anglo residents of certain Vancouver areas because of the 'monster house' issue, the media conspicuously mobilised these processes and their resulting stereotypes. The controversy evolved when established residents blamed newer ones for changing the tone and value of their neighbourhoods. According to Kathryne Mitchell, the new Hong Kong residents exacerbated their neighbours' consternation by removing significant trees, building very large homes, and generally disrupting the existing local environment. She states that racism accompanied these concerns because the anxiety was not because of the changes as such, but because it was felt that the changes resulted in a neighbourhood in which they no longer felt comfortable. Mitchell also writes about the *Meet with Success* seminars held in Hong Kong by the Canadian Club of Hong Kong on a twice-weekly basis for people with visas to emigrate to Canada:

> In an effort to offset the increasingly effective mobilization of the Anglo homeowners of these neighborhoods, the wealthy transnationals of both Hong Kong and Vancouver society attempted to lessen the neighborhood friction by educating and disciplining (in the Foucauldian sense) the future Hong Kong middle-class homebuyers of cultural norms for the area ("Hong Kong" 288).[2]

Although these efforts to smooth neighbourhood relations (a form of pre-immigration assimilation) are seemingly admirable, they occur alongside the creation of a new batch of orientalist stereotypes following the well-established and exploited 'Model Minority' mould. These are destructive coercions in the long term, considering the difficult task of breaking down what is behind the desire to stereotype (or scapegoat) Asian communities in the first place: fear of difference and fear of absorbing that difference. The perceived need by the Canadian Club of Hong Kong to groom future (Asian) Canadians to be good, unobtrusive citizens concretises the previous individual pressures on new migrants to conform and not make a fuss. The process begins before they even set foot in Canada and, with regard to the *Meet with Success* course, they are forewarned that they will not be welcome if their behaviour deviates from those of "positive Chinese roles" like those of the "'bridge-builder' and '*homo economicus*'" ("Hong Kong" 310). These clichéd images reinforce what is often touted as the primary function of Asians in Canada, that of economic facilitator as opposed to contributor within the nation. Internalised racism renders these subjects self-monitoring and, indeed, this regulation extends to others in their community. The 'Yacht people' events are mapped out against a background including 'boat people' landings and subsequent furore about asylum-seekers and deportation. Lily Cho is "doubtful of claims to the new, to something which too easily divorces itself from an ugly past of state-sanctioned labor exploitation and legalized racism" ("Serving Chinese" 32). She argues that "the desire to make the past past risks relegating what might be considered old diaspora subjectivities into the dustbin of Chinese diaspora history rather than thinking through the ways in which these identities not only haunt modern diaspora subjectivity but are constitutive of it" (31–2). Given the emphasis on new subjectivities and 'progressive' representations of diasporic Asian identities, critical concern must accompany the sometimes celebratory cosmopolitan 'transnationalism' of certain class fractions and their subjects.[3]

In an environment of continued Anglo-European dominance and control, non-Anglo groups and individuals have difficulty achieving validation as citizens or enfranchised participants in Canadian political or cultural systems. This situation is changing slowly, but eroding and opposing racism on various levels and working towards equity in society remain active and daunting tasks. Specifically addressing levels of engagement with racism and racialisation, Sneja Gunew argues for a further distinction between the Canadian and Australian situations:

> within Canada, the notion of racial difference is subsumed within multiculturalism in ways that are not easily applicable in Australia. I think that is why the Aboriginal Canadians find it easier to be a part of multicultural politics and to position themselves in relation to multicultural debates, and why they always include notions of racialization, the problems of racism, in ways that are not dealt with, say, in relation to multiculturalism in Australia ("Postcolonialism/Multiculturalism" 211).

One of the historical moments that distinguishes Canadian racial politics from those in Australia is the official apology by the government to Japanese-Canadians for their internment during the Second World War. This entailed a prolonged struggle by Japanese-Canadian groups for the recognition of wartime injustices, rejecting the partial and half-hearted gesture by the Bird Commission in 1947.[4] The National Association of Japanese-Canadians (NAJC) campaigned for the acknowledgement of, and compensation for, the Second World War grievances due to Canadian government policy. They succeeded in this endeavour in 1988, on the heels of a similar United States government/Japanese-American settlement. The most important step, according to Audrey Kobayashi, occurred when the "NAJC remained adamant that the principle of redress must be the compensation of individual *Canadians*, not because they were *Japanese* Canadians, but because their rights as individuals had been abrogated" ("Japanese-Canadian Redress" 5). This step confirmed the positioning of Japanese, and by extension Asian, citizens within Canada, and this influenced the evolution of contemporary cultural politics in Canadian arts activism.

The differentiation between generations of Asian-Canadian groups is becoming more marked as the communities become more defined, confident, and audible. To have the confidence to challenge the government and demand redress requires a basic sense of belonging and a certain assurance of community sanctioning. The Canadian settlement followed the United States' acknowledgement and served to underscore the legitimacy of Japanese individuals as citizens of Canada and the United States. Yuko Shibata states that the redress arrangement "prove[d] to be an important psychological experience, especially for former internees. Time after time, interviewees had spoken of how the apology had made them '*whole persons*'" (in Cook vii). In addition, Kobayashi frames this step as testimony to the "power of coalitions" ("Japanese-Canadian Redress" 7) and "not the conclusion of struggle, but a precedent for social change" ("Japanese-Canadian Redress" 14). Having set this precedent, Asian-Canadians affirmed their status as authorised participants in the public sphere. Japanese-Canadians appealed to, and successfully validated, a merging of two modes of multiculturalism: They applied to the government on the basis of a breach of civic ethics and mobilised the movement by using the utopian model and the energies of group activism. Kenda Gee describes a similar step that Chinese-Canadians are taking to claim compensation for the head tax levies, incidents that are even further back in Canada's history than the Second World War internment (Interview 1).[5] In an article which rereads the 'racism' of head tax, Cho suggests that it is not enough for Jean Chretien to "reenact the scene that Brian Mulroney played in 1988 where redress becomes the site of a self-satisfied national political consolidation" ("Rereading" 81). Whether the head tax redress movement will have the same 'success' as Japanese-Canadians remains to be seen. Whatever the outcome, however, that there is community and political impetus to engage in this way is significant in itself.

Following the assertion of their status in Canada, the experience of protesting and lobbying for change for the 'Model Minority' group lends future projects impetus and promise. The initial Redress compensation agreement and publicity did not, however, guarantee follow-through for the principles of the settlement. These steps are more difficult to negotiate after the initial excitement of the Redress settlement. In the Race Relations Foundation, this has been particularly problematic. Its role is ostensibly to combat racism and to gather information about race relations in Canada, but complex political issues continue to impede its effectiveness. Moreover, according to McFarlane, five years after their 'success', the NAJC was still lobbying for redress on behalf of "both Canadians of Japanese ancestry entrapped and stranded in Japan and prohibited from returning to Canada in the period between 1941 and 1949 and also Canadians of Japanese ancestry born in exile as a direct consequence of their parents' deportation from Canada" ("Covering *Obasan*" 410).

Asian-Canadian independent filmmaker, Midi Onodera, presents another issue associated with the aftermath of the politicisation and profile of the Redress movement. Federal funding agencies rejected her application for a film project and, on a provincial level, the grants office told her that she was "ineligible for funding" because "Japanese-Canadian history could only be perceived as political and not as cultural" (149). This narrow categorisation of what a community's experiences might be speaks to an inadequate understanding of what diversity can denote and, more importantly, it is a failure to understand the process of intersecting ethnicity with artistic endeavour.

The complications involved in current 'ethnic' categories for establishing the eligibility of an artist's work are demonstrated by the career of Asian-Canadian multimedia practitioner Paul Wong. Wong has an unpredictable style, with multiple identifications and no ultimate rendition of the self. His productions are symbolic of the larger Asian-Canadian cultural scene, with changing priorities and multiple affiliations. His work is consistently politicised and spans multi-cultures, genres, and different types of medium. Wong's retrospective, *On Becoming a Man*, demonstrates this range. His work broadly addresses forms of identity and draws from "performance, body art, punk counterculture, and the documentary" (Jean Gagnon 13). His twenty-year career as a multimedia and community artist refuses any easy labelling, and some of his work has even more impact today than when he first conceived it. An example of this is Wong's first colour film foray, a five-minute piece called *60 Unit Bruise* (1976). The short video shows Wong and his co-director Ken Fletcher with a syringe. Fletcher draws out several millilitres of blood from his own arm and injects this into Wong's back:

> The camera closes in on this, observing the slow response of the immune
> system as the skin turns red and purple. What was originally intended as
> a sort of ritual uniting the young men as blood brothers, with implicit
> reference to drug use, has become a disturbing and dangerous act twenty
> years later, in an era when AIDS evokes our deepest fears and anxieties
> (Paul Wong 56).

One of Wong's more recent works, *Blending Milk and Water: Sex in the New World*, combines many strands of contemporary political contention. It challenges sexual definitions and the assumption of moral high ground implicated in the blame surrounding AIDS rhetoric. Gordon Brent Ingram summarises *Blending* as a work that "compiles excerpts from a Pacific Rim future that is increasingly bound to be one part *Blade Runner*, one part 'information superhighway' and one part unstable political economy" (19). Considering the breadth of Wong's style, its defiance of singular definitions, and Onodera's difficult situation with funding, the complexities of negotiating pre-set expectations of 'ethnic art' are considerable. Only when racial minority artists and writers are read as both inside and outside these categories can the imposed essentialisms that keep them marginalised, restricted to certain kinds of funding, or in tokenistic positions, start to lose their hold.

Many explorations of being on both sides of the border (or the hyphen) take place in critical and fictional arenas and, in demonstrable ways, they maintain the notion of building Asian-Canadian identities through continuing and permanent processes. What has been particularly significant in the Asian-Canadian activist movement, and a twist on the 'both sides of the border' analogy, is the stimulation gained through alliances with, and precedents set by, Asian-American groups. The tension for Canada in avoiding engulfment by American cultural influences has long been an object of analysis. As Laura Mulvey describes it:

> The question of Canadian identity is political in the most direct sense of
> the word, and it brings the political together with the cultural and
> ideological immediately and inevitably. For the Canada delineated by

multinationals, international finance, US economic and political imperialism, national identity is a point of resistance, defining the border fortifications against exterior colonial penetration (in Turner, "'It Works'" 645).

This determined differentiation from those across the border is a national trope, as Williams comments, "the correct answer to the question, 'What are we?' is that we are not Americans" (6). He then stresses the differing political implications of stressing being 'not-American', especially for Native Canadian groups "for whom maintaining a difference from Americans is perhaps not such a priority as it is for Anglo-Celtic Canadians" (6). When it comes to minority group mobilisation, the policy and activist trail blazed by Asian-Americans and the establishment of political and community-affirming Asian-American streams of study meant that their Asian-Canadian counterparts had ready-made networks of experience and contact for their endeavours. However, these coalitions can be fraught with problems of co-optation or generalisation, especially with the significantly larger movement of Asian-American criticism and activism and the development of Asian-American Studies as a recognised and dynamic area of study. An example of this co-optation is the automatic inclusion of Canadian authors, like Joy Kogawa and more recently Kerri Sakamoto, as 'Asian-American' authors. This is a practice that is only now, in the last decade or so, being critically questioned and its politics deconstructed.[6]

Although similarities exist between Asian-Canadian and Asian-American concerns, and it is often politically wise to cohere for common causes, national contextualisation is necessary to avoid the homogenisation of diasporic Asian and national groups. Even within the one nation, the strategic mobilisation under the banner of 'Asian-Canadian' smoothes over important differences and particular community interests. Across nations, a diasporic Asian identity can come to mean very little if offered without further socio-political contextualisation and specificity. With the overwhelming volume of work taking place in the United States, it is also important for Asian-Canadian critical work to demarcate its own issues and priorities. As Tomo Hattori comments, studies in 'Asian-Canadian' cultural production will not thrive if they are merely a "branch office" of Asian-American studies (1). One portion of defusing the lopsided association is to contextualise the literature and its socio-historical positioning in national literary politics. Guy Beauregard posits that it is not just a situation for 'relabelling' or correcting, however, and prefers to focus critique on "why Asian American literary studies, with its history of cultural nationalism and a stated desire to 'claim

America', would seek out and attempt to incorporate Asian Canadian texts" ("What Is at Stake" 222). His conclusion that the North American comparative literature axis needs to go 'beyond' and engage with transnational cultural economies is certainly supported by the dynamism of other diasporic Asian literary studies.

Asian-Canadian literature benefits from ongoing self-definition because of the breadth and depth of perspective that results from intense discussion and public disagreements surrounding identity politics. The debates that ensued from the accusations of racism against *Writing Thru Race* garnered strong scrutiny and provoked much controversy. The decision to limit certain sessions only to people of colour caused a furore that resulted in the withdrawal of major government funding. Whether or not the organising committee was correct in choosing to do what it did is almost beside the point when discussions of the event have succeeded in exposing the racialised gaze of mainstream media coverage of the event and the mostly elided constitution of 'white' privilege in Canada.[7] Associated with the *Writing Thru Race* controversy, novelist Evelyn Lau wrote a piece damning the organisers of the conference for participating in reverse discrimination. Lau is known for her reluctance to be identified, or have her work categorised, as specifically 'Asian-Canadian'. Her well-publicised statements regarding the conference led Vancouver-based writer Sky Lee to comment, "it is not enough to poise oneself above and beyond politics. Everything is political, from the way one abstains to the way one focuses on and privileges 'talent' or 'being an established writer'" ("Writing Thru Race" 8). Lau's history of rejecting categories of identity (beyond universalist ones as writer and artist) overlooks the importance of deploying cultural citizenship as a tool and not only suffering it as an ascription. The contingent identifications of various artists of colour with certain communities or groups in Canada demonstrate the flexibility of politicising the self. Far from putting the writer into a straitjacket of cultural essentialism, it can clarify the overlapping networks of available support and empower writers to work across or in-between cultural, political, and community borders.

The often-tokenistic roles occupied by Canadian artists of colour are still issues with which to contend, but the political climate of Canada does seem to foster a doubled movement towards building an Asian-Canadian profile within the category of national literatures. This 'doubled' movement stems from the ongoing publication of Asian-Canadian authors, often supported by government grants and brought out through smaller alternative presses, as well as the critical work performed on these texts.

In part due to the Asian–American growth in literary work, and a general heightening of awareness about the politics of diversity and multiculturalism in Canada, the publication of Asian–Canadian work has risen in the past decade such that there is a discernible profile of racial minority writers in Canadian literature. Local communities hold writers' workshops and short conferences with regularity (and continue receiving funds for them) and the Canadian government encourages a small number of assorted first publications through funding for the writer and/or publisher. Presses such as Sister Vision and Theytus dedicate themselves to publishing Native Canadian and other racial minority texts. They are, however, still dependent on government funding and have limited publication rates because of this. A few, like NeWest Press and Press Gang, were proving the viability of 'multicultural' publications with their authors winning literary prizes and being in the public eye.[8] One spectacular exception to the pattern of publication by smaller or independent presses is Kerri Sakamoto's experience with Knopf when publishing her first novel, *The Electrical Field*. Many of these texts are now on university and high school reading courses, boosting sales for the publishers and, for students, hopefully offering a start on questioning structured concepts such as 'Canadian' and 'Asian-Canadian'.

'Grass–roots–level' workshops, readings at day conferences, or writing and community festivals foster increases in literary publication. The significant East and South Asian populations, particularly in British Columbia and Ontario, contribute to the dynamism of the Asian–Canadian 'scene'. Terry Watada, author of interlinked short stories about internment in Canada, *Daruma Days*, remarks, "[t]he Asian-Canadian literary scene is quite exciting at the moment. There is a great sense of optimism, a feeling that an epoch has been born" (Interview with Khoo). Watada also attributes part of the momentum of Asian-Canadian literature to community support and encouragement, especially within organisations like the Asian-Canadian Writers' Workshop (ACWW).

The ACWW focuses on encouraging creative energies and political alliances within the Asian-Canadian community of authors. Historically, the group began as a Chinese-Canadian writers' group. Since those founding years, the ACWW membership has grown and changed dramatically. The initial forays into literature and radio developed into strong networks of young and established writers who met regularly. The organisation now has branches across Canada, in most of the major cities, and represents both East and South Asian writers. Jim Wong-Chu, long-time Asian-Canadian community activist, stresses the goals of the group:

> Our mandate is simple: to assist our members to publish or showcase
> their work and talent. We aim to provide a supportive and culturally
> sensitive environment for writers from a common Pacific Rim Asian
> heritage, a place for more established writers to guide emerging writers
> through the difficulties of the publishing field. We are committed to the
> accessing of new performing and publishing venues and relevant
> information on behalf of our writers ("A Brief History" 1).

This statement has practical manifestations as proactive campaigns and
events, including the dissemination of information to the literary and
performing community. The ACWW's first issue of the newsletter *Rice Paper*
was published in 1994, a vehicle for publicising readings and future
publications, conferences and events for Asian-Canadian writers, and articles
concerning the effects of various funding moves. The newsletter is
published regularly and has its own website with selected articles (http://
www.ricepaperonline.com). The pages advocate global coalitions between
diasporic Asian organisations and are a valuable source of information about
Asian-Canadian activism and creative production.

In the years since its official inception in the late 1970s, the ACWW
has participated in several pioneering publications including *Inalienable Rice*
(1979; an anthology of short pieces by the Powell Street Revue and the
Chinese-Canadian Writer's Workshop) and *Many-Mouthed Birds* (Lee and
Wong-Chu 1991), a collection that is arguably the cornerstone of
contemporary Asian-Canadian literature. Lien Chao claims that *Rice* and
Birds are "landmark publications" that "help to reclaim community history,
and to define and redefine Chinese Canadian identity in a dynamic
community" ("Anthologizing" 166). Kamboureli describes the versions of
identity that emerge from the writing in anthologies as participating in
another balancing act, "substantiat[ing] the need for the ethnic subject to
articulate ethnicity at a specific historical moment, but offer[ing], despite a
certain common ground that they share, no cohesive 'grammar' of ethnicity"
("Canadian Ethnic" 17), an observation that reflects the aim of most Asian-
Canadian artists, that of being read outside and inside their community
contexts. The statements by Chao and Kamboureli emphasise the importance
of claiming space in national cultural spheres while not conglomerating
communities or expecting a single representative voice.

Most examples of Asian-Australian or Asian-Canadian literature reveal
marked resistance to a singular ethnic identity, directly opposing official
formations of 'ethnic communities' as homogeneous units that can be
approached for a group viewpoint or reaction. The current boom in Asian-

Canadian publishing and writing is, according to Chao, a result of collective efforts by the Asian-Canadian community to establish a literary presence and "to transform the historical silence of the community into a voice of resistance" ("Anthologizing" 148). The 'silence' in publications has possibly been a result more of neglect and systemic devaluation of these kinds of text rather than a lack of voice or dearth of people writing about it. That said, the community basis of ethnic groups should be invoked strategically and with consciousness of possible generalisations. As demonstrated by various Asian-American instances including the Asian-American Writers' Workshop, the political powers of coalitions between Asian groups are effective for pooling publishing experience and gaining political momentum.

The ACWW and its anthologies illustrate this point well. Chao, as mentioned above, attributes the current 'boom' of Asian-Canadian writing and publishing to the collective efforts of the ACWW, and the selection of anthologies as vehicles to promote 'generations' of Asian-Canadian writers ("Anthologizing" 147–8). Perhaps the most valuable facet of anthology publishing is the jostling of viewpoints and interpretations from various Asian-Canadian groups that would be more difficult to gain through single publications or isolated short stories in journals. Chao's work stresses the value of forming specific forums for Asian-Canadian literary work, as this then leads to 'springboards' for more serious consideration under 'national', 'Canadian' banners. Further, as Kamboureli argues, "by remapping the margins they have inhabited as the centres of their own cultural production, they realign the blueprint of power relations" ("Canadian Ethnic" 16). Many of the authors who were published in these early anthologies went on to publish novels and books of poetry. One of the largest changes since the publication of these two anthologies is the number of 'other' Asian groups of authors who are publishing works of contemporary Canadian literature — Korean, Filipino, Vietnamese, and Singaporean just to name a few. These 'newer' writers are making their presence felt as part of the dynamic Asian-Canadian literary community.

The ACWW had a reputation for fostering the work of new or 'emerging' authors, providing resources and other types of support including grant application information. This kind of facilitation in gaining the material means to finish or focus on literary work allows the establishment of a wide cross-section of 'first-time' writers from different cultural groups and generations. When this is considered alongside readings at festivals or writers' conferences, further publications, and the critical work that ensues, Asian-Canadian literature becomes a distinct and energetic discipline.

The growth of the Asian-Canadian profile has not only been in publication and attendant book launches or reviews but also in Asian-Canadian literature as an area of critical study and scholarship. The number of conferences which have dedicated panels to interrogating the terms of Asian-Canadian literary and cultural studies signal a marked move away from umbrella 'multicultural' events to more culturally and community specific foci. An example of this is the 1998 one-day conference held in late April at the University of British Columbia, "Diversity, Writing, and Social Critique: An Interactive Forum." Many, if not most, of the papers focused on Asian-Canadian issues, also emphasising North American Asian writing in general. The context of the papers was specifically Asian-Canadian but bridged historical and contemporary perspectives. The ability to focus specifically on the contemporary literary issues facing Asian-Canadian writers advances research beyond merely justifying the area of study.

As well as these public forums for discussion, several literary journals have published special issues which focus on Asian-Canadian literary criticism and fiction,[9] including the Vancouver-based journal *West Coast Line* which published a special issue on East Asian literature and which has consistently featured Asian-Canadian criticism, creative fiction, and artwork. For example, Issue 30.3 highlights the symposium (held in Vancouver) addressing the transfer of Hong Kong to China, focusing on diasporic concerns for immigrants and those staying behind in Hong Kong itself. The symposium included academics from Canada and the United States and was particularly pertinent for Vancouver, which has a high number of recent Hong Kong immigrants. Issue 31.2 of *West Coast Line* includes an Asian Heritage Month 'sampler', tying the publication together with the literary events at this annual cultural festival. These crossovers between academia and creative or activist performances nurture the area of Asian-Canadian studies by introducing and maintaining dialogue among artists, academics, community workers, and others. Furthermore, in a focused academic work, Chao published the first extended critical monograph about Chinese-Canadian literature in 1998, *Beyond Silence: Chinese Canadian Literature in English*. Her work concentrates on the historical contextualisation of Chinese communities in Canada and the significance of racist discourses and discriminatory structures on their contemporary fiction. The area of literary criticism develops extended analyses of racial representation and the politics of Asian-Canadian identity, the complicated functions of 'creativity' in multicultural work, and the erosion of any set assumptions regarding Asian-Canadianness. On the one hand, this ongoing agitation and reformation of Asian-Canadian subjectivity weakens the political impetus of claiming a particular minority identity while, on the other, it strengthens group power because it then represents communities more equitably. This somewhat contradictory balance is a necessary one which needs to exist in order to maintain interrogative energy.

The Asian-Canadian literary situation is not without complications and problems, of course, and has a continuing if not growing need for anti-racist and anti-essentialist strategies to remain active in the face of increasingly conservative politics and the backlash against support for racial minority initiatives in Canada. The fickleness of politics in supporting multicultural or diversity issues means that groups cannot remain complacent that existing grants or projects will endure.

For the moment, Asian-Canadian literary studies is a developing and vital field. The well-publicised launch of Kerri Sakamoto's first novel, *The Electrical Field*, took place in May 1998. Press coverage of the novel, brought out in Canada by major United States publisher Knopf, was intense. It won the Commonwealth Prize for Best First Novel (Canadian and Caribbean regions), the Canada-Japan award, and was shortlisted for half a dozen other prizes. Reviewers wrote enthusiastic reviews praising the novel as "sure-footed and sophisticated" (Govier D10), and it was noted that the novel had "international interest" and created "a buzz before [it] was even published at home" (Turbide and Bemrose 74). Sakamoto is kept busy on both the literary and academic talk circuits and will publish her second novel, *One Hundred Million Hearts,* in August 2003. If the progress of *The Electrical Field* is any indication, perhaps Asian-Canadian literature can look forward to quite a few more years on the 'menu' to consolidate its position within Canadian literary studies.

Japanese-Canadian author Hiromi Goto predicts that the present predilection for racial minority texts is a passing one, and that once multiculturalism and a "quick taste of the 'other'" becomes less popular, authors of colour will go back to struggling for publication and funding for their work while publishers will return to what are 'safe' texts to sell: "a little exotic fare, then back to the good old meat and potatoes" (Interview 3). The often sensationalist approaches to novels, and especially autobiographies, by more mainstream reviewers justify Goto's wariness of the ephemeral nature of mass media 'interest' in Asian-Canadian writing. The current sentiment that there are 'too many' autobiographies by Chinese women on the market is an example of the generalisations to which these texts are subject. While this interest may be short-lived, it does not mean that the gains for the field made in that time cannot benefit future Asian-

Canadian creative work. Richard Fung asserts a similar point to Goto's: "[t]he problem with race as a special event is that like all specials — lunch special, special of the day, flavour of the month — they are, by definition, not the staple, not the norm. On the other hand, without such events, the issue may never be raised at all" ("Conference" 38). This latter point of creating a starting point, and building on it, is crucial to this current stage of Asian-Canadian literature. The alleged 'boom' in publishing and writing can only improve the standing of the field in the larger arena of Canadian literature.

Whereas Chapter 1 delineates the difficulties for, and growth of, Asian-Australian activism and development, this chapter outlines the slightly more optimistic situation in Canada. Successive decades of multicultural policy and a dynamic Asian-American studies discipline across the border have produced a distinctive climate for Asian-Canadian studies. This encompasses not only publication but also readings, links with critical scholars working on this field of literature, and broader avenues for funding these initiatives. The empowerment of communities and individuals through this raised awareness and engagement ushers in further critical work and flags an energetic phase for Asian-Canadian studies.

3

Colouring In: Possibilities of Nationalism in Diaspora

Third Worlds have appeared in the First World and First Worlds in the Third. New diasporas have relocated the Self there and Other here, and consequently borders and boundaries have been confounded. . . . the flow of culture has been at once homogenizing and heterogenizing.

(Arif Dirlik, "The Postcolonial Aura" 352–3)

For me, Utopia is a place where as a member of a visible minority, I'll be neither singled out nor ignored.

(Kerri Sakamoto, "The Perfect Place" 1)

From historical to contemporary times, representations of Australian and Canadian citizens or national 'bodies' in literature are indelibly white and generally male: variations on the figures of 'tamers of wild frontiers'. These traditional images disavow and disallow Asian faces and bodies in national semiotic representations. If Asian characters are included, they are mostly in the form of ridiculed bit-players or as maligned figures.[1] Thus, historically entrenched constructions of a Western (white) citizenry in opposition with its threatening, most often coloured, Others, complicates an Asian person's configuration as a citizen in Australia or Canada. The 'Utopian' space desired by Sakamoto in the epigraph to this chapter is apparently not yet viable. This primacy of race as a point of irreconcilable difference and socio-cultural erosion or explosion informs readings of foundation narratives in this chapter's interrogation of various texts.

Australia and Canada have recognised Asians as citizens for only a short span of each nation's history. In Australia, the Commonwealth refused to naturalise Chinese until 1956. In Canada, Japanese-Canadians did not gain full voting rights till 1949, and the government did not give the franchise to Chinese-Canadians till 1947. Prior to this, individuals and communities of East Asian descent were variously controlled, rejected, and deemed unsuitable to be members of the majority Christian, White nations. Much more than being merely undesirable, East Asian people were epitomised as the perpetual Other in Australia and Canada. However, this did not mean consistently negative representation. For example, Cho finds that Chinese workers were viewed by some as perfect labourers whose cheapness and docility made them essential to 'young' Canada's plans for expansion and growth ("Rereading" 68), and David Walker notes that Australians often feared Asians for their 'positive' (racial) traits as much as for their more rabidly publicised negative ones.[2] Negative representations of Asians emphasised the potential corrupting and infecting qualities of the Asian races, and versions of this xenophobic rhetoric continue to surface in contemporary discourses surrounding immigration and welfare issues.[3]

To be granted citizenship legally by a nation's government is one matter. To be recognised by general society as a citizen, with attendant rights and opportunities, is another. The conventional meanings of citizenship evolve and alternate between two main perspectives. Gilles Paquet details that "one emphasizes a conception of citizenship as a status and is couched in a language of entitlements; the other emphasizes citizenship as practice and gives rise to a language of duties" (71). Ideally, it includes the right of political freedom to protest, vote, and be affiliated with national bodies.

A growing number of critics address the complicated issue of diasporic identity formation, affiliation, or, more precisely, what states of 'diaspora' mean for Asian-Australians and Asian-Canadians within particular national contexts. The invocation of 'confounded boundaries' by Dirlik in the first epigraph to this chapter aptly describes the situation of Asian communities in Western nations, and boundary studies has become a fertile and dynamic research area. How these issues manifest themselves in the production of, and reading strategies for, creative arts such as literature, however, is relatively new and under-researched.

Critics such as Aihwa Ong describe an emergent "multipolar world" (*Flexible* 29) of transnational trajectories where Western discourses should not influence non-European communities as in the past. She clarifies that her work is interested in "how the privileged half lives, exercises, and reproduces its domination" (30). Ong's work does bring valuable insight to the situation of certain class fractions and their activities. I would argue, however, that Ien Ang's ideas of "together-in-difference" (vs. "sameness-in-dispersal") brings a broad, functional materiality to discussions about diasporic Asian groups in Canada and Australia (*On Not Speaking*, Conclusion). Though Ang's arguments are self-avowedly urban-centric, these are arguably the spaces in which literatures are usually circulated, consumed, and critiqued.

Sanctioned attributes of 'good' and 'bad' citizens trouble the placement of hyphenated Asian citizens in Australia and Canada. Behaviours of 'bad' citizens could include protest and activism. Most established communities view these as extreme forms of civic participation, especially ill-suited to those who are persistently cast as 'Model Minority' citizens. Politicisation is a traditionally dangerous path for immigrants, because legislation regarding residency status in Canada and Australia often included clear stipulations about 'neutral' political records. That is, the desirable immigrant has no history of protest or arrest, and while awaiting permanent residency or citizenship papers, he or she could be deported for participating in workers' protests or rallies (Jamrozik, Boland, and Urquhart 92). This was particularly pertinent for non-white workers in Australia, since national unions were notorious for deliberately keeping competition away from their (white) workers: "[o]ne of the main motivating forces for the formation of Australian unions was to keep the Chinese and other groups, such as Aborigines and Kanakas, out of jobs such as shearing or wharf labouring" (Giese, *Astronauts* 78). Under restrictive conditions of forced, prolonged detention, asylum-seekers in various countries, including Australia and Canada, have protested through riots, acts of self-harm, and appeals to national media. The assumed desirable qualities for assimilating quietly are subverted, to a certain extent, by these situations in which 'boat-people' have started demanding basic health and housing needs while awaiting consideration in detention camps or other quarantine zones. The holding of refugees is almost always cast in disease/infection rhetoric, hence the use of the term 'quarantine' to signify attempts by Australia to inoculate itself from potential pathogens. In a Filipino holding camp at Bataan, one interviewee observed that the in-between-nation status, complicated by the 'Amerasian Homecoming Act' of 1987,[4] left them unable to continue with life while there is no progress in their applications to stay: "it's a problem, this real suffering in a not-real world" (Gourevitch 56). Moreover, Australian critic Brett Neilson asserts that the refugees are "commodities traded for political ends in Australia's cultural and economic relations with 'Asia'" (22).[5] Trapped indefinitely in 'holding' camps, their lives become static and the society outside more inaccessible: Being in-between nations has meant acquiring in-between lives.

As Paquet delineates above, concepts of citizenship always negotiate several levels of belonging at once, of "complex multiple rootedness" (Radhakrishnan n.p.). Asian-American theorist Lisa Lowe further specifies that a citizen inhabits "the political space of the nation, a space that is, at once, juridically legislated, territorially situated, and socially embodied" (2), but being an immigrant or visibly different can immediately displace a person from accepted national narratives. She argues that "the contradictions through which immigration brings national institutions into crisis produces immigrant cultures as oppositional and contestatory, and these contradictions critically politicized in cultural forms and practices can be utilized in the formation of alternative social practices" (172). More distracted and often divided versions of subjectivity, then, signify contemporary formations for diasporic citizens. Lowe does not posit an always positive perspective on this distracted subject but does contend that the ongoing dynamic between definitions of self and society is where "alternative social practices" emerge.

This chapter examines the framing of citizenship and national belonging in Asian-Canadian and Asian-Australian literature and investigates how Lowe's 'alternative social practices' manifest themselves in representations of racial minority citizens within majority white populations. The analyses demonstrate the possibilities of transforming social perceptions between these groups, within their literatures, and how these alternative social practices erode exclusionary categories of history and national belonging.

Literary Activism and the Internment Experience

This first subsection interrogates discourses of nationalism and citizenship through fiction that elucidates Japanese-Canadian perspectives on wartime displacement and discrimination. Joy Kogawa's *Obasan* and Kerri Sakamoto's *The Electrical Field* create a rich dialogue with and around the issues of the long-term social and political effects of internment within Canada. The analysis focuses in particular on interventions by Japanese-Canadians in the creation and maintenance of national identities and civic roles. The importance of Kogawa's book in Canadian cultural history foregrounds the potential radical place for literature in shifting perceived figurations of citizen, nation, and history. Reading Kogawa alongside Kerri Sakamoto's 1998 debut novel extends constructively the complicated and sometimes contradictory processes of national belonging and mediating life after internment.

Obasan enjoys the kind of canonical status which undermines rigid classifications of what is national or multicultural literature, classifications which are usually considered mutually exclusive. The novel also broaches broader issues associated with the institutionalisation of literature. Kogawa's novel, first published in 1981, delves into the then unacknowledged past of Japanese-Canadian communities, exposing elided histories of internment and intense discrimination during the Second World War. Roy Miki states that Kogawa is "one of the first [Japanese-Canadian] writers to name victimization" (*Broken Entries* 32). The ensuing critical and social discussion has reached considerable volume and profile. Much of the writing dissects the representations (literary and otherwise) and consequences of internment, discussing what loyalty, citizenship, and community could mean in Canada. *Obasan's* enduring prominence and its positioning on secondary and tertiary educational curricula assures the dissemination of this particular Japanese-Canadian voice and experience, presenting a narrative which gives depth to, and differs from, mainstream versions of Canadian history. This insertion into the canon can also be read as an attempt to provide a resolution and an 'ending' for Canada's racist past in its 'multicultural' present,[6] a "necessary hermeneutic operation" (Palumbo-Liu, "Introduction" 2) which has been discussed by Beauregard and Miki, among others.

Sakamoto's novel is set in 1970s, pre-Redress Canada. The focus on stifled emotion and the shame of being societal outcasts is the prime force in the characters' lives, complementing the more overt political edge of Kogawa's text. It is precisely the trope of leading in-between lives within the boundaries of one's own country, where one is supposedly a citizen, that East Asian Canadian history steadfastly transforms versions of contemporary Canadian literature and society. *Obasan* is a work of fiction which engages directly with the political implications and negotiations of Japanese-Canadian citizenship. In comparing Kogawa with Mena Abdullah, an Indian-Australian author, Diana Brydon argues that:

> Although neither [Kogawa or Abdullah] is migrant . . . neither is fully accorded native-born status. Ironically, despite their racial classification as 'visible' minorities, their non-European cultural origins have combined with their non-immigrant status to make native-born Asians peculiarly invisible, even in the field of ethnic studies (94).

While Brydon's observations may have been true once, conditions in Canada for ethnic studies and multicultural literature have changed to such an extent that Kogawa is arguably the most high-profile Canadian writer of Asian descent in the ever-diversifying category of Canadian literature. Her novel is especially difficult to cordon off in multicultural literature as it is understood in the more traditional sense, because of the book's direct address to ruptured forms of 'Canadianness' in the national context and the way in which this is intertwined with the accepted war histories of Canada.

The concentration of Asian-American scholars addressing Japanese-American internment and redress is much higher than the numbers found in Canada, and the range of literary representations of this period also reflect this disparity. In 1995, Korean-American critic Elaine H. Kim admonished Asian-American writers and critics to move "beyond railroads and internment camps" (18). Although Kim's call might be a little premature, considering the general ignorance of these facts about North American history, her aim of creating, as opposed to only restating, the present is a cogent one. Kim's preference for actions beyond reactive politics heralded a confidence in the stage of awareness reached in rewriting American history. For Canada, these rewritings are relatively recent phenomena and certainly would not be considered prevalent.

The vehicle of Kogawa's distinction is an exposing narrative about the injustice of Japanese-Canadian internment during the Second World War, 'authorised' by quotations throughout from official Canadian government documents and edicts. These set her literary text directly in the domain of political activism and protest. The novel was published before any substantial recognition of the Japanese-Canadian internment issue, and Kogawa's direct participation in the subsequent Redress movement serves to underscore her active political engagement with these issues. Teruyo Ueki contends that reading *Obasan* "evokes a political consciousness among its readers, leading them to active involvement in social reformation" (3). This 'real-world' effect of a literary text is further supported by Arnold Davidson who states that Kogawa was "'instrumental in influencing the Canadian Government's 1988 settlement with Japanese-Canadians for their loss of liberty and property in Canada during World War II'" and describes how parts of *Obasan* were read out in the House of Commons during redress announcements (14). The historical internment of Japanese-Canadian citizens during the Second World War emphasises the provisional citizenship rights of Asian-Canadians: "[t]he abrogation of citizenship and the subsequent degradation of subjectivity would have devastating effects on a community that had already suffered some fifty years of racism and exclusionist policies on the West Coast" (Miki, "Asiancy" 140). The complex body of literary criticism alternates between close textual readings of *Obasan* as rhetorical achievement, and the co-optation of the novel as an overtly political and revolutionary specimen.

The Nakanes and the Katos embody the hyphenated doubleness of Japanese-Canadian identity, the 'not-quiteness' that affects racially different citizens of majority white societies. Kogawa makes reference to the white privilege of 'belonging' in Canada through her Japanese-Canadian characters who are faced with questions like 'where do you come from?' or 'where did you learn to speak English?' Naomi observes that it is "[t]hese icebreaker questions that create awareness of ice" (225), marking out Asian citizens in Canada while re-establishing the right of belonging and the hegemonic power of Anglo-European citizens. Silence permeates the lives of the Nakane children, surrounded as they are with the 'old' ways of Uncle and Obasan and the refrain of *kodomo no tame* ('for the sake of the children'). The encounter with the visiting Barkers just after the death of Uncle epitomises this ingrained discomfort with undefined, unspoken difference (222–6).

Fearing these 'enemy aliens' in their midst, the Canadian government relocated whole communities of Japanese citizens to remote camps, also confiscating their material possessions. A similar campaign of forced removal occurred in the United States and, on a smaller scale, in Australia. Kogawa's novel traces the Nakane family's experiences of the steady banishment of whole communities through bureaucratic and military channels. The Canadian government made exiles of the Japanese-Canadians in their own country, as many of them were born and raised in Canada. The government shifted them to the rural margins, particularly in British Columbia and Alberta, effacing them from urban spaces and networks while making the 'wilds' of the interior a zone of ostracism and regulation. As Aunt Emily states, "the message to disappear worked its way deep into the Nisei heart" (184). Karen Quimby argues that Kogawa's novel attempts to reclaim the erased sites of Japanese-Canadian national spaces by emphasising the closeness to landscape of the protagonists, with the 'book-ended' introduction and conclusion of Naomi on the coulee. She points to the double dismissal of Japanese-Canadians from the Canadian socio-scape, stating:

> The Nakane family's exile to Slocan, a former ghost town in the Canadian Interior, implies the recurring theme of erasure not only by the idea of inhabiting a ghost town but by the erasure Naomi discovers when she returns to Slocan twenty years later and finds that "Not a mark was left. All our huts had been removed long before and the forest had returned to take over the clearings" (265).

After the war was over, another solution for Canada appeared to be trying to send as many Japanese as possible 'back home', while those who wanted to stay continued to be treated like criminals on probation and liable to restrictions on their personal and professional freedom.

The novel deliberately makes visible many racial and justice issues and, from an early stage in 'writing in' this part of Canadian history, offered a range of Japanese-Canadian voices. The main characters of the novel — Obasan, Uncle, and Naomi — surround themselves in numb, constant secrecy to try and negate the effects of past persecution. Uncle's consistent baking of the overcooked, black 'stone bread' metaphorises this attitude.[7] The exception to this silence was Aunt Emily, who became a crusader for Redress, as "[f]or her, the injustice done to us in the past was still a live issue" (34). The calls for redress after the Second World War initiated growth in Asian-Canadian activism and the community's social profile, energising the reaffirmation of civil rights at the heart of their compromised citizenship. While some members of the Japanese-Canadian community lobbied for compensation, some remained caught in the trap of self-effacement, of proving they were worthy citizens. Obasan and Aunt Emily represent the two extremes of negotiating postwar figurations of belonging as citizens in Kogawa's novel: "[o]ne lives in sound, the other in stone. Obasan's language remains deeply underground but Aunt Emily, BA, MA, is a word warrior" (32). Growing up through their teens in the internment camps, Naomi and her brother, Stephen, are 'Canadian-ised' to the extent that they find their family's cultural habits odd or distasteful.[8] This is truer of Stephen than Naomi, as he escapes the bounded community for an international, 'borderless' profession — a musician who plays concerts in Europe. On visits home to Uncle and Obasan, Stephen "is always uncomfortable when anything is 'too Japanese'" (217). The invasion of Aunt Emily's activist rhetoric into the quiet space of denial at the Nakane household initially fosters bitterness more than interest from Naomi. Naomi's gradual adoption of changed perspectives on internment and redress, however, symbolises the struggle Audrey Kobayashi identifies for Japanese-Canadians "to shed a sense of themselves as marginalized, that is, a sense of their racial inferiority, if they were to assert their legitimacy" (3). Naomi describes the initial resentment she felt when Aunt Emily seemed to be continually raking up the past:

> She's the one with the vision. She believes in the Nisei, seeing them as networks and streamers of light dotting the country. For my part, I can only see a dark field with Aunt Emily beaming her flashlight to where the rest of us crouch and hide, our eyes downcast as we seek the safety of invisibility (31).

Replaced by a growing awareness of the meanings of injustice and the need to find more answers, she figuratively dons her activist aunt's coat (246–7) at the end of the novel. A. Lynne Magnusson reads this as "an acceptance of her aunt's world" (66), and Ueki takes this further by stating that Naomi now has "new determination to don the language of Aunt Emily, to commit herself to transmitting the legacy of history" (10). The appearance of *Itsuka* (1991) several years after *Obasan*'s publication confirms Naomi's future as one in which she takes up Emily's mantle.

The end of *Obasan* reveals the experiences of Grandmother and Mother while in Nagasaki at the close of the war. Kogawa further stretches and subverts the demarcation between enemy and citizen by bringing closer the tragedies that befell Japanese civilians during the American B-52 bombing raids and the subsequent atomic bombings of Hiroshima and Nagasaki. The character of Mother is absent and considered by some as only an allegorical figure (Gottlieb 38). However, even considering this distancing of the Mother character and the time that has elapsed since the letters were written, the 'closeness' of the suffering to sites in Canada and to our protagonist, Naomi, still lend the revelations impetus. The personalised version of the aftermath provided by the grandmother's letters counter what Peter Schwenger calls the "Disneyfication" after the war of the American bombings. Schwenger argues that the need for Americans to turn the bombings into "an exercise in special effects" (326) has its "psychological uses; for any spectacle implies spectatorship and therefore distance from what becomes a sublime drama, removed not only from reality but also from responsibility" (327–8). In representing America's actions as part of a dramatic narrative, the devastating results are easier to discount. The symbolism of opening the cardboard folder of letters from Grandmother, and thereupon learning the secrets that had been kept from Naomi and Stephen for decades, indicates the subsequent 'opening' of the internment issue and the agitation for redress within Canada itself. The novel leaves us at this point, one that gestures to a recovery of sorts for Naomi now that her past is exposed, and for the Japanese-Canadian communities once they break their silence about that period of history and rediscover a sense of civic belonging that was usurped by internment. This partial healing and recognition, however, is by no means the 'end' of the issues Kogawa broaches: structural discrimination in Canada and the ongoing racialisation of Asian-Canadian groups and individuals.

In turning now to Kerri Sakamoto's 1998 novel, *The Electrical Field*, I want to position it as complementary to *Obasan* and discuss how it presents, in substantial depth, the psychological implications of internment for

Japanese-Canadian citizens. *The Electrical Field* initially caused a stir in Canadian literary circles because it was listed with a major German firm, List Verlag, even before it found English language distribution (Turbide and Bemrose 74). Publishing houses in the United States, Britain, Holland, and Canada quickly added the novel to their lists. Having such a successful first novel is noteworthy enough, but what Sakamoto chose to write about in post-Redress, 1990s Canada, deserves closer examination. Beauregard describes the novel as having a "quiet tone – along with its jagged undercurrents" ("Unsettled" 191). Indeed, Sakamoto moves the effects of civic and social marginalisation on Japanese-Canadian psyches centre stage in her novel, offering readers a study in limitation and blame through her muted, sparse prose.

In *The Electrical Field*, she focuses on a small community in 1970s Canada, before the Redress movement had significant momentum in Canada or the United States, before internment was written into Canadian history. The socially stunted characters populate houses that face each other across the electrical field, testifying to the lingering effects of incarceration and displacement decades after they were 'liberated' from the internment camps. Aside from the physical and social uprooting, the postwar period meant negotiating the impoverishment brought on by government confiscation of most Japanese-Canadian assets during the war and the inadequate compensation for these once people were allowed out of the camps. Addressing the political implications of internment in Canada obliquely through the character of Yano, Sakamoto does not produce a text as overtly politicised as Kogawa's *Obasan*. Instead, *The Electrical Field* furnishes details of the social and psychological costs involved in the process of recovery: Asako Saito's deliberately muted life and how she fights to retain control of her environment, her brother Stum's limited opportunities and dependency, Yano's futile activist meetings and deep-seated unresolved anger, and the impetus for the novel, Chisako Yano's escape from a family and life she does not want anymore. The central narrative in *The Electrical Field* involves the murder of Chisako and her lover, Mr Spears. This mystery is solved almost at the beginning, but Sakamoto draws out the ways in which the main characters, Asako and Sachi Nakamura, are implicated on various levels in the 'crime of passion'.

I want to concentrate primarily on Asako and the thin line of sanity she treads. For her, it is not so much the social outcast positioning from which she shies away, but the demands of a continuing life, one that insists she move on from her memories and take on new experiences. The neighbourhood of *The Electrical Field*, huddled at the base of ironically named Mackenzie Hill,[9] conveys the impression of stalled, decaying, and socially isolated Japanese-Canadian families. Viewed through Asako's eyes, the community surrounding them is peopled only by occasional alien *hakujin* and the other two *nihonjin* families that she observes across the empty electrical field and through whom she has her limited contact with the rest of the world: the Yanos and the Nakamuras. Her social environment is confined to these families and their habits, as her confusion and asocial behaviour at Detective Rossi's or Angel's presence reveals. Even so, the interactions between Asako and other characters in the novel are always difficult and embedded with her anxieties and memories. At one stage, when Sachi is in her bedroom, Asako views the space through an outsider's eyes and acknowledges "the dowdiness of [the] room, smelling the musty lifelessness, the meagre stillness" (78). However, she is also the one who works all day to keep anything from changing. The Saito household exists in a closeted, almost fossilised, space where stimulus and differences in routine are filtered out deliberately. This is quite literal for Asako's father, because he is bedridden after a stroke and needs all-day care, but Asako, who does not have any significant friendships in her life besides the somewhat ambiguous ones with Chisako and Sachi, has seemingly mapped out her own isolation. She tries to forget the past and the artificiality of internment but, because she closely associates that period of the last days with her dead eldest brother Eiji, she is "ravaged by memory" (Turbide and Bemrose 74). Her need to hold on to him compounds her paralysis in life and stalls her abilities (or inclinations) to build any sense of her self except through others and a numbing routine which she alternately hates and cherishes.

The tension in her personal sense of shame and self-blame for Eiji's sickness and death, Chisako's murder, and for Yano's murder-suicide, is linked with an equally disturbed Japanese-Canadian community that persists in believing that it is "dirty, bad and possibly even evil" (Govier D10). The laying of blame for the murders and, in turn, for the dislocation of Japanese-Canadians is made more complex and difficult because of "a belief in [Asako's and others'] culpability for the events" (Govier D18). An extreme interiority inflects her opinions about people and situations, a predicament which leaves her frustratedly not-knowing about (or not admitting) instances like Stum's new girlfriend Angel, his nascent 'friendship' with Yano, or her own feelings for Yano which Chisako airs in conversation. Sakamoto subtly exposes the biases in Asako's perspective through descriptions of Yano. From the beginning, where she notes that: "[h]is hair was more unkempt than when I'd seen him that morning, and he was perspiring, as usual. . . . A scent filled my nostrils; it was a mingling of Yano's pungent body odour and the not-unfamiliar smell of fried fish and daikon" (114), to later in the novel when she has formed an odd, never fully explained attachment to him: "[h]e was not so ugly to me that day. He wore fresh, clean clothes; even his fingernails, habitually long and dirty, had been clipped. He was a different person. Almost handsome" (256). The contrast is significant enough for readers to begin doubting the verity of Asako's narration by the end of the novel, drawing readers into the issues surrounding what is the 'truth' and a wariness about whose perspective is being revealed to them at any one time, especially when the protagonist keeps information from the reader for most of the novel.

Asako dwells on lost opportunities and the contemplation of a life in which things all went wrong, caught on the enduring hook of internment and its consequences. Her need to blame herself for Eiji's sickness and death keeps her resistant to Yano's desperation for support in his agitation for redress. She dissociates herself from what she assesses are social risks, much like Naomi hiding from the political possibilities of Aunt Emily's 'flashlight'. Asako waits and watches others, never initiating contact, traits which align her with the 'Model Minority' behaviour of many in the community who do not want to give the government any opportunity to single them out again. At the end of *The Electrical Field*, however, which Katherine Govier chooses to read as optimistic, Asako makes an unguarded joke with Stum and Angel: "[t]hey both laughed at that, at the little joke I'd made. On a whim, without pausing to ponder how funny my remark might be, to wonder if I'd make a fool of myself" (305). But the fact that Stum and Angel went on laughing "a little too long" (305) gestures to the enduring social discomfiture that she causes in others and in herself. In another bizarre social relationship, Asako's 'friendship' with Sachi consists of Asako trying desperately to know all of Sachi's activities and to control her. She was supposedly trying to care for Sachi when the girl's parents did not understand her. In the end, the odd and inconsistent behaviours of Sachi contrast too sharply with Asako's fossilised routine, pushing her to the limits of tolerance and sanity. Because of this, the diminishing of her obsession with Sachi at the end of the novel is perhaps a more promising sign than Stum's imminent 'escape' with Angel from the old farmhouse near the electrical field.

Kogawa's and Sakamoto's novels broaden the range of narratives about various 'bad' Asian-Canadian citizens. They conjure voices for those who participated in grounding themselves within Canada's citizenry and protesting their wartime displacement. The Redress movement turned accusations back upon the Canadian government and legislators who participated in exiling them and who oversaw the confiscation of their property. Japanese-Canadians used the same system which alienated them to absolve their communities. Yano's attempts to stir up a Redress movement are all the more poignant because the movement does eventually happen but, in so many ways, too late for the Yanos and the other families in the shadow of Mackenzie Hill. Referring to the redress moment when Prime Minister Brian Mulroney received a standing ovation, Cho argues that "[i]n a moment when the Canadian state publicly acknowledged its racism, it also achieved a moment of political solidarity" ("Rereading" 79). The eclipse of Japanese-Canadians in a moment which was meant to be for and about them[10] underscores the importance of vigilance when it comes to gauging the purposes to which this kind of acknowledgement is put. 'Internment' fiction is not a neatly presented package of Canada's history but examples of complex and durable racist processes that are still a part of contemporary society.

Chinese-Australian National Inscriptions

This second section shifts from fictionalised moments of erased history to the general absence of Asian-Australians in Australian history thus far. Their virtual invisibility as participating members of foundational narratives means that Chinese-Australians are more easily cast as non-citizens and 'Othered'. Diana Giese's oral history books, *Beyond Chinatown* and *Astronauts, Lost Souls and Dragons*, could be said to function in similar modes to Kogawa's text. Giese's work sites Chinese citizens within Australian historical landscapes through their physical presence and cultural influences. Given the genre, the primary text of interviews usually carries a higher load of authenticity and supposedly offers a direct 'voicing' of Chinese-Australian experience. Giese's creation of relatively new historical links between Australian nationhood and its Asian citizens are further strengthened by the narrative representations of Asians in pioneering, rural communities. These readings interrogate the category of 'Chinese-Australians' as presented by the structure and content of Giese's collections. The ways the participants present themselves in the books are a telling indication of how they want their communities and families to be perceived in Australia. Focusing as much on what has been excluded from their narratives as what has been included is valuable for assessing the politics of Chinese community in Australia. Giese's books are among the first to give voice to Chinese-Australians, differing from the other historical and demographic work that precedes them.

The 'in-between' status of Japanese-Canadians pre- and post-internment contrasts with the contemporary 'in-betweenness' of immigrant 'astronauts' from Taiwan and Hong Kong in Australia and Canada. Focusing in particular on Australia, Giese's oral history/interview books script Chinese-Australian narratives into Australia's historical foundations. Citizenship is depicted most often as a status to be earned, a status that is extended by the 'host' nation[11] on a conditional basis dependent upon continued good behaviour or adequate contribution to the surrounding society by the 'citizen' involved. Critics of the text should consider the deliberate 'face' shown in these representations of history and, in particular, what is not included.

Ang describes diaspora as "transnational, spatially and temporally sprawling sociocultural formations of people, creating imagined communities whose blurred and fluctuating boundaries are sustained by real and/or symbolic ties to some original 'homeland'" ("Migrations" 6). Especially for hyphenated Asian citizens in Australia and Canada, the economic configuration of the 'Asia-Pacific Rim' constructs their positioning in the West as usefully linked to 'homelands' as networks of capital. In some instances, the cultivated economic ties have meant that communities maintain familiar contact with others in Asian countries. This situation becomes one which disputes, to some degree, Vijay Mishra's contention that "one of the overriding characteristics of diasporas is that diasporas do not . . . return" ("New Lamps" 75). As these international relations receive more attention, others in diasporic Asian groups within Australia or Canada find it even more difficult to establish their particular nationally based identities. Within Giese's texts, these diasporic linkages are further strengthened by Chinese-Australian community trips 'home' and an ongoing, somewhat skewed dialogue with the 'Chinese' side of the hyphenation.

In the reworkings and recoveries of oral or archival history that have been performed in the past decade, evidence is overwhelming that Chinese-Australians were forced into much lower status jobs and faced discrimination in the workplace, with government and bank dealings, and in education. The citizenship of Chinese-Australians, then, is demonstrably not a 'natural' (white) right. The greater project at hand of recovering the dismissed and erased history of Chinese-Australians is, as Giese stresses, "a re-humanising one" (*Astronauts* 291). In particular for Giese's project, it is a process through which Chinese have shifted "[f]rom being perceived as sojourners whose allegiance was to other people" to "a picture of good Australian citizens who built up this country" (*Beyond* 39). Most of the successful families portrayed in *Astronauts* have made stereotypical economic gains in Australia: owning property, becoming professionals, being in positions to contribute (money) to their surrounding Australian community. The questions and answers in the interviews emphasise the prerequisite for acceptance in Australia of being necessarily *good* citizens: not neutral, certainly not bad, but evidently and materially good. These repeatedly expressed and vehemently upheld values of a few speakers serve to propagate Asian immigrants' stereotyping as the 'Model Minority'. Thus, low levels of political or social protest and no complaints for unfair treatment can become proscriptive community 'values'. Shirley Tucker comments that *Astronauts* is "celebratory in style" and serves as a "soothing rejoinder to Sang Ye's prickles" (83). Tucker is referring here to Sang Ye's compilation of confrontational interviews, *The Year the Dragon Came* (1996). This is a collection that raises "parochial Australian anxiety levels" (83) and provides some uncomfortable moments when 'ungrateful' Chinese-Australians from a variety of homelands speak frankly about their reasons for being in Australia and the conditions under which they live.

The continued and often revitalised antagonism towards peoples of Chinese descent, and the social distancing which results, contributed to the historical formation of 'Chinatowns'. These sites formed initially to protect displaced 'sojourners'[12] and to provide an area to access familiar foods, social activities, and languages: a retreat from the discrimination and open hostility of many white communities. As well, the withdrawal of the Chinese population historically served a greater social good by allowing easy discernment of where 'the Chinese' were and where one could go to partake of Chinese culture and spectacle. Reflecting the middle-class aspirations of many Asian–Australians, however, these areas steadily become less and less 'authentic'. As the Chinese population gained assets and established itself in other arenas of community, they moved to the suburbs: The owners and operators of shops and services are rarely based in Chinatown itself these days.[13] *Beyond Chinatown* focuses specifically on the establishment and growth of Darwin's Chinatown and its associated Chinese community. This book and the later publication, *Astronauts*, is part of the larger Chinese-Australian oral history project undertaken by the National Library of Australia. *Beyond Chinatown* opens with a series of excerpts from European documents 'looking in' on Darwin's Chinatown. Giese chooses to juxtapose comments which 'rehumanised' the tightly-knit Chinese community from that period of history. One observation adds a novel twist to the usual comments about Europeans and Chinese: "In the light galvanised iron house sat Chinese families, men with wives and a flock of pretty little slant-eyed children. They were happy. They had religion, sympathy, and unity. But the Europeans of Palmerston had very often no home, only a house" (1). The comparison between the Chinese families' sense of belonging and those of the Europeans' contingent residence is striking. More often, representations are the other way around, the Chinese viewed as unnatural communities within Australia and Europeans as rightfully belonging.

Beyond Chinatown traces people's movements 'out' of Chinatown after the initial establishment of communities and building of city centres, following them into the many civic and political areas into which they have moved: "[Chinatown] existed for years: from the time 186 Chinese workers arrived in 1874 by ship from Singapore, right up until World War 2. Then it disappeared" (2). Significantly, however, this 'disappearance' was not the result of the process of assimilation into surrounding suburbs but because Army troops destroyed many parts of Darwin through "'looting, burning, and bulldozing'" (31). The rebuilding of postwar Darwin led to the 'Territorians' becoming a more consolidated community, and the scattering of Chinese-Australians after the complete destruction of Chinatown assisted in their later appearance in a wide range of professions and in positions on civic boards. Giese's study is similar to the establishment narratives of other immigrant groups but, at present, because Chinese-Australian perspectives are relatively unrecorded and hardly disseminated, it is a pioneering project. *Beyond Chinatown* functions on several levels, one of the most obvious being the inclusion of Asian-Australians into the historical landscape and shared national moments such as Darwin's battering during the Second World War and Cyclone Tracy in 1974. The subsequent cross-community efforts to help each other out and rebuild the city forged stronger public ties and diminished the boundaries between groups. It was also during these times of 'pulling together' that Darwin citizens' identifications entrenched the notion of being a 'Territorian' even further, particularly because of the conflict with the Northern Territory's administrator, Canberra. This process of becoming identified with what is threatened iterates the group dynamics of Asian-Australians in history and in present times.

While both *Beyond Chinatown* and *Astronauts* tell the previously untold story about establishment sites and communal dynamics, Giese acknowledges the problems associated with oral history memories which are self-censoring:

One informant may see another as exaggerating, over-colouring, sensationalising, their stories as scurrilous and subversive. Those who wish to talk of scandal or failure may be tactfully silenced, or discredited as rumour-mongers. . . . The community's licensed storytellers may close ranks against someone with another story to tell, a discordant one (*Beyond* 13).

In Australia, it is even more important to realise the limitations or bias of this 'good face' that communities try to show, because there is no body of 'Chinatown' literature to present different renditions of the sites, peoples, and relationships between them. The current range of historical resources and representations is somewhat narrow. This is changing slowly, as organisations such as the Chinese Heritage of Australian Federation (CHAF) project testify. The CHAF website offers searchable databases of historical civic and press documents and a growing archive of scanned materials.[14] On a comparative scale, Canada has an established and ever-growing list of this type of fiction and non-fiction,[15] as well as the beginnings of a complex core of Asian–Canadian social history and literary criticism.

In the past, and still today, the fulfilment of various voyeuristic desires for the exotic Eastern Other is embodied in these Chinatowns and their activities. Kay Anderson notes that "[f]rom the late nineteenth century until the present day, European groups . . . have held the power to define and fashion Chinatowns in ways that reveal more about themselves than the 'ethnic attributes' of the East" ("Otherness" 70). Much has been written about the imposition of state regulations and cultural restrictions on the populations of Chinatowns. There is an increasing amount of criticism surrounding the issue of agency in Chinese communities and a form of 'writing against the silence' apparently imposed by the focus on European structures of discrimination and exclusion. Wing Chung Ng writes that Anderson "conveniently finds [among the Chinese themselves] an absence of initiatives and conscious motivations, except for the internalization of imposed categories and exogenous characterizations, which shows their subjugation to a Western cultural hegemony" (6). While I would point out that Anderson does include consideration of the communities themselves, albeit in their complicity with 'self-orientalisation' ("Otherness"), Ng's emphasis on the active and resistant elements of Chinatown communities does offer new perspectives on 'familiar' material.

While in contemporary Canada and Australia the exchanges between Chinatowns and their surrounding communities are on a different scale from at the turn of the twentieth century, the popular imaginary which

'Chinatown' inhabits is still active. The contemporary political effect of having Chinatowns, towns within cities, is often to acknowledge a different culture on a folkloric (food and clothing) level, while eliding larger, difficult political or social questions like how racial minority communities address or experience racism and discrimination. However, especially in post-Hanson Australia, political motivations for identifying as Asian-Australian strengthen and revitalise community links, particularly when their validity is called into question.

So far in recording Asian-Australian history, discussion around the axes of gender and class is scant. Aside from *Survival and Celebration* (1986) by Morag Loh and Christine Ramsay, little research delves into the 'culture' of Asian women in colonial Australian spaces.[16] Short histories listed on the CHAF site document lives of specific women in early twentieth-century Australia (under the title of "Women and Families"). From these, an understanding of the women as socially and physically removed, often burdened with children, housework, and cultural expectations from their own and the white community begins to emerge. For the majority of the interviews in Giese's book, the interviewees hardly address, if not completely dismiss, gender issues in the close Chinese-Australian communities. In discussing these selective group 'values', Gillian Bottomley attributes the constant conservative portrayal of 'good' women in ethnic communities to "petit bourgeois dominance of ethnic organisations and 'community' representation" (*From Another Place* 161). She also states that maintaining social 'face' has "to do with the kind of 'fixing' of time that often occurs in migration, and with a desire to be respectable, in the absence of other forms of cultural and symbolic capital in a new and ethnocentric society" (162). Charles See Kee, a member of the Ethnic Community Council in Darwin for many years, emphasises this freezing of time and cultural mores. He arrived in Darwin from Shanghai in 1941. Giese details his first impressions as:

> The sophisticate from cosmopolitan Shanghai found the little bush town 'backward', its people ignorant. As a young man, a dandy, seeking refuge in Darwin with his black sheep brother, he remembers how appalled he was at the drab conformity of European Australia. Nor was he impressed by the Chinese community, by their apparently docile acceptance of second-class citizenship (*Beyond* 19).

See Kee's admonishing of the Darwin Chinese for their frozen ideas of 'Chineseness' highlights the complications in negotiating imagined and 'real' homelands for Australians from elsewhere. Near the end of *Astronauts*, when discussing the massive task of documenting whole scattered communities' oral history and the gender aspects that have not been addressed thus far, one of the interviewees declares flatly, "The wives didn't do anything." (254) The roles of Chinese women also received damning praise from Paul Campbell when he says "Maybe the wives didn't do anything special or significant", but he still believed that it is valuable to document "ordinary lives" (254). Although the women's movement over the past few decades has accelerated the breakdown of public/private spheres and emphasised the valuation of domestic labour as a form of 'work' (albeit one without much political cachet), Giese's respondents made no reference to the domestic work, certain isolation, and the ostracisation of Chinese women running households in these often small, industry-based towns. While male Chinese were viewed as threats to the Australian way of life (and by extension its white women),[17] female Chinese are almost invisible in versions of history thus far. A further distinction would be that female Chinese within traditional family structures whose roles were wives, mothers, sisters, daughters, are the truly invisible ones. Australian historian Ray Evans and scholar in Japanese-Australian studies Yuriko Nagata have written about Asian women in the sex industry of colonial Australia. Both researchers have discussed the establishment of brothels serviced by 'imported' Japanese women in towns that had high concentrations of Chinese or Kanaka labourers. These places were labelled 'Little Yokohamas' and provided the workers with sexual services which white prostitutes, by government decree, could not be allowed to perform for fear that it would demean them.[18] Evans questions this problematic, constant convergence of sexuality and the figure of the Asian woman in colonial administration, and very little research exists at the moment that focuses on the historical situations of Asian women in Australia.

To counter the idea of a 'good' citizen in *Astronauts* as one who builds only on assets and civic participation, Giese turns to the work of various artists and writers to illustrate different ways of contributing to an 'Australian' way of life. She includes a section on Chinese-Australian artists and the growing recognition and understanding they are receiving in Australia and elsewhere in the world. The listing of 'artists' comprises writers (for example, Moni Lai Storz, who wrote *Notes to My Sisters*), dancers (Susan Wang), television professionals (Annette Shun Wah, who was associated with SBS), and filmmakers (Clara Law, who directed the film about a Hong Kong family's migration to Australia, *Floating Life*). These stories detail their expressions of creativity and how these have allowed them to be 'successful'.

An artist in Giese's collection whose work stirs up key critical issues that intersect with citizenship, Aboriginal and ethnic politics is Zhou Xiaoping. Zhou is a Chinese artist who visited Aboriginal communities to draw and paint. Included in the book is a photo of Zhou and Jack Davis, Davis's portrait by Zhou hanging in the background. The juxtaposition of an iconic Aboriginal figure with the 'newcomer' who portrays him offers the stark contrast of Zhou against the 'bush' artists who traditionally render Aboriginal images onto canvas. As well, the companionable presence of Davis with Zhou suggests a form of 'approval' for the portrait. Giese notes that while Zhou's exhibitions in smaller centres have been quite enthusiastically attended, "[b]ack in urban Australia, [Zhou's] attempts at understanding are not necessarily well received. There are those who would deny Zhou, as a Chinese man who has been in Australia only eight years, the right to paint Aborigines at all" (69).[19] The oddly hierarchised racialisation that permeates this kind of judgement warrants closer examination. Apparently, Zhou, as a Chinese man who is always inherently alien to mainstream white Australian society, will never be granted by some critics the 'right' to choose Aboriginal portraits as subjects.

The attempted repression of the subjects of Zhou's painting emphasises the highly commodified and complicated arrangement of 'rights' surrounding indigenous artistic issues[20] and the misguided liberal response of attempting to defend the 'poor Aborigines' from Zhou's representations. Marian Boreland responds to this reaction by stating, "[t]his 'sentimentality' invested in the figure of the Aboriginal is in itself a manifestation of 'white guilt', which displaces the history and effects of colonialism in Australia onto multiculturalism" (180). The relationship between Aboriginal and multicultural groups is often presented as fraught with tensions, many imposed by the (invisible) hegemonic structures of grants, in which "the symbolic politics of the semi-welfare state compelled groups to compete for most favored victim status when they sought governmental redress and social benefits" (Goldberg 207). In many situations, the groups are seen as in opposition or open conflict. For example, Mudrooroo:

> pointed to a lack of interest on the part of both these areas [policy and academia] to historicize and contextualize Australia with reference to an Aboriginal history, and stated that both so called 'white' and non-indigenous Australians are complementary kinds of colonizers. . . . [He offers the] idea of multiculturalism as simply another form of oppression and colonization (Boreland 178).

Comments by Ruby Langford Ginibi and Eve Fesl iterate Mudrooroo's charge against multiculturalism of eliding Aboriginal concerns. They consider their claims belittled by multicultural policy because it puts them 'under the umbrella' of ethnic claims, as just one of the ethnic groups.[21] Class stereotypes are prevalent in polemic against Asian-Australians as new colonisers of Aboriginal people in Australian society. Kay Anderson argues that the Asian middle-class business populations are the 'haves' who are sometimes complicit with the maintenance of dominant values and hierarchies ("Otherness"). Meanwhile, other groups, such as the refugees or 'boat-people', become competitors for the welfare dollar.[22] The majority privilege of white Australians who control the terms of definition usually remain absent from the debate.

This racial strategy of 'divide and conquer' is not unique to multiracial Australia. Asian-American cultural theorist David Palumbo-Liu discusses the 'symbiotic' relationship between Korean-Americans and Anglo-Americans in the 1990s as an example of this creation of self-destructive divisiveness. He uses the incidents surrounding the 1992 Los Angeles riots, after the Rodney King trial, to emphasise how "Korean-Americans were represented as the frontline forces of the white bourgeoisie" ("Los Angeles" 371), protecting their goods and property, being part of the capitalist programme which enables them to become asset-rich 'Americans'.[23] Most images and reports elided the presence of white Americans (in downtown south-central Los Angeles), whereas that of Black Americans was amplified. Ruth Frankenberg suggests that "racist discourse . . . frequently accords hypervisibility to African Americans and a relative invisibility to Asian-Americans and Native Americans" (12). Palumbo-Liu states more specifically:

> [t]he locating, real and figurative, of Asians in between the dominant and minor is made less tenuous and even rationalized by a particular element which situates Asians within the dominant ideology, and frees them of the burden of their ethnicity and race while retaining (for obvious ideological purposes) the signifier of racial difference: the notion of self-affirmative action ("Los Angeles" 371).

The basic desire to be accepted/assimilated into the majority white society of Australia has meant that, in some instances, Asian citizens are complicit with the promulgation of certain stereotypes of themselves, as well as taking on what Ellie Vasta terms the "racist stereotypes of Anglo-Australia" (51). As Anderson points out: "[i]n the case of Chinatowns . . . certain traders and investors of Chinese origin have themselves participated in the orientalising of Chinatowns. Certain class fractions of the Chinese-origin population have joined state and local governments in commercialising 'Chinese' difference" ("Otherness" 75). Vasta suggests, however, that "[u]ntil Aborigines and immigrants form their own alliance outside any state apparatus in order to combat racist structures and cultures, then the struggle against racism will continue to be fragmented" (52). The historically different manifestations of repression for various ethnic groups and Aboriginal communities do not have to cancel out other political priorities such as eroding and changing discriminatory structures in Australian government, fostering wider acknowledgement and encouragement of community/cultural networks, and dismantling frameworks that contribute to racial discrimination in society.

Most representations of Chinese/Aboriginal relations are "ignored or oversimplified" (Yadong Li in Giese, *Astronauts* 39), probably because research thus far has not afforded much importance to the contributions of Aboriginal and Asian communities in the building of Australian towns, society, and industry. That said, this is an area of research which has attracted much interest and gathered momentum in recent years.[24] In an attempt to address this issue, Giese intersperses stories throughout *Astronauts* of Chinese-Aboriginal relationships and mixed-race families. She interviews the children and parents from these relationships and investigates the overlapping spaces they occupy as Others within the colonial imaginary, as well as in contemporary figurations of Australian society. In doing so, these accounts also heighten the interconnectedness of communities in Australian history and subvert their too convenient, and ultimately limiting, conceptualisations as discrete groups. On a broader scale, this erosion also applies to the category that the collection is premised upon, that of Chinese-Australians. Giese's work strikes a somewhat contradictory balance between focusing on a racial minority group and dispersing that same group by concentrating on the different stories and the people within them.

Voicing the histories of Chinese-Australians disseminates long-repressed perspectives. These communities, of whom 'good' citizen behaviour is an expectation, must flesh out their narratives to make their forebears "human and not heroic" (Soo 1). This process aims to include the stories of Asian-Australian failures and disappointments as well as those of success and recognition. Otherwise, the Model Minority stereotype endures, and Asian-Australians remain trapped in its perimeter. Leaving behind figurations of a White Australia, these recreations and interventions into Australian history enable Asian-Australians to configure themselves as part of national histories. In addition, the circulation of texts such as Giese's encourages the generation of a broader definition for Australian citizenship, and this introduces more flexibility and inclusiveness into who can be 'Australian'.

Other Ways of Inscribing Nation

Using William Yang's photobiography, *Sadness*, and Fred Wah's biotext, *Diamond Grill*, this third section concentrates on the discursive possibilities in writing Asians into their respective national histories. Both of these narratives have their origins in small towns, and Yang and Wah each deploy artistic and poetic methods to signify specific selves against the national representations of the Anglo-European majority. I deploy Avtar Brah's idea of the 'homing desire' while siting nationalism alongside elaborate negotiations of diasporic citizenship within Australia and Canada. Brah has stated that "[t]he *concept* of diaspora places the discourse of 'home' and 'dispersion' in creative tension, *inscribing a homing desire while simultaneously critiquing discourses of fixed origins*" (192–3). It is in this frame of "multilocationality" across various borders (194) that I examine Wah's and Yang's texts. In locating East Asian citizens within Australian and Canadian communities and national histories, their works offer ways to break down multicultural binaries and establish the grounds for a more porous, dynamic consideration of national literatures by diasporic authors.

Diamond Grill and *Sadness* confuse the already indistinct boundaries of national identity through their innovative 'autobiographies' and meld various components (for example, photographic and poetic) in their endeavour to convey more particular versions of themselves. These representations of narrators' multiple subjectivities/nationalities succeed in contradicting perceptions of citizenship as a stable category while grounding their texts within the local and historical.

As the previous section indicates, restructuring cultural space for Asian-Canadians and Asian-Australians starts on a basic level, having different versions of their experiences included as possibilities for 'national narratives'. Many texts convey historically or socially suppressed perspectives about pioneering moments in Australian and Canadian histories in challenging forms and inventive textual configurations. The tensions between individuals and their respective communities are evident in the retelling of various stories and observations about 'the way things were' in what could be termed community establishment narratives (Wah in Nelson, British Columbia; Yang in far north Queensland).[25] On this point, Anna Johnston observes that "individual autobiographies inscribe individual life-narratives, which accumulate to inscribe a national discourse. Thus autobiographies come to 'add up to' a community of narratives — and a narrative community" ("'Memoirs'" 75). Their works are complicated by their national and diasporic Chinese memberships, as well as their engagement with, and partial use of, what Johnston terms "value-added" narratives (" 'Memoirs' " 75). For the most part, the two texts invoke these 'value-added narratives' in casting Chinese families as 'pioneers', including them in the establishment community, and in the discourses of war and patriotism. Content aside, however, the innovative formats of *Sadness* and *Diamond Grill* are examples of what Miki calls "the baffled textual screen characteristic of minority writing in its interface with dominant society" ("Asiancy" 145). This section examines the ways in which Wah and Yang interrogate their positioning within national literary arenas, with particular emphasis on mediating 'minoritisation'.

Wah's literary reputation in Canada rests on his sixteen volumes of poetry, his involvement in avant-garde Canadian literary movements,[26] and his significant body of critical work. *Diamond Grill* was his first prose work and it had "the largest initial order for any book ever published by NeWest Press" (Beauregard, "Rattling" 171). Of mixed Scots-Irish, Chinese, and Swedish descent, Wah narrates a life in which he can 'pass' as white in most situations until others trip over the stumbling block of his surname, a name that "is enough of a shade to mottle an otherwise transparent European background" ("Half-Bred" 61). In recognition of his otherwise 'passable' self, he offers the wordplay to which junk mail distributors have treated his name while trying to 'genericise' his identity:

> [he receives items] addressed to Fred *Wan*, Fred *Way*, Fred *Wash*, Fred *Wag*, Fred *Wan*, Fred *What* is always a semiotic treat. The one that really stopped me in my tracks though was the Christmas card from a tailor in Hong Kong addressed to Fred *Was* (169).

This playfully reflects the 'almost-but-not-quite' nature of his multiple subjectivities, a fractured self that also permeates the structure of the text. Wah's *Diamond* is a seemingly scattered compilation of impressions, half-memories, and blunt observation about race and acceptance in Canadian society. The biotext is an extension and development of Wah's "Elite" series in his *Waiting for Saskatchewan* collection (1984). Readings of *Diamond*, and any other autobiographical multicultural text, incorporate the critical perspective of hearing the previously unheard or unsaid. These new perspectives on establishment narratives contest already accepted versions of history. Their definitive terms undercut not only "the private act of a self writing" but "the cultural act of self reading" (Gunn, Janet 8). On various levels of representation, Wah 'reads' the placement of his family and its business on the map of small-town Canada while engaging with the highly personal stories of growing up in a mixed-race family. Joanne Saul writes of biotexts as "focus[ing] on the process of writing life — the ruptures, gaps, and workings of memory; the fictionalizing that reconstruction requires; the communal nature of the task" (2). Throughout *Diamond,* Wah text-hops and creates and fills 'gaps' in characteristic wordplay. The text is 'authorised' by Wah as both authentic and inauthentic:

> I wish not to offend any of my family or any of the Chinese-Canadians who have known and experienced some of these stories more tangibly than I have. These are not true stories but, rather, poses or postures, necessitated, as I hope is clear in the text, by faking it (Acknowledgements).

The experimental, non-linear form of *Diamond* replicates his 'mimicry' of various ethnicities within the text. This style contradicts the traditionally realist autobiographical one and especially contravenes the assumed realist mode of most multicultural writing. He satirises the futility of quantifying a person's family background and declares sardonically that in his family "we have our own little western Canadian multicultural stock exchange" (83). In his reference to the stock exchange, and its connotations of commodification and 'trading up', Wah ironically invokes the shallow contemporary discourse of 'difference for differences' sake' which is fuelled by some definitions of multiculturalism and the multicultural as merely recognition and signposting of difference. The Chicago Cultural Studies Group defines this concern as "the problem of losing the subject to a mere noting of this difference, with no 'power' attached to differences in practice" (538).[27] In literature as elsewhere, real social change, as opposed to mere illustration of where inequalities or differences lie, only occurs when the power disparities inherent in facets of diversity are examined and defused or dismantled. Wah's biofiction appears to expand understandings of small-town Canada beyond being unassailably white and, therefore, goes some way to dismantling the 'alienness' of racial minority individuals in Canada as citizens.

Diamond continues to build up with precision the layers and types of racism that the Wah family encounters in setting up and running the café:

Carl

from the customers, schoolmates, family, and government. The text is full of recollections of the café in Nelson where his family settled. Wah conveys his memories to the reader in great detail, down to counter displays, jukebox buttons, changing menus, and flavours of milkshakes. Growing up among many ethnic groups, and not feeling that he belonged properly to any of them, Wah creates spaces in his text that are zones of comfort or familiarity in the face of adversity. He analogises the swinging door of the Diamond Grill as "the wooden slab that swings between the Occident and Orient", and then speaks of riding the silence that is "a hyphen and the hyphen [that] is the door" (16). This negotiated hyphen is what Guy Beauregard stresses as Fred Senior's strongest trait. In "the apparently simple but increasingly heroic act of opening the café", Fred Senior's "historical agency emerges as the ability to move noisily *through the hyphen*, to unlock the doors that separate outside and inside" ("Rattling" 172). His facility in interacting with the spheres on both sides of the kitchen door allows him to become to the kitchen staff and his son "the centre of our life, with more pivot to the world than anyone I know" (61). Conversely, Fred Junior uses the area of the café's kitchen as a retreat, preferring "the meaningless but familiar hum of Cantonese and away from all the angst of the arrogant white world out front" (63). Ironically, he would rather listen to and absorb words he cannot understand than be a part of the customers' buzzing conversations in English. In a subversive twist, language becomes reduced to familiar sounds and tones, and not necessarily existing for communicative purposes or for dialogue. Wah uses the term 'code-switching' to define the layering of language mixtures with which he operated on a daily basis. The family's use of their own words equates with having "the power to own but not be owned by the dominant language" (Mary Louise Pratt in Wah 68). A characteristic example of this is his grandfather's use of the word 'high muckamuck', a word with roots in a First Nations dialect, which also has a genealogy over several Wah family groups in which connotations mutate and become something new for each succeeding generation (68–9).

Alongside observations about language and its fluid directions is the much more material issue of being a racial minority in small-town Canada and, for Fred Junior, internalising anti-Chinese sentiments (Beauregard, "Rattling" 172). During his childhood, Wah writes that he took the side of the white team rather than joining the Chinese team because he knew he was "white enough to be on the winning team" (53). His adulthood engagement with the Chinese and indelible part of him, however, alters this straightforward desire to 'be on the winning team' with the realisation that:

all my ambivalence gets covered over, camouflaged by a safety net of class and colourlessness — the racism within me that makes and consumes that neutral (white) version of myself, that allows me the sad privilege of being, in this white white world, not the target but the gun (138).

Wah was in the unusual position of being able to choose, to a certain degree, which 'team' he wants to be on, an option unavailable to most people of Chinese descent. As a boy, Fred Junior does not even think of himself as 'Chinese': "[u]ntil Mary McNutter calls me a Chink I'm not one" (98). More specifically, when young Fred does not think of himself as 'Chinese', it is not so much that he does not know he has a varied family background (knowing already that his father is not wholly a white 'Canadian'), but he wants to refuse the denigration and negativity that can be implied by the term.[28] Significant in these situations is that realisation of, and negativity about, their ethnicity is precipitated by external sources; of becoming "ethnic [only] through the eyes of another; the labelling is never one's own" (Brydon 94). Quite literally, their ethnic identities materialise only through the style in which they are named.

About his ability to look 'not-Chinese', Wah writes: "[p]hysically, I'm racially transpicuous and I've come to prefer that mode" (136). The creation of the word 'transpicuous' signifies Wah's ability to be categorised as part of many Other groups. Through dissecting the word, Wah could be viewed as 'transparently conspicuous', with a name and surrounding relatives that differentiate him from Anglo-European Canada; or the term might be interpreted as 'trans-conspicuous' with his 'foreignness' noted across several levels. Wah comes to choose 'Chineseness' out of all his "straits and islands of the blood" (22) because of its threatened nature, overtly engaging with the issue of contradiction apparent in being grounded in Canada but culturally resident in several spaces. The geographical analogy alludes to his identity mediations and the recognition of his known, but 'unmoored-at', 'islands' of identity. Chineseness and its unacceptability have led him, in adulthood, to deliberately and contrarily wear the sometimes uncomfortable "haircoat" of ethnicity (Kogawa, "Heart" 26).

In contrast to Wah's latecoming to interrogating his diasporic ethnicities, Yang has adopted overtly and self-reflexively his 'Chineseness' as a career. His friend, director Jim Sharman, comments that Yang "adopted his Chinese background" with "'an *awful* lot of fervour'" (Baker 21). Yang is best known in Australia as an artistic photographer, having had several exhibitions, performing his slide shows at Australian and overseas festivals, and being the focus of a retrospective at the State Library of New South Wales early in 1998.

His slide shows[29] have proven immensely popular. The book of his slide show, *Sadness*, is a glossy, slim volume, divided into theatrical 'Acts' with text and photographs. His typed monologue is combined with handwritten photo captions that lend the work a personalised air. During the performed show, the private nature of telling his life's story is melded with "an utterly contemporary version of the old-style Australian slide night" (Gerster 24). To extend the 'naturalisation' of Yang as an Australian and as a 'bard', to have the right to tell his story, Robin Gerster feels compelled to compare him to an iconic Australian poet and writer: "Yang writes as he speaks, with a terse sardonicism that is sometimes reminiscent of the dry-as-dust drollery of Henry Lawson, the Lawson of 'The Union Buries Its Dead'" (24). The co-optation of Yang as somewhat 'hyper-Australian' is contradicted by his Chinese features. His visible difference posits a challenge to the iconic Lawsonian images with which Gerster is associating him. The comparison is made easier, however, through Yang's high-profile projects of photographing Patrick White and displaying quintessential Australian scenes during various photographic exhibitions, particularly the striking landscape shots in *Sadness* and *The North*. Candida Baker states that Yang's ability to capture "such a wide-angle view of Australia" lies "in the dichotomies that have always surrounded his personal life and work" (21). His work covers urban and rural Australia, which lends him an all-round Australian focus. Even so, amidst this well-established role in Australian photojournalism, Yang himself comments: "I look Chinese, and because of that people tend to take no notice of me. It is often as if I am not there" (Baker 18). He is 'invisible' because of his Chineseness and this, he claims ironically, contributes to his success as a photographer.

In *Sadness*, Yang pursues the mystery of his uncle's murder in far north Queensland, noting that "[m]y mother regretted telling me [about] this detail because I'm the sort of person who talks about that sort of thing in public too" (21). The ostensible journey to find out about Fang Yuen fragments into a series of side journeys: into family history and the coming of the Yangs to north Queensland, vignettes of cousins and other relatives, and the background to the final holiday with his mother before her death. Through these stories, he touches on topics which make up the historical centre of Australian history: the opening up and establishment of cane fields (rural pioneers) and the input of Chinese and other minority labourers into these plantations, examples of his cousins serving Australia during the Second

World War and the community roles that Chinese had in the small towns of rural Queensland. This latter point is similar to Wah's siting of his narrative in the family's café in Nelson and his father's participation in the small rural town, writing themselves into that particular history.

The mutability of his narrative show is made clear when he introduces the book version of *Sadness* with an outline of the editing and cutting of slides which occurs according to the kind of crowd, city, or format for which he is performing. Yang had to cull the 600 slides that comprised his 'live' show to about the 100 that funds would allow for the book. His juggling of slides and formats is analogous with his changing personal presentation and which 'sides' he decides to emphasise. An unfortunate loss from transferring the performance to a textual form was the intriguing set of food photographs. While the book still has isolated images of served meals and the tinned crabmeat with Sao biscuits his Aunty Kath puts before him, one of the most humorous and ironic series of images is that of the grading Yang performed on the roadhouse meals he consumed during his trip north. In the slide show, he graded the gradually enlarging steak and potato combinations according to their level of 'Australianness' until he gave First Prize to a steak that almost would not fit on the plate, accompanied by (among other things) a huge pile of mashed potato and a floret of deep-fried cauliflower. Yang's judging of the authenticity of roadhouse food inverts the common practice of judging Other groups through their exotic dishes, an aspect of what Stanley Fish has called "Boutique Multiculturalism": "the multiculturalism of ethnic restaurants, weekend festivals, and high profile flirtations with the other in the manner satirized by Tom Wolfe under the rubric of 'radical chic' " (378). During the performance, he procures the gaze and makes the proverbial 'meat and three veg' an alien and increasingly bizarre occurrence.

Yang merges images and stories of his childhood, youth, and visits to far north Queensland with his friendships in the gay and lesbian scenes of Sydney and Melbourne. One perspective is that of rediscovering and reinterpreting his Chinese past while the other encompasses the coming-out of Asian homosexuals and meeting the friends he is losing, or has lost, to HIV/AIDS. These two subject areas and subjectivities seem to clash, considering the historical and continuing denial of homosexuality in Asian communities. Russell Leong argues, "[t]he domain of the Asian-American 'home' is usually kept separate from the desire of the sexual and emotional 'body'" ("Home Bodies" 5). Nevertheless, as Yang points out: "[i]n the end, I just threw the stories together, they were both my stories . . . I was the glue" (iii). For Asian homosexuals, Dana Takagi explains, the categories of 'gayness' and 'Asianness' are not similar: "[w]hile both can be said to be socially constructed, the former [is] performed, acted out, and produced, often in individual routines, whereas the latter tends to be more obviously 'written' on the body and negotiated by political groups" (25). Yang's 'social' membership crosses over family borders and gay and lesbian associations, and often these instances of 'crossing-over' are multidirectional. Tina Faulk even describes Yang as "an Australian photographer who is an ethnic Chinese homosexual activist" (62). Yang's belonging to the majority white Australian gay and lesbian scene includes his close involvement with the still-forming Asian Lesbian and Gay Pride Group (ALGPG), and he describes the usually excluded homosexual in Asian communities as "a minority within a minority" (12). In his family, he has a nephew who is also 'out' and in the ALGPG. The traditionally maintained separateness of Asianness and homosexuality is contradicted by Yang's very presence and narrative voice, yet reflected in the episodic nature of *Sadness*, which switches between following the murder mystery to far north Queensland and introducing his gay and lesbian friends to the reader/audience.

As a gay man in Australia, Yang occupies a particularly unstable discursive space as an Australian citizen and member of the Chinese ethnic community, albeit fifth-generation. His 'orientation' is complicated by his race and, barring Gerster's enthusiasm to claim Yang as typically 'Australian', by the heterosexual masculine imagery in most national representations.

National legislation has made an HIV condition one that excludes a person from gaining entry, let alone citizenship, in many countries. These kinds of sanction throw into doubt the apportioned rights that most citizens are granted, as well as destabilising the tenets of universal human rights. The taboo nature of HIV/AIDS representations in visual media means that the photographs of Yang's HIV-affected friends are more confronting in their shock value.[30] The prose and images of *Sadness* contest accepted and acceptable portrayals of this disease, rehumanising the undeniably debilitated bodies of his friends by juxtaposing them with earlier shots of younger, more optimistic times. Theorising the confrontational images in Eric Michaels's AIDS autobiography, Johnston contends that:

> [t]he photographs of Michaels, pre- and post-AIDS, challenge our ideas
> of bodily propriety and the role of the spectator of the diseased, sexually
> transgressive body. This body is not a passive vessel which will embody
> the spectators' narratives, whether they are narratives of liberal sympathy,

medical diagnosis, or aesthetic revulsion. Instead, Michaels meets the gaze of the observer and challenges it to enter his own self-consciously performed narrative ("unbecoming" 67).

In a similar manner to the way Michaels's challenging gaze usurps the power of the camera and his own positioning as 'object' of photography, Yang's HIV-affected friends maintain an active relationship with the photographer and the camera, imparting an ever more powerful 'ending' when, for example, the audience is shown the image of Nicolaas van Schalkwyk immediately after death. Yang creates a constant tension between life and death in the series of photographs portraying the poignant decline, and confronting deaths, of his friends. Joel Tan in "Communion", writes of his "family of gay men of color and other 'queer families'" who are "also bound by blood and history" (202). Tan's analogies, iterating yet skewing Wah's 'straits and islands of the blood', overlap with Yang's narratives, blurring even further the borders of 'family' and 'nation'. Yang's work in *Sadness* and his next show, *Friends of Dorothy*, challenge society's euphemistic representations of HIV/AIDS and the marginalisation of homosexuality. Although he has a dedicated audience and a high profile, Yang still admits that he would not take a 'gay' programme to smaller towns in Australia. He only took *Friends of Dorothy* to capital cities because he is not "that much of a crusader" to take the show to "places where there isn't a supportive community" (Litson 16). Although Gerster is quite willing to bring Yang into the yarning realm of Henry Lawson, perhaps the overall package of Yang's race and sexuality still renders him not-quite acceptable in mainstream versions of Australian citizenry.

Through all his shows, Yang frames his work, necessarily, from an 'Asian-Australian' perspective and 'philosophy'. At the end of the book of *Sadness*, Yang places a photo of a shrine at which he prays, explaining how he copes with the deaths around him of friends and family. Yang emphasises the influence of Taoism on his life many times throughout the monologue. In the performed version, Yang finishes the show by kneeling before a Taoist shrine and lighting several sticks of incense, performing a ritual to the dead while performing a show for his dead.

Pursuing the 'true' story surrounding the murder of his uncle many decades ago, Yang uses the quest to re-meet family and to allow them to embroider the mystery with their tangled versions. In the end, he finds the bloodstained documents his uncle had held, clears up the motive for murder, and discovers the racist reasons why the investigation proceeded so slowly. Contrasting with the photographic 'truth' of his dying friends with AIDS, the thread of finding out the secret of Fang Yuen's death is open to nostalgia, faulty memory, imagination, and restrictive discretion. The latter thread, however, offers a more traditional sense of closure when Yang's mother dies and the murder case is solved. In contrast, his depictions of gay friends and their subsequent deaths remain intractably open-ended, emphasising the onslaught of the disease and its current 'unsolvability'.

Inflecting the writing of both *Diamond* and *Sadness* are the obstacles encountered when creating a personal history/present. The members of one's own family or community, who are still present to contradict or judge the publications' veracity, mediate the process constantly.[31] This is not an issue specific to writers from the Asian population of Australia or Canada but in countries where the profile and numbers of Asian authors are relatively low, each depiction of, for example, a Chinese-Australian or a Japanese-Canadian perspective may become or be assumed as representative of the community perspective. Garrett Hongo, an Asian-American writer and critic, describes this assumed judgement of community reaction as that of a relatively "immature" culture within a culture because this group

> is so unused to seeing cultural representations of itself that, whenever representation does occur, many respond with anger because of the pain released. It is as if they recognize *their* story in the outlines of the story one of the writers is telling, but feel even more alienated rather than absolved because that story isn't theirs *exactly*, or doesn't present the precise tone and tenor of their inner feeling regarding the experience they feel the writer, as an Asian-American, should understand (17).

Although this is becoming less true of Asian-American literature, because of the sheer impetus in publishing and the demographics of the possible readership, it is still true of Asian-Canadian and Asian-Australian literature. For these latter two areas, the narrow perception of correct or incorrect representations may be changing slowly as more group-specific naming of East and South Asian activist groups agitate for change and become more confidently vocal in the larger public sphere. Examples of this civic agitation and raising of racial minority profiles as citizens include the Japanese-Canadian Redress movement in the 1980s, and in Australia the 1990s instance of the formation of the Unity Party in Sydney.[32] Yang's and Wah's texts succeed in 'asianising' the foundational narratives of Australia and Canada, installing Chinese families in rural towns and organisations. The authors' use of criss-crossing genres of fiction and non-fiction continue the blurring of boundaries between 'real' history and personal recollection or manipulation. In doing so, they destabilise the assumed coherence of historical narrative or memoir, perforating national histories with hyphenated Asian interventions. Moreover, Yang's membership in the gay community complicates even more the attribution of 'belonging' and, especially, renders notions of acceptance by others in the Asian–Australian and general community more intricate.

Conclusion

Through literary 'rehearsals' and restagings of diasporic identities and more traditional national citizenship, the texts examined in this chapter demonstrate the tensions between literary production, mediating multiple citizenships, and the porosity of multicultural nationhood. In contemporary Western society, writers of Asian descent still struggle against being 'visibly different' while remaining hegemonically 'invisible' and mostly inaudible when it comes to shifting specific educational, social, or governmental imperatives. Asian-American poet and activist, Michiyo Cornell, attempts to bypass formations of marginalisation from a 'desirable' white mainstream by claiming that she "live[s] in *Asian-America*" (83). The desire for viewing of 'parallel cultural societies' within larger hegemonic societies is a critical area largely yet untheorised, perhaps because it requires narrowing the focus at a time when this focus is considered still not broad enough. The published works of Asian-Australian and Asian–Canadian writers encompass different genres and, as a body of literature, they broaden concepts of nationhood and citizenship by implementing versions of Lowe's 'alternative social practices' mentioned earlier in this chapter. Lowe is speaking primarily about those practices used by a "'class subject' of transnationalism" (172) in negotiating new patterns of capital exchange, but her statements apply as well to the formation of critical literary subjectivities for hyphenated Asian citizens within Canada and Australia: "[they] cannot be politically or ideologically unified in a simple way but may be 'unified' according to a process based on strategic alliances between different sectors, not on their abstract identity" (172). The inclusive establishment of Asians within Australian and Canadian histories serve the dual purpose of diluting white myths of who gets to 'belong', as well as interrogating the necessity of 'belonging' in the first place.

While citizenship remains a seemingly conditional and contradictory status for Asian–Australians and Asian–Canadians, examination of their increasing literary production, and critical engagements, in both countries will allow critics to determine whether they are merely 'adding to' or "*add[ing] up to* national narratives" (Johnston, "'Memoirs'" 87). Lien Chao draws similarities between Asian-Canadian literature and the pioneering roles that Asian-Canadians filled in the earlier days of Canada's history, creating what she calls "the 'epic struggles' on the contemporary cultural front in order to help build a multivoiced Canadian literature" ("Anthologizing" 166). The crossovers between historic and literary manoeuvres in Chao's statement emphasise the citizens' rhetoric of entitlements and rights. Although the historical placing of hyphenated Asian histories is a necessary step, filmmaker Richard Fung warns against *only* establishing a presence:

> The Asian-American movement, one of the many social movements inspired by the civil rights struggle, has similarly adopted a strategy of based on a reclamation of historical space and many American films and videotapes center on putting Asians into Americana. Indeed, many productions draw on a disturbingly uncritical endorsement of American ideology in claiming their slice of the pie ("Multiculturalism" 18).

In lumping Yang with Lawson and "The Union Buries Its Dead", Robin Gerster enacts precisely the kind of 'disturbingly uncritical endorsement' elucidated by Fung. Gerster's endorsement of Yang ignores the specific history in Australia of anti-Asian sentiment and, indeed, Lawson's own racism. Alongside the impetus for more and different narratives from Asian-Canadian and Asian-Australian writers, then, is the gradual production of work that supplements the layering of generational perspectives in these texts. Vietnamese-American critic and filmmaker, Trinh T. Minh-ha, expresses the necessity for 'multivocality' in this way: "[t]he more ears I am able to hear with, the farther I see the plurality of meaning and the less I lend myself to the illusion of a single message" (30). It is through this depth of literary and historical representation that citizens of Asian descent in Australia and Canada establish community and national chronicles and a range of contemporary political subjectivities.

4

"At Home in Your Embarrassment": Boundaries of Community and Ethnicity

[T]here was something jagged underneath my waves, and I realised suddenly that I'd been jagged inside for years, jagged with shock and apprehension. Jagged from years of being judged but being unable to express my own judgements.

(Lazaroo, *The World Waiting To Be Made* 261)

to tell the truth
I feel very much at home
in your embarrassment

(Jim Wong-Chu, "How Feel I Do?" 17)

Inevitably tied up in discussions about representation and racial minority literatures are issues of community. This is not to say that 'community' is an issue but to highlight the overlapping, sometimes contradictory, perspectives of creative writers, their perceived audiences, and literary critics. While previous chapters outlined negotiations of cultural meaning within larger structures of diaspora and nation, this chapter maps the limits, breaches, and strategies of 'community' boundaries in and for Asian-Australian and Asian-Canadian literature. It interrogates how the writing community and the texts themselves intersect in their strategies for more broadly representing hyphenated Asian community identities. Where the previous chapter focused on how Asian-Canadian and Asian-Australian literatures transform notions of civic belonging and 'national literatures', this one examines how writers and their works operate on more localised levels of community identity formation and resistance. Asian-Australian and Asian-

Canadian authors' complicated anxieties about belonging to various groups produce individualised accounts that are challenging to generalisations. The axis of community upon which I base discussions is described by African-American critic Audre Lorde in this way: "[w]ithout community there is no liberation, only the most vulnerable and temporary armistice between an individual and [their] oppression. But community must not mean a shedding of our differences nor a pathetic pretense that these differences do not exist" (159). This chapter's readings interrogate the spaces between belonging to a community and alienation from it, leading to "the heart-of-the-matter questions" (Kogawa, "Heart" 27) for hyphenated Asian writers and literary reading practices in Canada and Australia. The interplay of different community values in literature is interspersed with sometimes difficult creations of individuality and independence in the work of Asian-Australian and Asian-Canadian writers. Their writing is mediated by socio-political perceptions of 'Asians' in their respective nations as well as the conditions of contemporary Canadian and Australian literary production. In particular, I argue that by viewing community coalitions as a series of chosen affiliations, and perpetually in process, the limits and modulations of ethnicity and community in literature are more thoroughly interrogated than if the analysis only addresses which side of the hyphen texts and authors seem to fall. The analysis specifically focuses on unpacking issues of 'ethnicity' as a potentially restrictive obligation or example of empowering coalition. The narratives in Hiromi Goto's *Chorus of Mushrooms* and Simone Lazaroo's *World Waiting To Be Made* detail the way in which internalised racism, sexual presumption, and the urge to assimilate influence Asian women growing up in white post-colonial societies. Both Goto's and Lazaroo's novels occupy what I want to call, after Wah's analogy in *Diamond Grill*, the 'hinges' of society, as opposed to the fringes. The latter term surrounds but connotes little movement from that space, whereas these texts provide an opportunity to swing from one perspective to another from a single position. This further emphasises the main point of this book: that reading and representational strategies for Asian-Canadian and Asian-Australian literature and its authors need to be broadened constructively. Their interventions in a range of community and national representations encourage further creations of distinct diasporic Asian subjectivities. Availability of options for how they situate their creative production combats the simplicity and ascribed values with which they sometimes have to contend. *Chorus* and *World* exemplify the contingencies and complications of identification with or against ethnic and other communities.

Because of the necessary deployment of Asian-American criticism in contemporary literary studies, an understanding of ethnic literary community relations and multiculturalism for Asian-Canadians and Asian-Australians needs to be juxtaposed with those of the United States. The civil-rights, activist-born Asian-American movement has a different developmental trajectory from those appearing in Australia and Canada. That said, however, the intercommunal negotiations — and how these overlap with decades of ethnic identity politics — provide Canadian and Australian researchers with ample, pertinent reference material while formulating their own nationally contextualised arguments. One of the most usefully fraught issues in Asian-American studies that correlates well with the current stages of Asian-Canadian and Asian-Australian developments is that of activism and scholarship. The overlapping goals of these two areas and their dissimilar modes of achievement can often be conflicting. The political relations between Asian-American communities and academics working in and with hyphenated Asians have always been tense. Because activism highlights and promotes change within racist or discriminatory structures, and critical scholarship by definition is one step removed from this, attempts to bring them together can be problematic. In Russell Leong's opinion, a pressing need remains for research in universities to return to the communities that shaped the information and provided the 'raw material'. He goes so far as to use the phrase 'academic pimping' to describe refusals to do so: "[a]cademic pimping . . . involves the following: utilizing the communities' 'bodies' as informants, studying, collecting and using community culture as material for research, publishing essays, articles and books based on the above — without giving anything back" ("Lived Theory" ix). Although Leong's comments are certainly valid in many fields, they do overstate the pertinence of 'community' reciprocation and liaison for other areas. Especially when theorising literary practice, this perspective, although useful in some instances, could lead to work *about* a community being conflated with work *for* that community. Arif Dirlik argues that, for Asian-American groups, "[c]ommunity represented . . . a basis for resistance to racial and cultural oppression, as well as the source of alternative visions of social organization for the future" ("Asians" 7). With Dirlik's comment in mind, Leong's concerns about losing political impetus in Asian-American studies are a genuine response to the increasing institutionalisation of the field in United States academies. I would also argue, however, that framing these literary studies only within community 'politicality' limits their discursive possibilities. 'Ethnic studies' schools appear to be on the brink of coming full circle: from establishing separate faculty operations and focusing closely on community-particular concerns (precisely to stop the conglomeration of 'ethnic' concerns as including Asian, Hispanic, African-American, etc.) to considering merging with the broad and cross-disciplinary area of 'American studies'.[1] It is this somewhat unquestioning application of 'community concerns' that requires further deconstruction.

Broadening a nation's possible 'membership' is crucial for eroding unequal hierarchies of belonging. Alongside this interrogation of the national are more specific layers of 'community' for individuals of Asian descent in Australia and Canada. The interactions of these groups perpetuate cycles of cultural negotiation and validation, in which Asian-Australians and Asian-Canadians face oscillating inter- and intracommunity tensions. Perceptions of diasporic Asian communities change with economic and political shifts, depending on how 'useful' they are seen to be. In community self-definition, the process of Asian communities or individuals talking to 'themselves' or their own community progresses issues beyond the need to always justify being able to talk at all. As Goto states: "[m]y vision of audience is changing. My audience doesn't have to be white" (Interview 1). However, the awareness of writing into a 'community' space can be both empowering and constraining.

The tension between being *seen* to be a part of a community and wanting to claim some form of individualised ethnicity is an ever-present one. The 1997 memoir of Korean-Canadian Yi Sun-Kyung, *Inside the Hermit Kingdom*, portrays 'Little Koreas' in Regina and Toronto as extremely conservative, almost feudal, communities. Describing the office of the weekly English newspaper for young Koreans in Canada, Yi portrays the publications and the workers as brimming with sexist and racist remarks, especially towards herself as a young, (unnaturally) single woman. Her book concentrates on exploring 'Koreanness', and Yi comes away disliking all of the 'Koreas' she has managed to find. She concludes with: "I'm not sure which Korea I'd been searching for — perhaps the one that had filled my imagination in my childhood" (237). The ironic twist in Yi's narrative is that although she fails to find the 'homeland' in the physical sites of Korea, representatives of that 'homeland' actively try to take away her manuscript, to stop her telling the 'truth' of her experiences which may be to their detriment. Yoon Kwang-Su explicitly states that she must "go easy on South Korea" (235), and attempts to appeal to Yi's sense of community and South Korea's need to 'save face'. Yi's text is quite specifically in a documentary style, but it is often the evocation of imagined homelands by Asian authors that is used to categorise writing about diasporic communities. This demarcation, however, needs to keep pace with contemporary Asian-Canadian literature because, in many ways, the area's increasing input is from Canada-born authors of Asian descent whose narratives do not fall within these areas. The situation in Australia, however, is currently one in which the majority of authors are first-generation migrants.

How ethnic minority artists and their work are perceived owes much to contemporary socio-cultural valuing of diversity and the range of acceptable 'multicultural' materials. The processes of government funding, community approval, and equity programmes mediate the work of non-white artists in differing ways. Although these procedures can strain community-artist relations, the ethnic community and government, through networked resources, grants, and publicity, can offer writers valuable starting points for their work. Like most artists in any society, hyphenated Asian writers are affected by many kinds of regulation. Government and community support offices grant arts funding while retaining the right to control and monitor events and publications. For many Asian authors, representative tensions between communities and an artist's creative self can seriously affect their work. The lack of depth or variety in representations of 'Asians' and the inability of many funding bodies to see beyond stereotypical definitions of 'community arts' also hinders engagement with the writing as 'literary'. Sneja Gunew observes: "[r]arely is the community as such seen as the repository of artistic excellence. Rarely are they seen as generating radical concepts or ideas to feed into the wider cultural debates" ("Ethnicity and Excellence" 5). Often these biases discourage, or disallow, readings of hyphenated Asian literature in national contexts, which is why this chapter, and the book in general, emphasises the terms Asian-Canadian and Asian-Australian. The 'either/or' binary — having to be either Asian or Australian — stalls dialogue and the development of new ways of framing these specific 'literatures'.

Yet the systems of literary production and author funding in multicultural Australia and Canada often encourage certain modes of affiliation. The passing of 'top-down' official Multicultural Acts in Australia and Canada in the late 1980s helped the establishment of specifically ethnic-identified community group profiles, often propagating racialised categories while being seen to manage 'the multicultural' without reference to race. Many critics have noted this elision of race while maintaining racial boundaries.[2] This contrasts with the overtly racialised dialogue of the 'multicultural' United States, which often collapses discussions of race with those of ethnicity. The United States' situation of conflating discerned ethnic communities with race results partially from the fact that for racial minorities common circumstances "consist in relatively permanent racial difference and nonincorporation" (Omi and Winant 22). This situation of being demarcated by 'same differences' is a double-edged predicament that can result in homogenisation as well as recognition of marginalisation by skin colour. For Australia and Canada, the association between ethnicity and racial difference is less direct, mostly because of the currency of the 'multicultural' or 'ethnic' term in postwar years when the majority of immigrants were from Anglo-European countries. The definitions of ethnicity for these two societies, historically, are more broadly applied and less tied to racism. Increasingly, however, the 'multicultural' has become associated with non-Anglo-European groups and their enfranchisement in the national cultural sphere, especially on the heels of Hansonism's call for a return to the white old days of 1950s' Australia, and the continuing growth of conservative rhetoric and promotion of protectionist policies in Canada.

Different national histories mean that various critics contest heavily the term 'ethnicity' and its use. In the widely quoted and influential article, "The Cult of Ethnicity and the Fetish of Pluralism", E. San Juan dismisses the "paradigm of ethnicity" as having nothing more than an "essentializing and ultimately apologetic function" (222). Further, San Juan characterises ethnicity as another form of racism (226) that should be eradicated. The term certainly has shortfalls and has been misused in certain contexts, but discarding it in the way that San Juan proposes overlooks its use in discussing cultural specificity within the larger racial minority groups. The danger of essentialising individuals or groups through the imposition of ethnicity is apparent. Indeed, Walter Benn Michaels asserts that this problem is even more pronounced in multicultural societies because "[t]he pluralist gesture toward tolerance (not 'better' but 'better for us') requires an essentialist assertion of identity; instead of who we are being constituted by what we do, what we do is justified by who we are. In cultural pluralism, culture does not make up identity, it reflects it" (683). Neither Michaels nor San Juan seems to allocate much value or opportunity in setting out complex, knowing ethnicities or the active claiming of an ethnicity. They seem to focus only on circumstances of majority/margin and neglect the complex interplay of negotiating ethnicities within cultural groups. Within the fields of art and literature, Asian-Canadian and Asian-Australian texts present not the voice of one community but a dialogue between individual authors, their community (cultural, social, or artistic), and surrounding frames of meaning. The knowledge that ethnicity, as a category, can be manipulated confuses identity ascription and works in concomitant ways. It can 'devalue' multicultural literature because of the view that the area cannot be trusted to offer a form of cultural truth. In contrast, this knowing manipulation can also leave space for alternative responses and challenges for identity and community politics.

Strategic subject identification has emerged as a useful way to move through paralysing and silencing social and political ascriptions. Ien Ang paraphrases Werner Sollors when she declares, "if I am inescapably Chinese by *descent*, I am only sometimes Chinese by *consent*. When and how is a matter of politics" ("On Not Speaking" 18). Ang's sentiments offer some way forward for hyphenated Asian authors: "from years of being judged but being unable to express [their] own judgements" (restating my epigraph from Lazaroo) to "assum[ing] responsibility for the frames of reference through which their subjectivities are reproduced in public discourses" (Miki, "Asiancy" 136). While one can gain a form of representational agency through controlling what is thought of as 'ethnicity' or how one is presented as 'ethnic', the category and its ascriptions are never hermetic. Anne Brewster concurs with Ang by arguing that "a postmodern and performative ethnicity, that is, an ethnicity that comes into being through the enactment of strategies and positions" (13) is what is needed in discussions of multicultural literature and interrogations of the terms 'ethnic' and 'community'. This perspective can sometimes fail to take into account that although ethnic community attributions are never only applied, they are not always enacted 'strategies' either. Viewing them as such underlines the lopsided consideration of which communities need to cater to others and which do not. Ethnic writers and communities are not the only ones who need to be aware of and manipulate their own representation — those who impose these classifications in the first place need to be part of the re-vision process.

Further to the idea of complex communities, strained relationships often exist between artists and their ethnic or cultural communities. The nature of artistic endeavour means that boundaries are necessarily pushed and overstepped. This tendency is more meaningful for racial minority artists, however, as approval from the community is sometimes required before funding applications are considered. The Department of Canadian Heritage requires that some submissions for its multicultural grants scheme for writing denote that they are "supported by individuals with the appropriate expertise and/or recognized community organizations, groups or institutions where necessary" (7). The processes of cultural authorisation that this entails could effect restrictions in the content and perspective of an artist's work. The government gives those representing ethnic groups the task of determining who is fit to exhibit or express their particular community. Potentially destructive dynamics between ethnic minority communities and artists/ writers emerge at this intersection of ascribed authenticity/authority and potentially curbed artistic creativity.

In Australia, bureaus or offices of multicultural affairs are where specific funding for multicultural work is usually sought. Most often, the funding categories follow guidelines of promoting cultural diversification or cross-cultural work. The multicultural initiatives influence definitions of Australia's cultural identity and international reputation, oblique versions of 'engaging' with Asia. Elizabeth Gertsakis comments that this is not necessarily a progressive agenda, as "the issues around the multicultural debate have been occluded and displaced to a degree by the newer, more glamorous component which has come to fulfil the twin-headed resource category of 'culture marching with economics' of the Asia-Pacific" (42). This is a lucrative, though somewhat nearsighted, trend that successive governments are keen to acknowledge as their own. Encouraged by government funding for cross-cultural work, Susan Wang, a dancer/choreographer who arrived in Perth in 1988, changed her technique so that she could dance "for Australians", in a well-funded Chinese-Australian style (Giese, *Astronauts* 287). Lynn Fisher, who has been studying Wang's work, observes that:

> such acceptance can be 'a golden trap' . . . . If Wang moves too far away from her Chinese heritage, becoming more 'Australian', she may no longer find acceptance so easy. . . . other Asian-born choreographers living in Australia cannot get out of being pigeon-holed 'cross-cultural' if they want to continue to be funded (in Giese, *Astronaut* 287).

Moreover, Gillian Bottomley comments that the system in Australia for consultation is too simplistic and exclusive: "[t]he current, or most recent, policy, multiculturalism, basically attaches ethnic 'groups' or 'communities' to the state by means of representations, usually middle-class men" (*From Another Place* 49). This gender bias in representation, coupled with the conglomerating tendencies of most ethnic designations, can narrow the artistic possibilities for Asian-Australian authors because of the lack of community and other support. Similarly in Canada, Richard Fung observes that a skewing of representation occurs especially with regard to the containment and defusing of race issues. He contends that "multiculturalism has produced a whole caste of 'community leaders' who have facilitated in the management of race politics. The relative peace in Canada has depended on other concessions that can't be guaranteed" ("Multiculturalism" 18). This sidelining of certain concerns exposes the construction of ethnic community affairs as supplementary to the 'general' populace. Their issues are most often read as community-exclusive, in the same way that racism is considered often as only being a 'problem' for those who are non-white. This narrowed range of interaction between ethnic groups and government bodies is made even more so by the generally acknowledged gender disparity, asserted by Bottomley, when it comes to those who head the organised community groups. This would certainly influence cultural events and priorities for funding concerns. Gisela Kaplan's argument that "[m]any women's organisations could not exist without government funding, and this dependency tends to restrain them from exceeding their social and advocacy role and becoming a contesting political opposition" (194–5) also holds true for the relationship between women's groups and (largely male-dominated) community organisations. Moreover, multicultural women's groups are even more 'indebted' to government funds, and therefore subject to a heavier onus to stay within guidelines and to remain acceptable. To lessen the power of *cultural* bias, Gunew suggests a list of possible directions for more responsible and equitable arts funding/encouragement, including requiring people sitting on funding bodies to be informed (community) advocates ("Ethnicity and Excellence" 6). These actions do not offset the gender biases mentioned by Kaplan, and these concerns are ongoing considerations when examining the priorities and results of cultural/community funding. Coming to terms with the fact that a few from a community can never represent fully the demands and priorities of their constituents is a start for finding other ways of framing racial minority groups. The 'inside/outside' nature of self-identification against another group's values demands constant reassessment and awareness of the crossovers for each category. This dynamism should ensure that literary criticism has the ability to interrogate constructively the hyphenated literatures in Canada and Australia.

The diverse communities to which hyphenated Asian writers can belong comprise more than racialised or ethnic affiliations, and they are never singular, static, or unproblematic. The Chicago Cultural Studies Group points out that now, employing "newer styles of postmodern anthropology", critics "emphasize (and indeed celebrate) the openness or permeability of cultural boundaries, the impurity of cultural poetics always infected by other cultures, and the multiply constituted nature of subjectivity" (538). This 'openness' has consistently been criticised for feting apolitical versions of diversity, rendering the subject a free-floating signifier who stands for all and nothing at once. The ability to 'take on' subject positionings has led Peter McLaren to argue: "[b]y positing undecidability in advance, identity is reduced to a form of self-indexing or academic 'vogue-ing'" (64). Attempts to be unpinnable and forever shifting negate the political efficacy of purposeful identification, otherwise known as the strategic essentialism proposed by Gayatri Spivak. The diluting of impetus suggested by McLaren's use of the term 'vogue-ing', the 'strike-a-pose' made famous by pop star Madonna, is taken further by Fernando Coronil who argues that deconstructing metanarratives

> produces disjointed mininarratives which reinforce dominant worldviews; reacting against determinisms, it presents free-floating events; refusing to fix identity in structural categories, it essentializes identity through difference; resisting the location of power in structures or institutions, it diffuses it throughout society and ultimately dissolves it (99–100).

In assessing the 'free floating' signifier, both the politics involved in the action of claiming and the politics behind valuations of certain types of identity must be examined. Hyphenated Asian authors are hailed by identifications surrounding intricate conceptualisations of 'subjectivity': a sense of self that encompasses politics, sexuality, gender, class, and race or ethnic considerations. Indeed, commentators remarking on identity politics in the past decade strive to lay to rest more specific possibilities for already generic, multivalenced terms such as hybridity and the multicultural.[3] This is a manoeuvre avoided by critics including Gunew and Bottomley, because they find it productive to persevere with shifting or recreating the significance of these terms, instead of jettisoning them altogether. Bottomley cogently argues:

> A critical reflexivity could disrupt unquestioned knowledges and open up possibilities of genuinely democratic processes — not the 'anything goes' attributed to postmodernism, but sophisticated forms of recognition of the cultural possibilities being opened up, of facing rather than effacing discomforting differences and of developing forms of multiculturalism that can move beyond ethnic pluralisms ("Identification" 47).

Similarly, Gunew attempts to shift discussions about multiculturalism away from Canadian and Australian governmental terms because of their tendency to focus on ethnic communities as "perpetuating the past in a petrified form" and as 'exotic spectacles' ("Multicultural Multiplicities" 454). Building internal community links and recognising the benefits of improved, dynamic interaction with their own and other minority groups dismantles the one-way "tribute system" (McFarlane, "Haunt" 24). Scott McFarlane's use of the phrase 'tribute system' emphasises the way in which he visualises the Multiculturalism Act as "explicitly concerned more with cultural *contribution* as opposed to cultural *relations* that produce race discourse. In fact, it understands the latter only in terms of the former" (24, emphasis added). To avoid this 'supplementary' status, of only contributing to the 'whole', is the challenge for theories about Asian-Australian and Asian-Canadian literary production.

With this in mind, writing provides an ideal forum for artists refusing to tithe to government or 'the mainstream' because "[t]he arts allow a social space in which it is legitimate to ask how things might be otherwise" (Rizvi, "The Arts" 66). Ironically, however, the main source of funding for publishing community, 'multicultural', or alternative literature projects in both Australia and Canada is from government grants. In the Canadian context, Lynette Hunter argues that "[f]or many, the Multicultural aid is a stepping-stone on the way from local papers and self-publishing to being published by more established presses with aid from the Canada Council or from Provincial Arts' Councils" (40). [4] This level of cooperation is more established in Canada, particularly on the West Coast for Asian-Canadians, than in Howard-governed Australia at present, though Australia has had a 'multicultural' agenda since the mid-1970s. Some of these Canadian-funded groups and events include the Asian-Canadian Writers' Workshop (ACWW) and the annual May 'Asian Heritage Month' activities in major Canadian cities (e.g. Vancouver and Toronto). The availability of resources for publicity and financial support results in constructive dialogue and joint projects between community and artistic groups, usually creating enough momentum for further collaborations.

That said, cultural and administrative politics have also overwhelmed and restricted some joint projects. The *Writing Thru Race* conference, held in Vancouver in 1994, is perhaps the most publicly embroiled Canadian example of this kind. Both the Writers' Union of Canada and the Department of Heritage pledged funds for the conference. Later, however, a significant portion of Department of Canadian Heritage funding was withdrawn by then minister Michel Dupuys after Reform MP Jan Brown provoked media reports that accused the conference of "reinventing apartheid" (Fulford n.p.). Monika Kin Gagnon characterises these developments as "hysteria in the mainstream media [that led to] a crisis in

cultural funding policy within the Canadian House of Commons"
("Building" 118). Gagnon is one of the few critics who chart the community
outcomes of the event in all its ambivalent disarray while considering its
eclipse by the 'apartheid' outrage. She states that "the conference did not
automatically produce a homogeneous politic with regards to self-
identification, self-definition, or strategy" (*Other Conundrums* 67). The basis
for the media and parliamentary controversy were conference sessions in
which organisers limited participants to writers of colour. This same
arrangement occurred in 1992 at a previous Writers' Union of Canada
conference but failed to come to the media's attention at that time. Fred
Wah explains the reasons for the policy:

> The writers of colour and first nations writers wanted, simply, to reserve
> a space of their own, for a total of seven and a half hours one weekend,
> free from the ongoing necessity to educate, report to, and soothe the
> dominant culture. They wanted not a separation, but a chance for a cross-
> cultural exchange where 'cross-cultural' isn't only a white-crossed-with-
> everything else exchange ("Half-Bred" 2).

An article by Aruna Srivastava and Ashok Mathur, "Preston Terre Blanche,
Snow White, and the Seven Deadly Disclaimers, or the Dos of Racism",
support Wah's attitude.[5] The piece sharply criticises the shallow level of liberal
motivation towards anti-racist strategies in Canada. Srivastava and Mathur
created the article from collected, verbatim comments made at six artistic/
literary functions, amply demonstrating the forms of maintenance of white
privilege and ensuing defensive moves should this privilege be challenged.
McFarlane cogently summarises these manoeuvres as "[w]hite guilt and its
various obstructionist narratives of worship, confusion, envy, fear-mongering,
going–Native, tearful apologies and so on" which "repeatedly occupy crucial
time at anti-racist gatherings" ("Haunt" 27–8). The tension between the
ways in which racial minority writers perceive themselves and how they
are represented/viewed by various community groupings is an ongoing one
as these authors shift between different clusters of 'community'. Gagnon
observes that the withdrawal of funding for *Writing Thru Race* exposed the
"Reform Party's ability to influence cultural policy in spite of its reductive
and uninformed critique" ("Building" 126). It is precisely this reductive
commentary, however, that succeeds continually in capturing popular fears
and prejudices — the similarities between Reform and One Nation appear
once again.[6]

Many Asian-Canadian and Asian–Australian literary narratives express the need to either escape or return to various localised communities and cultural mores. These anxieties about community borders are heightened when authors and their narratives continually extend, redraw, or breach perceived social and cultural boundaries. According to Australian author Brian Castro, the repeated crossing of boundaries/genres by his writing serves a purpose: "[m]y thesis is that cross-genres relieve the schizophrenic pressures upon the dichotomy of authenticity and inauthenticity. If you cross borders regularly, you don't really have to defend them" (*Writing Asia* 36). Although Castro's comment sharply focuses attention on demands made of 'Native Others' and his methods of slipping past these imposed categories, he elides the dynamics of power implicated in 'crossing borders', physical and metaphorical. These dynamics extend beyond the act of 'crossing' itself to encompass the problems of access and mobility for various people in different communities, the connections and politics between sites on either side of a given 'border', and whether or not the crossing is a crossing over (to the other side) or a process of border erasure. By invoking this fluidity as an unmitigatedly positive condition, Castro risks becoming an individual "segregated from the collective sites of history" (Krishnaswamy 126). Far from being liberating, the act of free-floating between 'established' locations could engender feelings of displacement and alienation from the centre, difficulties with social and civic participation, and internalisation of negative representations. Rey Chow's delineation of the "politics of admittance" ("Politics" 5) argues, further, that to be let in is both a process of "recognition and acknowledgment" and "an act of repentance, a surrender of oneself in reconciliation with the rules of society" (6–7). These tensions are manifest in Goto's novel, *Chorus of Mushrooms*, which shades the borders between genres, exposes the subjectivity of oral storytelling, and the folly of believing in a singular version of ethnicity or authenticity. Throughout the novel, she deliberately combines writing styles and languages. Patrick Rengger describes it in this way: "[the book] segues into Japanese at times, creating a borderland the English-speaking reader can enter but cannot fully understand" (C2). Goto's play with language implies more than just turning expectations around. She re-forms the power of language through its multiple applications, not aligning multiplicity with dilution or lack of purity but with empowerment through its canny cultural possibilities. Through the narrative and its structure, Goto redefines ways of existing in community and creates a flexible ethnicity that remains true to its political motivations.

Since *Chorus* won the Commonwealth Prize for Best First Novel

(Canada/Caribbean regions) in 1994, Goto has been a frequent guest speaker at various feminist, Asian-Canadian, and alternative cultural events. Her publications in 2001 include *The Kappa Child* and the young adult novel *The Water of Possibility*. The setting of her first novel *Chorus* on a number of literature courses broadens her readership, as does the travelling of the publication overseas. The novel challenges many levels of representation for Japanese-Canadians, women, and cultural 'homes', while providing complex, blurred demarcations between fiction and biography. Goto's other written work, both academic and creative, engages with the politics of ethnic identification ("The Body Politic") and with contemporary feminist 'fables' ("Tales from the Breast"). The judges of the Best First Novel Prize stated that they were "utterly taken with [the novel's] ability to negotiate between cultures, with the lyricism of its prose, with the clarity of its feminist vision, and with its imaginative commitment to Alberta's landscape and culture" (McGoogan 1). Goto herself states that her sense of place in community does not necessarily come from a geographical one 'of the prairies', though Betty Quan describes *Chorus* as "prairie fiction from the Sinclair Ross School . . . get[ting] a twist" (45). Rather, Goto feels that her 'community' consists of "people, mostly women of colour writers, feminists, anti-racist allies who live all across Canada as well as in Calgary, where [she] now live[s]" (Interview 2). This invocation of a political and creative community overshadows any sense of 'ethnic' community for Goto. The lack of primary affiliation, however, does not negate her consideration of how the Japanese-Canadian community may receive her text. She warns in *Chorus's* Acknowledgements:

> [i]n the process of re-telling personal myth, I have taken tremendous liberties with my grandmother's history. This novel is a departure from historical 'fact' into the realms of contemporary folk legend. And should (almost) always be considered a work of fiction (vii).

Goto's comments ready the reader for a non-traditional text, and the style of the novel soon confirms this. The book, dedicated to Goto's grandmother Kiyokawa Naoe, includes rewritten creation myths and skewed feminist anecdotes. *Chorus* filters the Japanese-Canadian experience through several generations, and meshes social satire with cultural discovery (as opposed to *re*-discovery, which presupposes an already existing object). The power wielded by the storyteller is an attribute not lost on Goto who, like her contemporary Larissa Lai, considers her writing a "tool for change" (Interview 1). She challenges readers to take the narrative apart and offers this encouragement both to readers and, one could assume, other members of racial minority groups: "[y]ou know you can change the story" (220). By doing this, Goto shares the power of her storytelling, and the reader is immediately complicit with the language games and recreations of myths.

One of the folktales which reverses tragedy is about an old woman in the mountains who was about to be abandoned by her poverty-stricken family. She turns the abandonment into a type of freedom unknown to those maintaining social mores, having her way even as she is cast out of the community (64–6). The main character's grandmother, Naoe, demonstrates repeatedly this vitality in older characters. She persistently toys with those around her and refuses to play the role of the quiet, unintrusive elderly relative. Marilyn Iwama describes her as "funny, bawdy, impatient, and sexual" (Review 17–8). Naoe covets subversive opportunities in her life, stranded as she is in her daughter Keiko's ordered household. She keeps and feeds the moths which Keiko tries to vacuum up each year, eats taboo Japanese foods in bed with her granddaughter Muriel, and declares that she feels "horny as a musk-drenched cat" (39) at eighty-five years old. The 'happy ending' that Goto affords in her novel details Naoe's final escape from the Tonkatsu household and into adventures which include an affair with Tengu and riding as the "Purple Mask" in the Calgary Stampede. The final images of Naoe as the "Purple Mask" ironically install a Japanese grandmother into a most incongruous arena, one full of cowboys, rodeo culture, and the associated cultural 'familiarity' of the long-established stampede.

Naoe and her narrator granddaughter Muriel, who she calls Murasaki,[7] form a bond in which meditations on what it means to be Japanese-Canadian offer a 'future'; one abandoned by Keiko. Keiko represents the assimilative generations, who hoped to disappear into the *gaijin* landscape even while knowing that they could never do so because of their racially marked bodies. She exhibits what Quan describes as "cultural aphasia" (45), a condition of "impairment or loss of memory of language [and culture]" (Sasano 12). In her desperation to be seen to be "the perfect rural Albertan" (Sasano 7), she suggests to Muriel's drama teacher that dyeing the girl's hair to play the part of Alice in a school play is acceptable. Muriel, appalled that she would "stand out like a freak" (177) if her hair was dyed, offers to play the part of the Cheshire Cat, who has slanty eyes anyway. Contrasting with her mother's attitude, Muriel rejects the 'want-to-be-white' perspective, though she is equally suspicious of relationships in which she is configured only as an 'Asian' girl.[8]

Through the voices of Muriel and Naoe, Goto blends generational and cultural observations with narrative time leaps and the pushing of community, gender, and family boundaries by the narrator. Isolated from the more concentrated urban Japanese communities, the Tonkatsu family live in the small rural town of Nanton, Alberta, a place Muriel describes as "cowboy purgatory" (124). The farm grows mushrooms and employs the cheaper labour of newly arrived Vietnamese immigrants who become the Others in Muriel's, and her mother's, eyes. They even resort to giving the workers new names because they deem Vietnamese ones too hard to pronounce. Her mother tells her, "[h]elp me think up of some nicknames for these people . . . their real names are too hard to pronounce and no one will be able to remember them" (34). They come up with names like 'Jim' and 'Joe' for the workers — alluding to, and complicit with, the process of 'anglicising' foreign names that occurred when people emigrated to the New World. When Muriel and her white Canadian friends run through the workplace, she sees it through a white 'Canadian-ised' perspective, making judgements about the alienness of the employees, convinced that they are laughing at her. She distances their foreignness from herself and is alarmed, even feels betrayed, when one of her white friends tells her that the Tonkatsu home smelt of "warm toes": "[s]omething so insidious tattooed into the walls of our home, the upholstery in our car, the very pores in our skin" (62). The way in which the Tonkatsu family earn their living undercuts Keiko's quest to remove all signs of 'ethnicity' from their home and persons. Cropping mushrooms becomes analogous with Muriel's aversion to Japanese 'ethnicity': something silently growing in the dark, kept from normal view, with the "fushigi" (Monika Gagnon, "Story" 17) smell of it clinging to you despite all efforts to hide it.

The multi-generational household is configured such that it presents clashing ideas about language and orality, reflecting each person's disposition towards their 'culture': Naoe speaks only in Japanese but listens in English, Keiko refuses to speak Japanese though she listens to it, Sam remembers how to read Japanese but does not speak it, and Muriel functions almost completely in English and cannot understand Japanese but wants to. After Naoe disappears, she and Muriel 'communicate' with no linguistic barriers at all, sliding from Japanese to English and back again in various (mental) conversations. Lien Chao presumes that latter generations of Asian-Canadians are necessarily 'hard done by' because they speak English and not Chinese, Japanese, or another "heritage language" ("Anthologizing" 150). She terms this loss a form of "linguistic dispossession" ("Anthologizing" 161). Such a prescriptive trope of embarrassment at the lack of linguistic authenticity, of bereftness because of some perceived loss of language,[9] is challenged by the characters' language games in *Chorus,* who present a more malleable approach to the complexities of language functions. To propose that 'losing' a heritage language is all that is involved in negotiating one's voice also overlooks the use of English as a first language and seeks to deny that English can ever, satisfyingly, be an Asian-Canadian's tongue.[10]

Further to this point of narrowly defining and emphasising the Other only in terms of language, Gunew remarks: "[i]n the drive towards universalism one cannot afford to admit that those oppressed others whom we hear as speaking authentic experience might be playing textual games" ("Culture, Gender" 5). What *Chorus* accomplishes successfully on several levels is the interplay between finding cultural 'homes' within certain activities and rejecting authenticity as an inconvenience and, in the novel, a bit of a laugh. Gagnon discusses this humorous edge that Goto gives to episodes of 'insidious and pervasive racism', mentioning specifically the irreverent surname of Tonkatsu ("Story" 17).

Chorus, read alongside Kogawa's *Obasan* and Sakamoto's *The Electrical Field,* produces a sharply contrasting rendition of Japanese-Canadianness that subverts accepted notions of this community even while re-inscribing new versions of them in the course of the novel. A marked divergence between *Chorus* and the other two novels is the way in which Goto offers "a resonant chorus of women's voices" (Gagnon, "Story" 17), whereas *Obasan* and *The Electrical Field* pivot on the uses and significance of silence and that which is repressed. Kogawa's and Goto's books display a similar satirical edge when it comes to naming authority figures, emphasising their hypocrisy or describing forays into community participation. In *Obasan,* the officer writing in reply to one of Aunt Emily's queries signs his/her name "B. Good" at the end (37): not 'being good' given as one of the main admonishments from the government for justifying the uprooting of communities/families during internment and the confiscation of homes and assets in the 1940s during the Second World War. In *Chorus,* Goto includes a passage about Pastor Lysol in Nanton,[11] detailing the consequences of courting social contacts within established local 'Canadian' institutions like the Christian church. During a Sunday service, Muriel contemplates the places where god(s) would exist and decided that they "would never linger in pews stinking with selfish guilt. With all those wads of gum" (99). Lysol's wife declares that she has been tempted by the Devil to masturbate (100–1), and her husband responds to this announcement by giving a sermon about the weakness of women. Goto's indictment of the double standards surrounding racism and other forms of discrimination in a small community's authoritative structures (including schooling systems) demonstrates why Muriel seeks validation of her self through newly mapped paths which combine elements of 'Japanese' cultural traits with 'Canadian' practicalities. She follows neither the examples set by her parents nor by her grandmother, though the latter has a profound effect on how she perceives of society and the relationships she chooses.

Aside from language and Goto's sporting with racist and sexist assumptions, one of the foci for the Tonkatsus' cultural changeover has been the determined alteration in eating habits, Westernised food being the only type provided. Naoe comments that her daughter has "converted from rice and *daikon* to wieners and beans" (13) and, in many ways, Keiko tries to make them eat their way into a new Canadian skin. Ostensibly, through the absorption of Western-style Canadian food, the Tonkatsus would achieve the goal of becoming one of 'them'. Using metaphors of cultural miscegenation, Muriel, as well as *Obasan's* Naomi and Stephen Nakane, are considered 'banana'. This usually derogatory metaphor is used by those within and without the community, across most racial and class groups, barring the embedded invisibility of whiteness. There are similar metaphors which denote the clashing (not melding) of races or cultures. For example, African-Americans who take on what are deemed white, middle-class characteristics, or who do not act 'like a black person should' are termed "oreos" (Dyson 222). Similarly, apples have been used to describe Native Americans and coconuts to individuals of Southeast Asian or West Indian origin.

The plethora of food metaphors links these models of hybrid identities with notions of cultural consumption and ingestion. Yau Ching, examining Ang Lee's film *Eat Drink Man Woman*, observes: "[t]hose close-ups of the kungfu of chopping and stir-frying constitute a postmodern version of the West's Chinoiserie. I felt like I was stripteasing, selling something that I didn't have" (31). Yau's positioning as a part of the 'striptease' offered by the highly detailed shots of food preparation is discomforting. The scenes are meant to be evocatively 'Chinese' and operate as cultural shorthand: "[f]ood thus serves as an index of the imaginary 'heritage' passed on, the racial symbolism, the alimentary sign of Chineseness" (31). This obsession with the minutiae of process and ingredients becomes a part of what Shu-Mei Shih calls a "porno-culinary genre", another way for 'Chineseness' to be observed, assessed, and ultimately consumed.

As pointers of racial/cultural doubling, the food markers mentioned above assume a constant social or mental bearing as 'towards white': white as the centre, as the most desired once again. The community or familial censure that this doubling encounters could be read as a start in eroding the assumed attractive power of being 'white', except that the judgements are based on essentialist ideas of what white/non–white means (in behaviour, talk, etc.) and their incompatibility. This mode of reasoning maintains that a subject must be one side of the hyphenated identity or the other. For the most part, the terms used to describe the 'whitened' Others are analogous with various versions of raw produce and organic perishables. Conversely, "[w]hiteness [is] often signified . . . by commodities and brands: Wonder Bread, Kleenex, Heinz 57. In this identification, whiteness [comes] to be seen as spoiled by capitalism, and as being linked with capitalism in a way other cultures are not" (Frankenberg 199). The condition of whiteness as embodying capitalism inflects various constructions of Western 'modernity' as well as the assumption of this kind of modernity as the logical state to which all nations and communities aspire.

The constant melding of competing races as food symbols contradicts the argument that food is but a surface facet of cultural identity, as only "a further lamination of ideology" (Morrissey 75) rather than an area of intense personal and political negotiation. Goto addresses this dismissal of food as only "a superficial means of understanding a different culture" (201) through the cooking/shopping sequences which allow Keiko to balance cultures and, obliquely, Muriel to heal after Naoe's escape. For Muriel, dipping into her culinary roots does not mean swaying to the Japanese side of the hyphen as much as balancing and challenging her hyper-Canadian upbringing.

In the latter part of the novel, Goto directly analogises the telling of stories and the sharing of folktales as another form of cultural 'food': "there must be a lot of people out there just starving for a filling story. Something that would leave a rich flavour on their tongue, on their lips. Lick, then suck their fingertips. Let me feed you" (201). Muriel learns the power of storytelling from her grandmother, whereas Keiko eventually starts telling her own stories by the end of the novel, a sign of her 'recovery' from a completely assimilative position. The office library maintained by Muriel's father epitomises the secrecy of the Tonkatsu's visible but suppressed Japaneseness. It exhibits Japanese books because the father remembers how to read the language but cannot speak it any more after many years' denial. He would need to 'glue his tongue back on', to protest the repression of his speech (Kogawa, *Obasan* 36). He perseveres in slinking into the Japanese grocery store to buy his clandestine food supplies as if it were a criminal act — a betrayal of Keiko, and of their 'Canadianness' which they had tried so hard to achieve. When Muriel claims her more flamboyant Murasaki identity, it is through a combination of food triggers, adapted folktales, and being able to understand Japanese once her grandmother has disappeared. As Guy Beauregard stresses:

> the stories Murasaki tells, like the food she cooks, are not attempts to reclaim an authentic identity from Japan. They are instead part of what Rey Chow calls the process of writing diaspora: negotiating, and not merely preserving, cultural identities outside of narrow ethnic, racial, and national borders ("Hiromi" 59).

Chorus openly plays with people's ways of interpreting and reinterpreting/ rewriting stories. Throughout the novel, Goto keeps the reader caught between being led by the narrative and having to reassess the 'truth' of what they were just reading. This situation is modulated, of course, by whether the reader is familiar with Goto's stories or is hearing them for the first time. Especially in conjunction with Goto's erosion of language as defining authenticity, her dismantling of who gets to tell the 'right' story also diffuses the burden of truth-telling and the educative potential of ethnic narratives. Retelling a story different ways every time is the way Naoe teaches Muriel the constructedness of narrative form and, metaphorically, elements of self-determination. Naoe gives Muriel the power to create and tell her own stories, and her own lies. Goto symbolically questions her own authorial power by having Muriel, the omniscient narrator, sprinkle her prose with double takes, asking whether she has forgotten or told the wrong story. Through redefining what ethnicity and community signify in *Chorus*, Goto's novel broadens the boundaries of what 'Asian-Canadian literature' can be.

For groups with less well-established presences, work that defines and redefines the range of available identifications helps in laying the bases for further constructive contestations. Although the publication of Asian diasporic narratives concerning mainland China has boomed, there is not the same level of exposure and dissemination of literature that specifically addresses, or is grounded in, the concerns of Asian-Canadian or Asian-Australian groups, however problematically these may be defined. Even so, the next reading generation of Asian-Australians and Asian-Canadians will be the first to grow up with a body of texts that 'hail' them and reflect, to varying degrees, their own experiences of living in a majority white society as parts of minority groups.

While the levels of representation for hyphenated Asian authors in national literatures is increasing now, an associated development required for building a more resilient and sophisticated area of study is the recognition of Asian-Australianness or Asian-Canadianness as validated identities. The term 'Asian-Australian' occupies a relatively new space in the critical imaginary, and momentum for Asian-Australian studies as a discipline is only apparent since the mid-1990s. In mainstream media and common community parlance, 'Asian-Australian' has yet to make an impression. Trans-Asian-community coalitions are relatively scarce, and certain groups that cohered during the growth of Hansonism are no longer in existence. Lazaroo's novel, *The World Waiting To Be Made*, maps some of the fictional contours of 'Asian-Australianness' through a mixed race narrator.

The narrator (who remains unnamed throughout the novel) recounts the transition for her family, from Singaporean to Australian society, detailing the compromises and challenges of growing up as a Eurasian woman in 1970s–80s' Australia surrounded by the very Anglo-Celtic suburbs of Perth, Western Australia. The family, with an Asian father and an Anglo-Australian mother, comes to Australia just after the abolition of the White Australia policy. The narrator is immediately embroiled in the quest to be more Australian and less 'ethnic/Asian', mostly brought on by the intense exclusion and discrimination surrounding her in the schoolyard. This takes her through a material rejection of foods and sweets, similar to Keiko's attempt to 'Canadianise' her family through its eating habits in *Chorus*. That she is never able to fully excise these from her palate signifies the enduring influence they have on her sense of the world and hints at ways in which she could partake of it. The novel progresses through the metaphoric *Bildungsroman* of the beach (à la *Puberty Blues*)[12] and the outback for some revelations but few recognitions. The narrator chooses to try and "map a new self in the perceived emptiness of [the Outback]" but found that "it only accentuate[d] the alienation of her position and the complications of finding space for herself that was not already overlapping, or outside of what was offered by the people surrounding her" (Khoo, "Someone Else's Zoo" 27).

The narrator feels desperately on the outside because of her racial and cultural background, with who she is falling short of the person she feels she needs to be. Throughout her adolescence, she tries to alter her features and mode of dress, to escape her home influences and become someone who did not cause comment or stand out. In a section subtitled "Changing Sides", the narrator comments that she turns up for dinner with the family one night "with everything red from either plucking, shaving or dyeing, the skin underneath my brows, the colour of my hair, my legs. A tandoori chicken" (99). It is through the accoutrements of 'young womanhood' that the path of change is read. The narrator's embarkation on the "itchified" trail of Australian femininity causes consternation and disapproval on her father's part. He labelled girls who exhibited signs of "ripening too early" (98) as 'itchified' — the narrator further hones this observation to whether to categorise girls as only 'itchified' or truly cool. What is apparent in her demarcation of these two categories is the combination of class awareness and levels of 'flaunting' sexuality. For her, coming from a lower middle-class family and without the benefit of the belonging white skin, the social group available to her "bought their uniforms secondhand, wore lace-up shoes and did their homework diligently. . . . We sat together because no one else would have us" (98). All the others in this group are not-white, not-affluent, and suffered similar experiences of derision and rejection.

The father's response to his daughter's grappling with the overwhelming adolescent need to belong is a textual example of the policing of 'good women' in ethnic groups as described by Bottomley. Hierarchies apparent in ethnic communities and their reflexively conventional mores project roles for men and women in the maintenance of the 'nation': "whereas men are invoked as leaders and citizens of the new nation, women are widely regarded as icons of national values, or idealized custodians of tradition" (Boehmer 224). In Lazaroo's novel, the narrator harbours deep resentment against her twin sister for being the good, Eurasian daughter, the one whose contrasting behaviour casts hers as all the more unacceptable. The protagonist's intolerance of her own sibling demonstrates the destructiveness of internalising racist values. She comforts herself with the fact that her sister is darker and therefore more recognisably 'Asian'. Her sister was also more of the 'back home' sort, one who is in the "waiting-to-be-asked" category (84) — fitting the Good Asian Daughter stereotype that the narrator tries so hard to shake off or disprove.

The discrimination and emphasis on her outsider status encountered during her schooldays and later at work also carried over into her personal relationships with others in the Chinese community, her lovers, and family. From her teen years, she sees her father 'trade in' her mother for a "frosted prospective wife, Dawn" (207), a literal projection of his need to be seen as truly 'Australian'. He goes through the process of finding the most 'Australian' house he can, a piece of real estate which soon becomes symbolic to his daughters of his desertion of the 'family' and the deterioration of their mother's mental well-being. Although his first wife is 'white' Australian, she is too much a reminder of where he came from and she is the mother of his brown children. These traits impede his embrace of the Australian way of life and his nurtured sense of sophistication which can only prosper when an immaterial and mysterious 'exoticness' attaches itself to him: "[i]n his Asian-ness, he seemed so detached and partially revealed, enticingly undiscovered" (137). He preferred the maintenance of this cultivated 'inscrutability' rather than the everyday reality of living as a racial minority in a discriminatory society. For him, the heightened cultural capital of appearing unreadable 'progresses' him through his search for an Australian lifestyle. He ascertains correctly that he must maintain an aura of exoticism while living a lifestyle that denotes 'cosmopolitanism' as opposed to 'multiculturalism'. The former term implies a sense of fluidity that the latter does not — multiculturalism grounds an individual in the context of nation and community in ways which cosmopolitanism specifically does not. The narrator sums up near the end of the novel that "ethnics like us had either to hold together with our own precious few in communal dagdom, or learn how to appear more knowingly and sophisticatedly international than other Australians" (199). The father's eager movement away from the people who know him prompts his daughter to observe that "change is the essence, for him" and that her parents' marriage was destined to fail because "[her] mother had stepped out young and full of hope onto the shoreline of his home, to find him gone, already looking for something else" (265). The suburban existence of his wife and children clash with his consolidation of Otherness and as exotica, representations that earn him the attention and unfixed, generalised identity he desires.

For his eldest daughter, however, this quality of 'difference' is a bane that seemingly manifests itself in a physical rejection of her own 'Asianness' (as she interprets her appendicitis attack). Her repression of everything that might make her behaviour differ from that of her school friend Sue and her group could not be contained physically. In her outward appearance, though, the situation is completely reversed and she becomes the repository for all kinds of exoticism. She became "any wog people wanted [her] to be" (81). Asian-Canadian writer Jam Ismail further details this feeling of genericism when she describes a character, Ban Yen, as being thought:

> italian in kathmandu, filipina in hong kong, eurasian in kyoto, japanese in anchorage, dismal in london england, hindu in edmonton, generic oriental in calgary, western canadian in ottawa, anglophone in montreal, metis in jasper, eskimo at hudson's bay department store, vietnamese in chinatown, tibetan in vancouver, commie at the u.s. border
>
> on the whole very asian (128).

Several instances in Lazaroo's novel reflect the process of Othering to which Ismail refers in her collection of cultural and political 'allocations'. The treatment of the narrator by her first 'serious' lover, Max, as well as her consideration of Eddie the 'Chinese Boy' are just two of these examples. Max is interested in her precisely because of her perceived exotic Asianness. He eventually breaks up with her and moves on to a relationship with a "little *Japanese* lady" (205), a move from which she has to refrain from "congratulating him on his multicultural approach to dating" (206). For her, the aversion to associating with Eddie is a result of her seeing the same 'negative' things in him which she is attempting to deny for herself: "[a]t school, Eddie had been the Asian no one had wanted to own, least of all me, so cowardly about owning my own Asian-ness" (204). These self-imposed barriers between members of similar racial minorities in Australia and elsewhere are repeatedly expressed in literary work. They refer, mostly ironically, to the 'dangers' of not trying to assimilate. The narrator in *World* refuses both Eddie and Franco as potential school social dates, as turning up with them at the dance would prove that she did not belong (85). In a similar way, Goto in *Chorus* indicates this reluctance to associate with other Others: "I knew that being seen with [Shane Wu] would lessen my chances of being in the popular crowd. That Oriental people in single doses were well enough, but any hint of a group and it was all over" (125). Later in her life, though, when the pressurised environment of school is over, Eddie corresponds with her while she is at her outback teaching post. His homosexuality and HIV-positive status affect her ability to talk about him with anyone else, though she recognises the compromised friendship she has conducted with him all these years as a self-protective measure against the denigration of her classmates.

Although the narrator comes to realise in the end that she does not have to take on the difficulties of her family's history, it is only through being forced to negotiate between their vision of the world, Uncle Linus's, and her own that she reaches these conclusions. In many respects, Eddie was someone who could not 'go home' in the same way as she does, because both his parents were dead. The narrator manages, however, to work through her identity crises by incorporating aspects of what she learns from the way her parents act towards each other, and on her trip back to Singapore.

Lazaroo's highlighting of class difference in community relations plays an important part in the narrator's depth of perception about herself, from her school days of comparing her looks and income[13] to those of Sue and her other 'friends' to the nasty beachside episode with another Eurasian woman. In these scenes, when she first meets Gloria, the Eurasian interior designer, the narrator is pleased to see someone of 'her' background so assured and confident, not hiding or afraid to have an opinion. This does not dissipate even in the face of Gloria's snide insults and patronising conversation, a major part of which relies on an affected superiority because of Gloria's more 'British' stock. Her first comment to the narrator, after finding out her last name is Dias, is: "[a]h. A lower class of Eurasian. From Malacca. Quite, ah, simple people. Quite. A different race really. Less British in their blood than my family. . . . Speech lessons would help" (192). The colonial legacy of shamefulness attached to being 'more native' is a trait of *World's* narrator all through school and her first teaching appointment, finally exploding itself during the festival parade in Broome where the organisers dress her in a mermaid suit as part of a determinedly multicultural float.

It is during the festival that one of the most significant identifications in the novel occurs. When she is being fitted for her costume, two men from the pub next door verbally accost her. They position her squarely as someone who is fit to provide 'Oriental sex' (as alluded to in Goto's *Chorus*) by yelling to her, "[c]an you do things the strippers in Thailand do with bananas?" (194). The fact that she had automatically smiled at them first, as she had been taught to do, curtails the ways in which she could answer the offensive comment. This meshing of the accrued, socially taught, feminine manners and the hailing of her availability/sexuality as an *Asian* woman exposes the social and 'cultural' barriers that she must mediate daily. She regrets her initial response of smiling at them, but then states, "[a]ll my life I had been practising disguises, and now I felt as if I was practising for some culmination of this" (194). Her resignation about the fact that 'this is what is expected of me' underlines the scepticism that Lazaroo writes into the farcical scenes in which Vic the PR man attempts to get Broome successfully 'multicultural' in the parade.

Ultimately, when the narrator makes a trip back 'home', the emotional revelations allow her to be accepting of being not-blond, not-blue-eyed, and 'not-cool'. Travelling to the origins of her life and her family's quirks permit her to lay them to rest and move on. Lazaroo's evocation of contemporary Singapore offsets any essentialist or clichéd solution to 'in-betweenness'. On the flight over, the loud musings of a nearby couple going on holidays in Singapore perplex her. They point out the war memorial to Australian soldiers they want to visit which, apparently, "looks nice and clean" (210), and this makes her complicit in the discourse as both a 'tourist' and a historically (but not really) sited 'local'. The travel blurb screened by the airline does not mention Eurasians as a distinct group in Singaporean history or contemporary society, and this excludes her and her family again, mirroring the way she feels excluded in Australia as a member of a racial minority group. Her perspective on the journey to Singapore is mostly as an outsider, as she remained unknowledgeable about language and custom, geographically inept, and unable to trade her ability to look 'belonging' into any feelings of confidence. In choosing what to buy from the overflowing shopping districts of Singapore, a process she called "search[ing] for other disguises" (219), she manages to shock her cousins and her aunt. They delve into her purchases surreptitiously and denigrate her for buying silk underwear (which she had purchased in haste thinking that they represented the "sophistication of both East and West" [220]). Their comments shifted from being appalled at her spending so much money when she should be saving up for her marriage, to assuming from her spendthrift ways that she would have friends who had died from AIDS. Even though her Middle Aunty is 'shocked' at her spending so much money on silk underwear, she had expected such behaviour from the narrator. The reason is that the family assigns to the narrator several stereotypes of the 'Western'/Australian woman, and it is this category in which the family most often installs her. From them, she does not find much comfort for her confusion about who she is and where she 'fits in'. The narrator is aware of her incongruent positioning in a society and country that is familiar yet altogether alien. The journey 'home' is not simple, nor is she instantaneously at ease. Her relatives are all strangers but for their names, and their deliberate family intimacies wear thin after only a few days in Singapore. The narrator's desperate shopping trips in Singapore for items that are not actually what she normally wears demonstrate her ingrained perception of what one does in Singapore. Singapore is full of hollow shopping temptations and family that disapproves of how she dresses, Malacca is steeped in history that she finds alien, and her stay with Tilly only emphasises the number of 'faces' she maintains in her life. Because she was hoping to overcome the excluded status she felt she had in Australia by going 'home' to where her roots were, the realisation that she was even more of a foreigner in Malacca and Singapore is doubly powerful.

Initially, then, the return to her roots appears clichéd but, in her ambivalent and contrasting evocations of contemporary Singapore and Malaysia, Lazaroo avoids celebrating homeland or any kind of cultural family. As Stuart Hall argues, the crucial point is not to confirm inherent cultural characteristics but to "insist that others recognize that what they have to say comes out of particular histories and cultures and that everyone speaks from positions within the global distribution of power" (in Ang, "Migrations" 15). In her individual characters and their overlapping ways of living in 'post-colonial' Southeast Asia, Lazaroo demonstrates the fine line between living with, and exoticising, Other customs, while estranging her narrator's version of normality. The assumptions that the relatives maintain about the narrator because of her Australianness stand as a paradox to the way she is perceived in Australia itself.

Because of her intention to visit Uncle Linus, she encounters resistance from various aunts who tell her various stories of Linus' supernatural powers or his assumed senility in an attempt to repel her. On meeting him again, her conversations with Uncle Linus elevate him to a role like that of an oracle. He speaks wise words about belonging, having personal integrity, trying too hard to belong, and consequently alludes to his astral journeys where he visits his family in Western Australia. The comfort the narrator derives from the audience with Linus seems to rest upon his ability to know her, and his lessons which were, in essence, about 'knowing thyself'. At one point, Linus mentions the numbers of in-between people in the world who are "unrealised in themselves" (259). The mystery attributed to his gifts of perception is deepened when the narrator herself reconfigures her younger dreams of travelling to other shores as a *bomoh* in astral travel, perhaps an allusion to a genetic spiritual trait.

The way in which Uncle Linus embodies the 'wise Asian' stereotype requires further examination here. Though the narrator fails to find a sense of self through interacting with her aunts and other cousins, she does discover it with Uncle Linus. In the novel, Lazaroo has offered readers two versions of the 'inscrutable Asian'. The first is the narrator's father when he deliberately fosters his image as exotic and elusively cosmopolitan, shedding the embarrassing reality of a wife and two brown children. The second is the figure of Uncle Linus, who subsequently offers the narrator the answer to her angstful queries of adolescence and adulthood. He couches his responses to her life's questions in formalised, sometimes cryptic, ways, much like those of a great sage or guru. On her problematic 'Australianness', he observes:

> Australians are very *emotional*, but afraid of real feeling. Australians are . . . afraid of informing their thoughts with real intelligent *feeling*. In this fear you have become Australian. And you do not smell Asian any more. You are not eating our curried devil anymore in Australia. You are dealing with other devils (258).

Linus's comments could be read as trying to distil the true essence of Eurasianness which has been lost from the narrator and, thus, allowing her to resolve some anxieties, even while she has doubts about Linus fulfilling her need to have them solved for her (260). Dorothy Wang reads Lazaroo as "showing how 'Australianness', and 'Asianness' and individuality are commodities to be bought and sold" and how, for the narrator, this is "inseparable from the activity of consumption and self-commodification" (49). The realisation after her uncle's death that she saw his son in the crowd at Broome during the festival parade seems to advocate this sentiment. For the narrator, having family sited in the previous spaces of discomfort recalls the difficulty of always wanting to be someone else, someone more Australian. She describes "their relationship to one another" as "overwhelmed by our longing to imitate this vision of Australian life" (275). But having understood what Linus meant and finding some sort of peace from her fervent search for a 'self', she can afford to 'recognise' members of her family within the alien socio-scape of Australia. No longer does she only see things with a "migrant's gaze" (274). In the movement between communities, Lazaroo stresses, there is always a compromise for making your own place, and these could be quantified either in loss or gain. In specifying the contingent nature of ethnic and community cultural negotiations in Australia and 'back home', the novel succeeds in moving the terms of identity politics onto continually shifting foundations. It is never a matter of only distinguishing which side of the hyphen dominates but how 'community' is formed and on what bases — political and social — it functions. These real-life situations and confronting prejudices emphasise the falseness of the 'free-floating signifier' who can slide between and over borders, as envisaged by Brian Castro. These cultural allocations have material repercussions and, in their texts, Goto and Lazaroo provide narrative trajectories for how these actions affect and compose certain senses of identity.

The complexities of exploring ethnicity are epitomised in the texts by Lazaroo and Goto. Goto, a first generation Japanese-Canadian woman, evokes the strangeness of being 'Canadianised' in Muriel's family, as well as the ways in which the narrator is considered only as a generalised Asian by surrounding white Canadian associates (especially in relationships where "Oriental sex" is sought [122]). Lazaroo's Eurasian characters are similarly categorised, complicated by the treatment of the narrator as a true 'Australian' by relatives in Singapore and Malacca. The two texts also demonstrate wariness about community participation in general and in ethnic community groups. Both Muriel and the narrator of *World* grow to recognise the advantages of choosing 'community' at certain times, whether they are cultural or social communities, but they also know that the activity of making choices does not stop. The novels also iterate the influences of different generations on each other. *World* has the narrator find solace in the words and mannerisms of her (Great) Uncle Linus, whereas Muriel is inspired by Naoe's actions and perspective on life.

While the older generations of Naoe and Uncle Linus represent sources of wisdom and re-vision, the parents of the two protagonists are consistently apologetic or caught in their own inventions of 'new selves', and the younger generation is left to piece together their own alliances and possibilities. In this way, the novels question more traditional 'search for identity' narratives by not offering a solid, straightforward ending. There is no closure. The endings are, admittedly, quite happy but this does not evolve from any sense of cohesiveness in the narrators' identities. They emerge more from the main characters' growing awareness of other people's fallibility and their own perceptions of how they had excised parts of their lives to better fit in. They find a workable balance by stopping the denial of their cultural pasts and scrapping the necessity of a perfectly assimilated future.

The multiple connections between individuals and their communities can function in both encouraging and restrictive ways. The example of the intercommunity controversy during the *Writing Thru Race* event confirms the answerability of most initiatives to governmental offices, and this often means diminished autonomy for community groups in setting the agenda. Aside from negotiating with dominant Anglo-European structures in government, Gagnon noted that the fractured concluding sessions of *Writing Thru Race* indicated a transitional cultural politics among racial minority writers and publishers themselves. Though it may 'look bad' to funding bodies for these groups to disagree, Gagnon deems it necessary and states that "[i]nitial optimism for a shared politic must give way to different, if more dramatically effective, crises of representation" ("Building" 128). Although she is speaking specifically of activist events and community anti-racist initiatives, the narratives examined in this chapter accord with the process of reaching constructive points after phases of uncertainty, discord, and rejection. For Goto, the revision of tales and lending them a feminist perspective allows Muriel to 'own' them. In Lazaroo's novel, Uncle Linus becomes the stuff of contemporary legend, occupying a Buddha-like role and setting the protagonist upon the enlightened path of self-knowledge. In separate ways, both Goto and Lazaroo use these myths and legends to rejuvenate their protagonists' relationships, their understanding of being visibly different in Western society, and strategies to meld their Australian or Canadian selves with their social and cultural communities.

The multiple positionings afforded by community and ethnicity demonstrate canny and playful possibilities for diasporic Asian fiction. However, the reality of discrimination and its material consequences tempers the propagation of this knowing manipulation as only a word game or a form of political point-scoring. The *Writing Thru Race* example proves that prejudice can set back community initiatives and even prevent their taking place. Australian feminist scholar Chilla Bulbeck argues that "[c]oalition work certainly does not advocate incorporation of the other. It means walking the tightrope of connection, distance and power" (221). The need to address racism at all levels underlines the necessity of transforming current representations and critical practices. This process includes new forms of coalitional politics that emphasise the prevalence of compound priorities, as well as the ability to read these literatures as creative, rhetorical strategies.

5

Patriotism, War, and Other National Desires: Asian Masculinities in Progress

> If I had replied, "Of course, I'd fight against Australia, fight against you Australians," they'd have found that normal behaviour for a yellow devil.
>
> (Sang, *Year the Dragon Came* 159)

> [Fanon's work] reminds us that identification is never outside or prior to politics, that identification is always inscribed within a certain history: identification names not only the history of the subject but the subject in history.
>
> (Fuss, *Interior Colonies* 39)

Tongue-in-cheek, Sau-ling Wong declared 1991 the Year of the Asian-American Man because of the number of successful literary publications by Asian-American men and the appearance of "an especially intriguing cultural artifact" ("Subverting" 1), the Asia Pacific Islander Men calendar that showcased the desirability and virility of Asian men. Her subsequent critique of the calendar and its priorities is a welcome artifact in its own right, as Asian male identity and sexuality have been arguably the most under-represented areas in diasporic Chinese and Japanese studies. This is particularly true of representational studies and critiques of cultural production. That said, diasporic Asian masculinity studies is currently an area with a fast-growing profile.

Ironically, the impetus to write against prominent patriarchal structures has led to research in diasporic women's studies and feminism, and gay and lesbian studies outstripping examinations of diasporic masculinities. That is, while there is significant overlap in some areas of gay/queer studies and diasporic masculinity studies, there have been few concurrent, overt engagements with both areas. Undeniably, the majority of research in diasporic masculinities is currently taking place in the American context thanks to the momentum of institutionalised Asian-American studies. Research into these particular formations of masculinity has permeated the debates (and their permutations) between and about Maxine Hong Kingston and Frank Chin, critiques of David Mura's *M. Butterfly*, and the 'invasion' of Hollywood by Hong Kong action filmmakers and stars.[1] The increasing publication of works that address diasporic queer and masculinist theory indicates an engagement with long-neglected aspects of Asian-North American society. Whereas statistical and sociological information about the Chinese sojourner population or interned Japanese communities is becoming readily available, the examination of cultural production about these (and subsequent) experiences from specifically masculinist perspectives is at an early stage. This is particularly noticeable in Western regions outside North America.[2]

He Says, She Says: Intra-community Gender Division

Kenneth Lee titled his article "Angry Yellow Men: Exploiting Asian Discontent" and emphasised the importance of recognising strategies of co-option and staged antagonisms — not just towards Asian communities but, in a much more destructive manner, *within* them. Knowing the strategies of division could prevent these tactics from swamping dialogue about the politics of gender and representations of sexuality. One of the foremost tactics for defusing the mobilisation of racial minorities is pitting groups within the movement against each other, particularly along gendered lines. For diasporic communities, this splitting occurs partly because of the hyper-visibility of the Asian Woman compared with that of the Asian Man. In the histories of Western nations such as Australia and Canada, diasporic Chinese and/or Japanese men are the figurative and material threats to the integrity of perceived Australian- or Canadianness. These perceived threats ranged from invasion and contamination scenarios and the enduring fear of the Yellow Peril 'stealing jobs' through their cheaper labour, to greedy nouveau riche, gangster or refugee stereotypes.[3] Ironically, these aggressive scenarios of diasporic men swamping and dominating society exist alongside equally hostile representations of them as 'feminised' or emasculated Others, completely alien and socially unacceptable in Western societies. The perceived docility of Chinese workers was certainly exploited in gaining cheap, amenable labour for Australian and Canadian nation-building projects such as building railways. Both Kam Louie and Jinqi Ling argue for attention to the differentiated consequences of referring to feminisation or emasculation, Ling specifically pointing to the men's feminised image as it is conflated with Model Minority traits (Ling 315).[4] Allan Luke describes diasporic men in the West as:

> hav[ing] all the characteristics of something Other, something more feminine in the normative eye of Western sexuality: slender and relatively hairless bodies, differently textured and coloured skin and straight hair. In Western public representations of masculinity we are defined in terms of absence, lack or silence. In this kind of sexual environment, we are invisible — not present, without a place or 'name' in the discourses and practices of white male sexuality (32).

More sophisticated cultural representations of diasporic masculinity (and, simultaneously, femininity) develop when conditions and hierarchies of nationalism/community are addressed in conjunction with those of gender/ sexuality. I deliberately entwine these concepts, because masculinity in many Western nations is a concept with historical and recurrent definitions strongly influenced by tropes of war and patriotism. Particularly with the advent of another Bush administration and post–9/11, displays of national unity/ patriotism and warmongering discourses appear fully merged.

This chapter addresses the contexts of diasporic male representation in Australia and Canada, occasionally making references to Asian–American critique. On this intersected axis of diasporic Canadian and Australian cultural production, the micro-politics of the individual thus inflect the macro-politics of globalisation and constructions of nationhood. To focus this chapter further, the texts I examine are by diasporic artists who use Western notions of nation and patriotism as points of departure for examining diasporic masculinities and the placement of Other citizens in these societies. Concentrating on the implications of Western discourse for diasporic communities and individuals highlights the dilemmas faced by those who have spent the majority of their creative lives in Australia, Canada, or the United States. In short, what is the socio-political context for discussing representations of diasporic Chinese and Japanese men in Australia and Canada? How can readings of these texts diversify, and give depth to, formations of diasporic masculinities?

Limited representations of Asian men circulate in disparate literary and other cultural discourses in Australia and Canada. Both of these societies and their structures are patriarchal and dominated by Anglo-Europeans, having circumscribed representations of non-whites in mainstream media and publishing channels. The persistent Orientalist image of 'Asia' as the feminine to the masculine culture (and proprietorial status) of the 'West' contributes to the restricted range of possible contemporary subject positions for diasporic men. Luke's remarks quoted above assert this lack of a profile, while Australian filmmaker Ayres argues more specifically that

> [i]n the heterosexual [Western] world, Asian women are coveted and fetishised. From Suzie Wong to the Singapore Girl to Gong Li, the Asian woman has crossed into Western consciousness, embodying a sexy blend of enigma, suffering and compliance. She is the epitome of femininity ... The same racial stereotype that makes Asian women desirable makes Asian men marginal ("Undesirable Aliens" 112).

Unpacking Ayres's use of the two-pronged stereotype, I would argue that the ways in which diasporic women are stereotyped are distinctly gender-based. Therefore, their application to diasporic men results in their feminisation and, in turn, leads to a version of exotic and 'freakish' maleness. This is initially not a process of erasure but certainly of "'deviant' masculinities [which] represent a tacit challenge not only to conventional male subjectivity, but to the whole of our 'world'" (Kaja Silverman in Savran, 127). Erasure and displacement result from the ensuing rejection of different forms of maleness or, indeed, other male forms that signify difference. Although there are specific issues with the unproblematised (though partly ironic) way in which Ayres invokes images of Asian women, his point about the double disempowerment of diasporic men in Western society is valid. Often, the women are considered as "socially *paired off* or *contracted*" to the white man (Chow, "Politics" 9), and most diasporic women's studies work strives to defuse, counter or work through this configuration. Rey Chow details the way in which women of colour could be considered "object[s] with exchange value" ("Politics" 9), and outlines the assumptions of "women 'succeeding'" as necessarily meaning "cheating and laying with the white man, whereas the [coloured] man's attempts to 'be white' are seen as attempts for justice and equality" (14–5). The idea that Asian women are less problematically included in Western society's discourses than men rekindles the gendered clichés of women as acquiescent and non-confrontational and men as more aggressive and competitive for social space.

Inflecting this argument is the prevalence of texts featuring diasporic men desiring and commodifying white women, particularly in North

American literature. Discussing certain Chinese-American texts, Sheng-Mei Ma configures this "longing for caucasian women" as "the disadvantaged (male) group's fallacy of assimilation" (66–7). This form of bargaining entry on the bodies of women, as described by Gayatri Spivak,[5] emphasises the deflection of overt engagement with diasporic men themselves. Embedded in the dynamic is the assumption that white women are the metaphorical keys to gaining entry to Western society, a notion that affirms the reification of women and their circumscribed 'femininity' as markers of cultural maintenance.

Women's studies, race and multicultural theory in general, and diversifying national cultural categories have so far accommodated critical studies in diasporic Australian and Canadian cultural production. Most of these, however, do not directly address the complications and representations of diasporic masculinity or the 'Asian' man. As noted earlier, critiques that address diasporic masculinity are still scattered and often focused on processes of intracommunity criticism (for example, Chin writing about Maxine Hong Kingston and Amy Tan; Luke examining Tan's *The Joy Luck Club*). The overwhelming amount of work on gender politics in diasporic writing is from women's perspectives and read through feminist frameworks. Although this work is necessary in reclaiming and establishing spaces from which diasporic women and their experiences can be expressed or read, it also means that diasporic men are spoken about but effectively silenced in the bulk of these writings. Sidelined by mainstream literary representations of 'Asianness', these masculinities are hyper- or under-represented in diasporic women's texts.

The recreation or recovery of a diasporic masculinity could be possible, according to Louie's *Theorising Chinese Masculinity*, if the *wen/wu* dyad was recast by diasporic men in these Western contexts. The emphasis for both Australian and Canadian icons of 'masculinity' is towards the *wu* [physical/martial] aspect of manhood, such as soldiers, pioneers and sportsmen. One common factor in these national icons is their traditional association with — indeed predication by — 'whiteness'. The diasporic Asian man's virtual invisibility on a discursive level has no easy or particular positioning against which he can register resistance or protest. This positioning has led some men in literary circles to attack those who seem to have gained public profiles at their expense. An example of this is the public debates between establishment Asian-American writers Frank Chin and Maxine Hong Kingston.[6] Although this example occurred in the United States, the tensions along gender lines within the diasporic Australian and Canadian writing communities also arrange themselves around questions of selling out or maintaining community/cultural integrity. In Canada, as in Australia, diasporic women writers are currently out-selling their male counterparts for various reasons. These include the appetite of the reading public for confessionals and exposé-type books by (mainly) Chinese women authors, many of which incorporate 'Confucian' gender exploitation and feudal sexual mores as major parts of the narrative. These stories are often written by an author based in the West. Chow considers this process to be "the *National Geographic* of the soul — the observation platforms and laboratories in which the 'perverse' others — the 'inmates' — can be displayed in their 'non-conforming' and 'abnormal' behavior, in their strangely coded practices and rituals" ("Women in the Holocene" 210). The complicity of authors recounting narratives from without could be read as an example of 'buying entry' into Western society: "[i]n so far as confession is an act of repentance, a surrender of oneself in reconciliation with the rules of society, it is also related to community" fu (Chow, "Politics" 6–7). For diasporic women authors to be seen to be acceptable, it seems they must physically renounce their 'homeland' and symbolically disavow traditional male control — in favour of the Anglo patriarchy in the West. Whether or not this is what their writing is doing, reviewers prefer to read them as most often denying their 'own'. Detractors from within their communities choose to (mis)read these women's texts as an attack on group cultural values. Chin, characteristically bombastic, declares:

> all of the Asian-American stuff was autobiographies that I despised. All pushing the idea that we're all victims, all pushing the idea of the Chinese family or the Japanese family in America as dysfunctional. Talking about the big change to become Americanized. That's the only kind of thing that had ever been published in Chinese America, the White supremacist autobiography saying how fucked up it is being Chinese in America, that it doesn't work ("West Meets East" 88).

Commentators such as Garrett Hongo saw this division as orchestrated and, in some ways, expected: "[w]hite academics had identified a gender war in mainstream writing, African-Americans had identified one in black writing, and, it seemed, we Asian-Americans had the mimetic desire to define one among our own writers" (Hongo 19). Further, the ensuing allocations of writers to authentic or unauthentic categories act as a "*policing* mechanism of the ethnic culture, governing the range of allowable literary production" (Hongo 20). This monitoring creates certain fixed types of community expectation/assumption when, on many levels, as Lisa Lowe points out, "Asian-American Literature" (and any other body of national literary work) is "an unclosed, unfixed body of work whose centers and orthodoxies shift as the makeup of the Asian-origin constituency shifts, and within which new voices are continually being articulated" (61). This process of community and cultural emergence is occurring in Australia and Canada as literary groups become more active, competitive (for funding), and creative from gradually stabilising political and social bases. Ironically, the stimuli for concentrated activist or artistic work for diasporic writers and critics are often also threats to their validity and roles in society. Chin's vitriol has a key function in drawing attention to fraught questions of representing community, gender politics, and what constitutes an author's 'artistic licence', but his determinedly simplistic readings of texts by other (female) authors detract from his critical work. Although diasporic Asian-Canadian and Asian-Australian disciplines are in their formative stages, it is useful for them to learn from, and participate in, this context of ongoing debates and fissures.

Cultural clichés of the Asian man in Australia and Canada range from the Yellow Peril rhetoric that was prevalent in the early gold-rush days of both nations to comic, peripheral, asexual figures in literature. This is particularly noticeable in some canonical works that have been studied widely in Australia and Canada. For example, in Australian writer A. B. Facey's widely studied autobiography, *A Fortunate Life*, the Chinese cook provides comic relief and a study in alien, eccentric Oriental behaviour. In Canadian author Robert Kroestch's *Badlands*, the caricature of Chinaman Grizzly occupies similar semiotic ground. Lien Chao describes Grizzly as "a constant, unchanging alien throughout the novel" ("Constituting" 339). Chinaman Grizzly is denied a speaking voice, literally, because he is mute and this fact, along with his relations with a Native woman, configures him as closer to 'animal' (nature) than 'man' (civilisation). The discourse of Asian men as the ultimate Others from nineteenth and early twentieth-century literature is exemplified by such "frontier, adventure stories" (Dixon 118) that "work to centre the nation by narrating the limits of its territory and civility" (119). The diasporic Other occupies these limits, and in fact often *is* the limit of 'civility' and relegated to representing a despotic, corrupt (and corrupting) people. Particularly at the end of the twentieth century, when the 'angry white male' backlash was in full force, the already liminal spaces occupied by racial minority individuals in Australia, Canada, and the United States are again under threat. In the process of reacting against the society in which they find themselves, whites who consider themselves 'victimised' by affirmative action and political correctness manifest their anger as blame.

Far from weakening gender bases, however, the eroding of stock perceptions of Asian men, and their diversifying styles and types, leads textual depictions towards an incompleteness that serves as a much more inclusive, dynamic, and potentially radical field. In these uncertain national masculine spaces, Luke contends that when diasporic Asian males are not being portrayed as "evil or exotic scenery" they may "turn up as non-emotive, repressed and desexed props" (33). He is referring here to both the 'external' depiction of diasporic men by non-'Asian' writers and filmmakers and to those by diasporic women.

This criticism was raised recently, and often repeated, about the film version of *The Joy Luck Club*, in which the men are objects of vilification and resentment, often depicted as cardboard characters. This is especially true of the younger male roles in Wayne Wang's film. The role of the father (an older, widowed male) is presented as asexual and therefore non-threatening. His wife is long dead but still mourned. Viewing these representations as an attack by diasporic women on diasporic men threatens to sink coalitions for racial minority group politics, and is a strategy of divide-and-conquer that focuses only on antagonistic relations. Peter Feng reads Tan's film/novel as reinforcing the perceived cultural unit of "WMAF (White Male, Asian Female)", stressing that "in these films, Chinese patriarchy functions mainly to shore up American culture as one in which women can flourish. Romantic relationships with white men provide the freedom that Asian unions would quash" (Feng 1). The high profile of Tan's work lends it the dangerous aura of representing 'Asian-America', rather than just being one narrative out of many. The tendency to create factional gender oppositions within racial minority groups is a longstanding issue when considering gender representations, one previously argued with reference to Chin's purposeful dividing of diasporic American artists. African-American literary representations of men and women underwent (and are still undergoing) a similar process. Parallels are apparent between the criticism generated by Amy Tan/Wayne Wang's film *The Joy Luck Club* and Alice Walker/Steven Spielberg's *The Color Purple*. Both brought forth accusations of betraying the political cause of the racial minority group to focus on women's issues or perspectives. Citing bell hooks' vehement rejection of the novel, Linda Selzer observes that "to many readers of *The Color Purple*, the text's ability to expose sexual oppression seems to come at the expense of its ability to analyze issues of race and class" (1). One interviewer even ponders whether Walker's novel has "come to symbolize Black malebashing at its worst" (Whitaker 1). These reactions to single narrative representations demonstrate the necessity of diverse points of view. The expectation that authors represent an entire community exposes the conglomerating tendencies of hegemonic concepts concerning Other groups. While positive gender role models can prove valuable to communities that lack significant mainstream representation, merely reading representations as 'good' or 'bad' examples of African-American or diasporic 'Asian' men does not contribute to dismantling discriminatory structures of gender and race. Breaking down the categories upon which these binary oppositions depend is a tactic often employed by authors who challenge the status quo of gender and national representation, and these challenges often take the form of rewriting masculinity and the structures that govern the male-identified trait of patriotism. For diasporic Asian men, the axes of war and nationalism regularly serve as socio-historical flashpoints. David Eng's discussion of the contrived demarcation between the Japanese "enemy" and the "friendly" Chinese (104–10) exemplifies this process. The changing renditions of Japanese and Chinese men as either 'good' or 'bad', given differing economic and political climes, reflects the ambivalent nature of the relationship between Western nations and their 'governable' diasporic citizens.

In order to examine versions of masculinity and patriotism in diasporic Canadian and Australian cultural production, I now focus on texts by Australians Tony Ayres (*China Dolls*, 1997), Hou Leong ('An Australian', 1995), Hung Le (*Yellow Peril from Sin City*, 1997) and Brian Castro (*Pomeroy*, 1990); and Canadians Terry Watada (*Daruma Days*, 1997), Wayson Choy (*The Jade Peony*, 1995), and Wayne Yung (*Beyond Yellow Fever* chapbook, 1996).[7]

The analysis contends that the ways in which these artists inscribe styles of masculinity, community belonging, and characteristics of national affiliation enable broader, less simplistic renditions of Asian men but also complicate issues of national loyalty. It is precisely this multiplication of possible masculinities that leads to cogent challenges for structures of nationalism and traditional perspectives on gender politics in racial minority cultural production. The emphasis is on the cultivation of possibilities for diasporic masculinities rather than an attempt to discover or recover a 'true Asian manhood'. *Pomeroy* and *Daruma Days* are texts in which uncertainties dominate and the elementary re-siting of characters' affiliations as Australian or Canadian is problematised and almost rejected. Even as they are rejecting current prescriptive styles of patriotism, the novels formulate new possibilities for its expression at the start of the twenty-first century. The discussion of the Australian paradigm of masculinity in this section also includes consideration of the possible resistances or interventions in other textual forms such as Leong's photographic work and Le's stand-up comedy text. Choy's novel contributes to the Vancouver 'Chinatown genre' and offers an intergenerational cross-section of Chinese-Canadian men's history.

The Australian Expat

Pomeroy is Castro's second novel and focuses on the Eurasian narrator, Jaime Pomeroy. The book presents a rigorous interrogation of Australian masculinity through invocations of expatriateness and the complications of Chineseness. Pomeroy is an expatriate resident who returns to Hong Kong to report for *ID*, a local tabloid paper. Castro's playfulness with ascribed personas surfaces in the telling title of the tabloid, and the gibe foregrounds the central dilemma of Pomeroy's character. The novel details how he escapes from the Gold Coast in Queensland because he needs distraction and distance after losing his love, Estrellita, to his best friend, Rory Harrigan. This romantic triangle resembles the Dickensian one of Pip, Estella, and her husband from *Great Expectations*. Pomeroy's international networks heighten Australian anxieties about the kinds of citizen who belong as, already, the contemporary coverage of issues about diasporic groups in Australia focuses on whether 'they' could possibly be one of 'us': "[M]oral panics fly around Japanese investment and Asian immigration in the language of patriotism, invasion and the evocation of danger. Here colonization, empire and race resonate with concern about our rightful sphere of influence, and indeed about who we are and who threatens us" (Pettman 69). Produced within these discriminatory structures and their contradictions, Castro's writing suggests "that what we do is largely a patchworking process of examining parts, discarding or refreshing some, and patching in or adapting new paradigms" (Deves 220). Castro's versions of (Chinese) Australian masculinity revoke role-model writing and, in fact, seek to unbalance the idea completely by presenting obviously flawed characters with few exemplary qualities. In an interview with Ouyang Yu, Castro configures the male writer's self as "under construction in a desperate, terrorised way" (Ouyang, "Interview with Brian Castro" 77). A symptom of postmodernity is often the encouragement to read the text as a dismantling of sorts, and the deliberate obfuscations and disintegrations in Castro's writing can be read as retaliations against the imposition of any kind of cohesive, traditional, patriarchal identity.

The narrative in the first half of the novel, as in much of Castro's work, is a study in 'expatriate'-ness, exploring situations such as Pomeroy returning from Australia to Hong Kong and mixing with an unflatteringly described group of debauched and insensitive Australian expats. The characters and the plot resonate with urban detective fiction markers: murky underworld allusions, hardened and cynical characters (in this instance, mostly journalists), and undercurrents of sexuality and possible liaisons between male and female characters. Superficially, the novel reads as an example of male-dominated, hard-boiled crime fiction in which, as Beryl Langer describes, the narrator is "the archetypically Australian 'smart-arse' whose quick wit, disrespect for authority, physical toughness, and fondness for a drink gives him both generic and national credibility" (239). Typically of Castro's 'heroes', or more accurately anti-heroes, Pomeroy has *almost* all of the traits Langer describes. He is physically capable but outmatched quite a few times in fights, he defies rules but immediately wonders what kind of trouble it will bring, and he manages a detached observer's perspective until the consequences of involvement overwhelm him with physical realities. Castro's hero is, ultimately, not very 'heroic' at all. Yet he still succeeds in stumbling across most of the clues that lead him to uncover the mystery of 'Boy' Wong.

Castro's invocation of the overtly masculine, traditionally sexist, and rather White 'Mike Hammer' style in the first half of the novel is highly satirical. As he states, "genres imprison you within certain things and unless you jump out and parody them, you're not really tackling any advancement in writing" (Castro, "Interview with Ramona Koval" 8). Accordingly, he creates as the protagonist a mixed-race (Chinese-European), somewhat gauche, individual whose scruples are ever changing. Pomeroy is an indecisive, non-confrontational man, who appears somewhat incongruously in the tough, masculinised genre of hard-boiled crime fiction. The narrator's voice is hesitant — more of a bystander than an actor in the novel. In contrast to the universal (male) voice that projects cohesion and certainty, Castro often uses an inconstant narrator whose viewpoints alternate between first person and third person from one paragraph to the next. Discussing Castro's novels *After China* and *Drift*, Ommundsen calls this "a 'prismatic' perspective" and argues further that "it is as if Castro ... mocks the very idea of 'identity' in writing. There is a general sense of loss of origin and centre, and a proliferation of traces" (Ommundsen 156). In *Pomeroy*, the narrator is somewhat more integrated than in other works, but Castro's technique involves the destruction, or at least unbalancing, of narratorial power. This act highlights the possibilities for renditions of Australian 'maleness' by its national Others.

As Pomeroy enters Hong Kong society (symbolised by the Van Ecks's reception), he rediscovers familiar groups of Australian expatriates and uncomfortably identifies himself as one of them: "[their] faces jowled and creased from rainbow-coloured hours in the Barrier Reef sun, too many cigars, anxious phone calls, and cut-lunch sex between beers and races" (43). Yet his closeness and similarity to the Australians is contradicted by his positioning as a returning Hong Kong expatriate. Tellingly, the expatriates Pomeroy refers to at the Van Ecks's party (from Australia and elsewhere) are all men, referred to by the power they wield in the 'colony'. This power is portrayed as racially divided, the governor surrounded by the "lesser lights, mere Chinese tycoons, the almost-but-not-quite British" (45). This metaphoric emasculation of Chinese men through colonisation, sidelined from the real power of Whiteness because of their race, taints Pomeroy's interactions with the expats even while they are the group to whom he gravitates while in Hong Kong. The portrayal of the expat population there as debauched and grotesque contrasts effectively with Castro's summation of Australia's attempts to be "in Asia" as "ludicrous" (Castro, *Writing Asia* 10). Castro underscores the insularity of Australia as a nation with a parochial population and sets Hong Kong up as a (still problematic) cosmopolitan enclave.

For Pomeroy to represent 'Australia' to most of the novel's characters upsets Australian "myths of nation" which "are not only masculinist, but ethnically restrictive" (Langer 249). Castro continues throughout the novel to present 'typical' characters, and then undercuts them with traits of doubt, hypocrisy and tinges of madness. The splintering of Australian-ness and the roles of men in Castro's cynical and ethnically mixed society highlights the ways in which discourses of masculinity and nationhood cross over. The effect of reading about Pomeroy and Rory's failed dreams is similar to the frustration that stems from their deliberately unsteady renditions of Australianness and their bizarre behaviour when it comes to Estrellita. Using the backdrop of the typical Australian outback, Castro writes an atypical narrative that erodes concepts of who the Chinese-Australian man might be. In fact, Castro seems to focus more on stressing who the Chinese-Australian man is *not*. As well, his twisting of perceptions in masculinist genres adds another level of critique to the category of maleness and disallows simple interpretations of his novels.

Castro's fictional revisions of Chinese-Australian masculinity and gender associations erode perceived cohesive images and inform them with his style of inconclusive humanity. This incompleteness and hesitancy defines Castro's method of presenting images of men who are constantly confused and uncertain about their roles.

Playing with Australian Icons

The differences between negotiating this mode of characterising Australian and Chinese masculinity in written text and the instantly powerful visual images of Hou Leong expose further the entrenched values of the 'Australian man' and his assumed Whiteness. Leong's series of photographs entitled "An Australian" subverts notions of Australian maleness by directly supplanting White Australia's most invoked icons with his Chinese presence. Traditional versions of Australian masculinity dominated by images of the Bushman, the Surfer, and the Digger,[8] an Asian-Australian man tends to fall into the category of villain more than hero. This is a situation that Leong exploits. He superimposes his own head on many white Australian bodies including Crocodile Dundee, a member of the Returned Services League (RSL), and the Ampol man. The photographs are effective because he not only uses highly recognisable personalities, but sites his Chinese face in situations that are the most characteristic of Australian male domains: the pub, sporting fields and locker rooms (cricket and rugby), and agricultural shows or rural spaces. In rupturing all-too-familiar representations of 'Australianness', Leong makes incongruity work towards emphasising entrenched ethnocentric notions of who is, or can be, considered Australian.[9] The photographs place the Asian face in the centre of Australian culture, as opposed to the usual surplus or supplementary state that multicultural citizens and their texts occupy. His action of appropriating the white Australian male body, too, challenges the hermetic qualities of national icons and, satirically, reverses the exploitation of the Chinese body. There is, however, another way in which these images could operate. For example, if the idea of a Chinese Crocodile Dundee remains comical and an object of ridicule, how does this affect attempts to have the term 'Australian' be inclusive of those with Chinese features? The incongruity that makes the work humorous and effective could also reaffirm the boundaries of white Australia and the improbability of Chinese-Australian men belonging in these contexts. Further, how far do we still have to go when this humour trades on the absurdity of a Chinese face on Australian icons?

Leong's technique of somewhat abrupt placement within these familiar and symbolic Australian images is taken further by Hung Le, a Vietnamese-

Australian comic. Working as a stand-up comedian, a profession seen as a mostly white male preserve, Le's show consists of anecdotes about his family, coming to Australia from Vietnam, and growing up in Australia as an Asian boy. The book *Yellow Peril from Sin City* contains segments of his stand-up show and was published in 1997. Fronting an audience of (mainly) Anglo-Celtic viewers, Le occupies an odd, even contradictory, position. Paraphrasing Homi Bhabha's argument about the colonised subject producing "mimic Englishman", Le's reproduction of the true-blue Aussie could be read as "resemblance and menace" (Young 147). As Robert Young explains, "the imitation subverts the identity of that which is being represented, and the relation of power, if not altogether reversed, certainly begins to vacillate" (147). The reaffirmation of group values which accompanies joking and humour is performed by someone who is normally positioned as the Other, culturally and socially. Additionally, Le's facility with very 'Australian' English (slang and broad accent) both emphasises group cohesion with the audience in Australia and makes him aurally recognisable as 'Australian' in other countries. Le has attended many overseas comedy festivals to 'represent' Australia, either individually or as part of a troupe. Being Asian-Australian, however, his designation through audience and humour recognition as 'one of us' (or 'one of those Australians') is more difficult. Le further complicates his persona by appearing in a tuxedo when he first takes to the stage, often accompanied by a vivid purple, orange, or red head of hair.

Tony Mitchell recognises that "[c]orrect English is the discourse of power in Australian society, and migrants of non-English-speaking background signal their difference and lower social status by a perceived inability to speak correct English" (120). Le's ocker mode of speech is a device that runs through the entire show and book, imbuing all his anecdotes with an Australian twang. Nick Giannopoulos, writer and performer from *Wogs Out of Work* and *Wog-a-rama*, recalls classifying Le as a "Vietnamese Paul Hogan" (*What's So Funny?* 1995). Admitting Le into the category of the archetypal Australian that 'Hoges' personifies could indicate an inheritance of Australian representational status for Le, or it might also imply that the only way 'multicultural' artists can gain some recognition is through performing a kind of hyper-Australian persona, that of the 'ocker', 'larrikin', or 'yobbo'.

The fine lines between these categories are regularly redrawn. Hogan has characterised himself as a larrikin in the past, a category which he takes pains to differentiate from 'lout': "[l]outs break windows and throw bottles, and they're brainless loons. . . . Larrikins tend to do things for fun" (Dunn and Ellis 1). The definition of what an ocker is has also changed since the term appeared almost fifty years ago. J. S. Gunn states that "our ocker has retained his sporting interest and some friendliness but gradually he has also become more loudmouthed, aggressive, and offensive" (92). Lisa Jacobson details "Ockerist rituals" as including "xenophobia, dogmatism and bigotry" (139). For Le to be seen to be taking on some of the manners of the larrikin and of ockerism, then, lends his performance a subversively 'Australian' edge. Although he narrativises similar subjects (e.g., sports, pub adventures, trying to get the girls), they are inflected with awareness of racialisation and displacement of previous categories. Especially with the sporting habit, Le makes it clear that he was contravening family wishes by becoming an Australian footy fan. This incident depends more on generational differences and the wide cultural gaps between 'old' world immigrants and the new generation that is being educated in Australia. The expectation of being a sports fan as part of mythical Australian masculinity prompts Le to be a participant in football, becoming metaphorically more 'Australian' because of his enthusiasm for the national sport. Further, it challenges the stereotype of Asians being bad sports-players and non-participants. In various cultural ways, Le departs from the family 'fold' at twelve for the beery support of the stadium and the extroverted ceremonies of Australian mateship on the sporting field.

However, Le's work challenges charges of only reaffirming or emulating white versions of masculinity. The performative nature of his work and his confronting material push the boundaries of what can constitute, or is understood as, an 'Asian-Australian male'. He reverses racist slurs when telling stories that address Asian male prowess and the colonisation of Vietnam. In a schoolyard anecdote, he talks of being chased around by two girls who were trying to kiss him. Finally, he capitulates and kisses them back, commenting: "coming from a French colony if there's one thing we learnt from the French it's 'Never say *non* to a *menage à trois!*'" Then he continues with how the girls were ahead of their time because "Asian boys are really in demand now because people have finally realised that once you've had a bit of Chinese, twenty minutes later you'll be hungry for more" (51). He recounts more excruciating amorous accounts throughout his book, blending them somewhat uncomfortably with blatantly racist encounters in nightclubs and bars. The ability to empathise with his adolescent angst is fractured when it comes to episodes of discrimination — the (reading) audience is then pushed into odd, complicit positions while still being on Le's 'side'.[10] His humour is successful because he is adept with being, and 'playing' Australian to Australian audiences.

The deliberate use of ANZAC[11] imagery by Leong, and the invocation and satire of the politically fraught Vietnam War by Le, fix on crucial moments in the definition of the 'national' and the 'masculine' for Australia. The ANZAC soldier myth is a part of the "national self-fashioning" in the "value-added" narratives of Australia (Johnston, "Memoirs" 75). Confronted with Leong's Asian face in an Australian army uniform, presumptions about 'enemy' and 'hero' are twisted together in the one body. The role of the Australian Digger (and the Allies in general) is called into question. A more traditional rewriting of Australian history to include the wartime involvement of Asian-Australians is Morag Loh and Judith Winternitz's *Dinky-Di: The Contributions of Chinese Immigrants and Australians of Chinese Descent to Australia's Defence Forces and War Efforts 1899-1988* (1989). This book is one of the few publications to highlight the scarcely documented roles that Asian-Australians played in both world wars. It takes a sociological, oral history perspective. *Dinky-Di* consists of interviews with different generations of Chinese-Australians who served during the wars (including Vietnam and the First and Second World Wars). Several times, the Australian army used special groups of Asian-Australian soldiers to infiltrate Japanese or Chinese lines, making the 'enemy within' work for them, albeit temporarily and somewhat grudgingly. Harassment and insults in the barracks and during training accompanied this 'acceptance' on the front line, but the opportunity to fight for their country emerges as a defining moment of perceived acceptance for most of the interviewees. Loh and Winternitz have compiled a document that recovers neglected history and personal stories at the same time as it seeks absolution for Asians in Australia as worthy citizens. The emphasis on Asian-Australian men's patriotism indicates an attempt to restore Asian masculinity through proving their bravery and desire to protect the nation. The epigraph from Sang Ye's *The Year the Dragon Came* evokes the demand on Asian citizens to prove their loyalties, and the scepticism with which this is met if they do indeed choose to 'side' with Australia. The expectation is for Asians to return to cultural roots where patriotism is concerned which prompted, among other instances, the pervasiveness of Japanese internment in Australia.[12] There is now a growing thread of research about Asian (mainly Chinese) soldiers who fought for Australia in the First and Second World Wars. This seems to indicate a high level of interest in locating Asian bodies within nation-building moments for Australia, validating their presence and, perhaps, proving their loyalty to Australian ideals.

Liberating Internment

The move to rewrite wartime history to include Asian citizens is an important step that goes some way to establishing historical and social legitimacy in Australia and Canada. Having participated in war, some Asian citizens hope that this 'proves' their right to belong. Loh and Winternitz's compilation is comparable to the Canadian publications *The Dragon and the Maple Leaf: Chinese Canadians in World War II* by Marjorie Wong (1994), and *We Went to War: The Story of the Japanese Canadians Who Served during the First and Second World Wars* by Roy Ito (1992). Both of these works relate the nation-building role of diasporic citizens in the Canadian armed forces. To contrast this empowerment through national participation for Chinese-Australians and Chinese-Canadians with the denial of citizens' rights for Japanese-Canadians and Japanese-Australians during the Second World War is particularly pertinent when discussing the evolution of diasporic masculinities in each country. The hierarchy of 'differences' during the war led to over-identifications with being Chinese (and therefore assumed 'safe') and rejection of being Japanese (and therefore open to displacement to inland camps). One type of identification meant possible participation in the war effort, albeit with hostility in some instances, and gaining for the community and the individual a sense of belonging. The other relegated whole communities to exile and ignominy as 'enemy aliens', a form of group emasculation as well as disempowerment on an individual scale.

The denial of citizenship rights to Japanese-Canadians is the background to Watada's collection of short stories, *Daruma Days: A Collection of Fictionalised Biography*. Watada presents readers with a wide range of narrators in the discourses of war and displacement within nation. These communities faced many repercussions in their forced role of 'enemy alien'. Watada's compilation is one of the first to meld the evocation of Japanese-Canadian internment life and the psychosocial effects of the forced move on the community. Kuan Foo points out that "though the spectre of internment lurks over the entire book, the stories largely concern themselves with the day-to-day politics of the Japanese community within the camps the character politics, the community politics, the sexual politics" (Watada, "Interview with Kuan Foo" 2). It is precisely according to this interned time, however, that the readings of masculinity and changes in male roles manifest themselves. Watada also discusses and elaborates on the pervasiveness of organised crime syndicates in the creation and maintenance of the internment camps, a part of Japanese community to which Kogawa refers briefly in *Obasan*.[13] Many historical and sociological books document the processes of mobilisation, the seizing of people and property, and eventual internment, but few literary representations have thus far been published. The beginnings of a literary core addressing the social effects of internment on Japanese-Canadians is forming around texts like Watada's, and works by Kogawa, Goto, and Sakamoto. Watada's work is one example of the ways in which detailed prose is 'filling the gaps' of the internment experience, particularly the roles of men and the consequences of broken family links.

Foo contends that the more work from authors like Watada, Kogawa, and Sally Ito there is out in the public space, the "better to educate mainstream readers, critics and reviewers to the fact that there is more than this 'cult of victimhood' that seems to have developed around the Asian-Canadian experience" (Watada, "Interview with Kuan Foo" 5–6). Following the necessary work of reclaiming and assembling that part of Canadian history accomplished by researchers such as Muriel Kitagawa, Roy Miki and Maryka Omatsu, most literary versions of wartime experiences follow the historic decision to recognise the injustices of wartime Canadian government actions.[14] Possibly the most well-known novel of all these texts, and one that preceded the official announcement of Redress by almost a decade, is Kogawa's *Obasan*. Kogawa's text achieved much when it was published in 1981, not least of which was putting the Japanese-Canadian experience back into Canadian national history and exposing the ongoing consequences of the internment period for the scattered Japanese-Canadian communities.

Uniquely, Watada's collection addresses the gaps in social perspectives of internment camps, providing stories that have no single voice but, instead, form a linked series across decades and families. As stated earlier, Elaine Kim called for Asian-American studies to move "beyond railroads and internment" (11) and, although it is important for subject matter and styles to diversify, the level of general knowledge about the anti-Asian pasts of Australia, Canada, and the US is still quite low. Perhaps even more insidiously, this kind of material is considered well and truly 'historical', the contemporary consequences or repetitions unacknowledged. The incidents in Canada are high-profile ones of recognition for civil rights abuses and racism in the country and serve as an important precedent for other minority groups (McFarlane, "Covering *Obasan*" 401). Watada's stories arrange themselves around the major upheavals in Japanese-Canadian social and political life while managing to also address spiritual matters and established superstitions, such as the significance of the *daruma* doll and the female fox demon. With particular resonance, the *daruma* doll (after which the collection is titled) indicates a wish that has been made, a sense of hope while waiting for the internment period to be over.[15]

Watada's narratives flesh out the often homogenised and faceless communities of the internees in isolated, abandoned towns. The hero figure of the pioneering European settler contrasts strongly with the presence of the interned Japanese communities. Many of the Japanese men served on work gangs or farms and were placed in separate camps from their families. The government sited these camps in the British Columbian internal 'frontier', often in old, abandoned mining communities. However, there is a difference, Kyo Maclear argues, between the romanticised portrayals of the interior and the way Watada and others "paint the outback as a politically charged space — where adversaries are less the ferocious elements and impenetrable bush than European settlers and hostile governments" (34). For Japanese-Canadians, the 'frontier' became a site of exile and shame compared with the heroic, even virile, connotations of conquering the wilderness that traditional Canadian literature presented.

The stories involve many overlapping, continuing characters and focus mostly on family relationships ruptured by the internment process. The narratives also go further than previous fictional accounts by providing details of the ensuing physical and psychological problems for some 'inmates' associated with camp life and their extreme living conditions. Most significantly for discussions of Asian masculinity, the text addresses the motivations and emotional tones of many displaced men while still writing them in as integral parts of their communities. The inclusion of gangsters in the camps, and the delineation of their role in influencing negative and positive changes in the lives of the internees, is a perspective that has hardly been explored. Although the presence of gangsters could be threatening and intrusive, the salvaged empowerment of being part of the gangs lent some men the semblance of dignity and position. The enforced exile of the communities by Canadian authorities revoked citizenship security and any professional alliances people might have had. Belonging to the syndicates was a way to live more comfortably and with a form of respect, although it was at the expense of exploiting the internees around them.[16] These groups were powerful enough to establish the terms of internship at some camps, and residents paid for various levels of accommodation at the sites. At Minto, for example, "[h]ome for Asao and his mother became a ten-by-ten-foot shack that had been dragged from an abandoned mine ... Most internees lived in comfortable cabins with indoor plumbing and electricity since they had bought their way into the self-sustaining camp" (83). It is in these situations that class and gender differences in the Japanese-Canadian community are exposed and sharply narrativised. The aftermath of internment was severe for all involved, but the ones who were most affected after the war were those whose living consisted of material (confiscated) belongings. The more professional or educated families, although stigmatised in postwar Canada, could afford to recover in cities farther east, like Toronto.

One of the most effective symbolic acts that Watada writes into *Daruma Days* is in the short story, 'The Brown Bomber', which tells of Toshiro building Lemon Creek's *ofuro*. The story addresses the issue of racism and hierarchy within the Japanese community and focuses on the Matsuba family. The Canadian government's classification of them as unacceptable and dismissible (consider the repatriation programme at the end of the Second World War) destabilised community and family relationships. Initially, Toshiro was sent to a roadwork gang, and Kimiko and her mother to Lemon Creek internment camp. Traditional Japanese masculine authority was non-existent in the face of RCMP officers' orders, and societal structures were dismantled. Having been stripped of possessions and status, emasculated culturally and socially, Toshiro regained some hope and sense of self by rallying his fellow internees to construct a bathhouse for themselves. The helpers on the *ofuro* project "even chuckled over constructing something so Japanese given their predicament" (142). Ironically, while symbolically allowing Toshiro to have a place in society and family again, the *ofuro* is also the cause of his death by drowning a while later.

Vancouver's China Men

Where Watada's prose serves as another way to address the *"blanc-outs"* (Maclear 35) in Canadian national history and within Japanese-Canadian cultural and social histories, Choy's 1995 novel *The Jade Peony* falls within the Chinatown genre of literature. The novel delves into the politics and social interaction in Vancouver's young Chinatown of the 1930s and 1940s, a subject that has already established something of a tradition (albeit early) in Asian-Canadian literature. Choy also contributes to this genre in *Paper Shadows*, a second book that fills the gaps of his adopted past. Only starting to write *Jade Peony* at age fifty-five, Choy observed that up till then he "had nothing to say" and realises this was a form of "internalised oppression", that he was struggling with his own "banana complex" (Deer 40). Choy sets out to "explore ordinary lives lived with decency" (41), deliberately countering popular sensationalist tales about Chinese families and communities.

Two of the sections in the novel are told through the voices of the second and third brothers (Jung-Sum and Sek-Lung), and the first is related by Only Sister, Jook-Liang. The three-part novel, for the most, draws on realist renditions of how growing up within the influence of ethnicity, hierarchies, and family affected each of the narrators. Although not participating in undercutting the processes of masculinity and nation to the extent that Castro knowingly does, nor recovering a group as in the case of Watada and interned Japanese-Canadian men, *Jade Peony* is of particular interest here because of the range of localised masculine voices to which Choy gives space. Notably, the axes of possible masculinities upon which Choy's narrators hinge their sections provide a fictional community and societal cross-section of the changing effects of Canadian socio-politics on these 'Chinatown' populations. In this reading of Choy's novel and its modes of representing masculinity, I am only addressing the sections concerning Jook-Liang and Jung-Sum.[17]

The first chapter presents Only Sister Jook-Liang's perspective, focusing poignantly on the relationship between Liang and Wong Suk (Uncle Wong), otherwise known as the Monkey Man. It is through her eyes that his character is given depth, his bachelorhood explained, and the community expectations about his duties rendered ambivalent. Considering his unmarried state, and his assumed lack of other responsibilities, he was the ideal messenger to travel back with a shipment of recovered bones (of long dead railway workers) to China. His job was simply to accompany them to their final resting place. Wong Suk epitomises the truncated generations in Chinatowns because of government restrictions on immigration and bringing family or prospective brides into Canada. Working for years on the Canadian Pacific Railway trail, he was the typical bachelor man who ended up alone in a boarding-house. This group of men, on becoming elderly or incapacitated, were cared for mostly by the Chinese Benevolent Association, as they had no kin of their own, a consequence of the Chinese Exclusion Act. Lien Chao describes it thus: "the Chinese labourers' initial separation from their families was institutionally prolonged and hence instigated the formation of the Chinatown ghetto as a kind of replacement for the family" ("Constituting" 335). Even with the help of this Chinatown 'family', Choy narrates in detail the dire consequences for the bachelor men when the Canadian government implemented the Chinese Exclusion Act of 1923 on

1 July, Canada's National Day, a day also considered by Chinese-Canadians as the Day of Shame. Choy writes:

> [i]n the city dump on False Creek Flats, living in makeshift huts, thirty-two Old China bachelor-men tried to shelter themselves; dozens more were dying of neglect in the overcrowded rooms of Pender Street. There were no Depression jobs for such men. They had been deserted by the railroad companies and betrayed by the many labour contractors who had gone back to China, wealthy and forgetful. There was a local Vancouver by-law against begging for food, a federal law against stealing food, but no law in any court against starving to death for lack of food (17).

These details in Chinese-Canadian literature serve as a foil for the usually positive stories of immigrant success that make up the bulk of representations. Resolution usually occurs in the form of settling into the new country and gaining financial stability. Thus, Wong Suk's hunched back and limping walk are fitting physical manifestations to represent the stunted Chinese-Canadian community that resulted from government restrictions applied over many decades. Eng argues for the possibility of reading these resultant bachelor societies as queer spaces that were "institutionally barred from normative (hetero)sexual reproduction, nuclear family formations, and entitlements to community" (18). This stimulating take on the otherwise faceless and asexual modes of representing Chinese bachelor communities is one rarely employed. For Choy's novel, Wong Suk represents the older generation of Chinatown, the sojourners, who considered their time in Canada temporary and the journey home preferable to dying in new, continually hostile lands.

The languages with which Wong Suk communicates also highlight this generational gap, in particular to Liang, who characterises the conversations between her grandmother and Wong Suk as "monkey-talk" (26). To her, he epitomises the Old China group and she configures him as the Monkey King in disguise. This classical literary allocation for Wong Suk underscores his authentic Chinese roots and his dedication to Confucian filial piety, as does his later fulfilment of duty by accompanying the recovered bones back home. In epitomising the initial wave of Chinese immigrants to Canada, Wong Suk also represents the old-world patriarchal values and obligations. The way in which Wong Suk leaves a lifelong impression on Liang reflects the aim of Choy's writing about the enclosed world of the early Chinatowns, which is to "[decipher] silent historical documents [and lives]" (Chao, "Constituting" 339). Even in the representation of Wong Suk's story in this novel, the little-known history only comes to us from the perspective of a few generations on. In writing the lives of the bachelor men, Choy's writing debunks the myth of hard beginnings but 'worthwhile' endings. For some, life after hard labour on the railways was a forced in-betweenness that resulted in debilitated lives and curtailed hopes.

In contrast to his depiction of Wong Suk and the introverted sojourner generation, Choy's next portrayal is of Jung-Sum, the Second Brother in the family. The contrast between the stalled bachelor men lives in Chinatown and their homeward gazes and the contemporary confrontations and social opportunities for Jung-Sum as a solidly Canadian-based Chinese boy is sharp. Liang's family adopted Jung after a tragic and violent early childhood in which his mother died at the hands of his stepfather. His new older brother, Kiam, protects him at school and later inducts him into the very male world of boxing gyms. From the beginning, the grandmother declares that Jung is different, associating him with the moon, or *yin*, which is traditionally the female essence. In this section, Jung realises that he desires one of his older brother's best friends, Frank Yuen. Frank is the boxing champion in their circle of friends and, "with his leather jacket half-opened, and his zoot pants tight at the ankle" (113), a respected tough with an alcoholic father and a dead mother. The effect of missing, dead, or abusive fathers on their sons permeates Choy's evocations of less than traditional parental/family units in *Jade Peony*. It also adds to reconfigurations of Asian masculinity and manhood beyond the Confucian ideal represented by Wong Suk. While involved in a spur-of-the-moment fight with Frank, Jung has a flashback about his own father beating him with a belt. As a result of being comforted by Frank during this episode, Jung felt that he was "suddenly lit with an unbidden, shuddering tension" (117) and characterised Frank as the sun (118). In representing gayness as a matching of male/female spirits, Choy indulges, to some extent, in the cliché of applying heterosexual norms to a homosexual relationship. Further, Jung only has the flashback because of the extreme emotions he experiences while fighting Frank. The acts of violence seem to induce Jung's homosexual awakening, and the only other time readers are privy to him being affected by Frank's proximity is when Frank leaves to join the US Marines and his friends hold a party for him. The friendship that Frank extends to Jung transforms into something else. It is, in fact, cast by Jung as a closeness that Frank wants to cultivate (120) but chooses to deny. Frank prefers "to let some darkness gently go" (117) and vanishes into a military life, one that reinscribes the incommensurability of being a 'real man' and homosexual as he plays straight and fulfils the heterosexual norms of being a soldier and a good Chinese-Canadian citizen.

He ends the night of his going-away party with "bawdy song[s] about girls in the back of cars" (121). The realisation of Jung's sexual identity is scattered across the fabric of his otherwise normal life. Choy does not linger on those moments beyond a few tactile images and an obvious lack of resolution or exposure of Jung's desire for Frank.

The merging of discourses of war and heroism in Frank and those of latent desire in Jung create an odd fracturing of the 'war sweetheart left behind' narrative. The nature of Jung's relationship with Frank is briefly acknowledged when Max offers him "deliverance" through telling him to "have courage" (122) as Frank leaves the country. In subversive or radical aspects to these representations, the gay relationship in *Jade Peony* exists only as allusion and implicit acknowledgement by Max and by his grandmother. Christopher Lee argues that "[f]amily unity and coherence is maintained through a collective investment in its discursive hierarchy, which includes an implicit (or explicit) agreement to keep certain aspects of family history secret" (21). Jung's sexuality stays submerged, and the challenge for the enmeshed Chinatown families, and by extension community, is defused. Lee also observes that Choy "is aware that the differentiation between oppressor/ oppressed is not necessarily synonymous with white/Chinese" (31). Given this latter point, Choy's portrayal of Jung and Frank in a same-race relationship, however unfulfilled, is significant. That Jung readily finds Frank desirable contravenes the stereotype found within some gay communities, and in Asian men themselves, that Asian men are unsexy.

"The Quintessential Enemy Within": Positioning the 'Gay Asian Male' (GAM)

This section examines representations of being gay and Asian in Australia and Canada. The texts discussed include Tony Ayres's documentary, *China Dolls* (1997), which consists of interviews with a cross-section of Asian-Australians, ranging from straight-gays to drag queens; and Wayne Yung's small circulation chapbook, *Beyond Yellow Fever*, one of the first texts to address specifically the emotional and social situation of an Asian-Canadian man who is in a mixed-race relationship with an HIV-positive partner. This chapbook was produced by the Vancouver-based, experimental arts group, the Pomelo Project.

The difficult situation of being gay in notoriously resistant and dismissive Asian cultural communities, and in discriminating gay communities, means that "many gay Asians are run over at the intersection of racism and homophobia" (Wat 79). The tension always exists between coming out and, perhaps, losing the support of their community or staying in and playing straight. Jung in Choy's *Jade Peony* voices these same concerns when he obsesses about the possibility of Frank finding out how he is feeling about their relationship and rejecting him as a Little Brother. Further, Eric Wat illustrates the cyclic nature of denial and rejection of homosexuals within Asian groups when he argues, "the perceived conservatism of Asian communities has often led queer Asians to turn their backs on their ethnic and cultural identities. The separation is hereby complete, and the paradox preserved" (77). Ayres mentions this separation when he describes having "done a Michael Jackson to his psyche" ("Undesirable" 112), carving it up to orient it 'towards white'. Across readings of Asian gayness in various texts are many similarities within the body of criticism on tropes of marginalisation, losing/finding community, and internalised racism. Especially significant is the applicability of much of the work that has been done in the United States about Asian homosexuality to Asian writing occurring in Canada and Australia.

Ways of figuring gay community identities shift from homosexuals as an ethnic group (Altman, "[Homo]Sexual Identities") to a form of reverse diaspora in which queer groups assemble from many different areas as opposed to dispersing to them (Sinfield). Specifically, Dennis Altman argues that, "[i]n some ways 'gay' has become another part of the multicultural mosaic, and events such as the Gay and Lesbian Mardi Gras can be easily encompassed as another ethnic festival" (108). While Altman's deliberate narrowing of definition for ethnicity and gayness to mean only folkloric markers highlights the shallow 'lifestyle' perceptions of marginalised groups in society, it fails to address the vastly different life experiences for racial minority and 'white' individuals. Alan Sinfield argues that gays within their own 'ethnic' communities are "perfect subversive implants, the quintessential enemy within" (281) because of enduring heterosexist assumptions. Further, Sinfield rejects the ethnicity model, contending that configuring gays as another 'ethnic' group

> encourages the inference that an out-group needs concessions, rather than the mainstream needing correction; so lesbians and gay men, [Didi] Herman observes, may be "granted legitimacy, not on the basis that there might be something problematic with gender roles and sexual hierarchies, but on the basis that they constitute a fixed group of 'others' who need and deserve protection" (272–3).

For Asian gay men, the intersection of race and gayness muddles further definitions of gayness as another form of 'ethnicity'. Associated with the difficulties of coming out to Asian communities is the stereotype that homosexuality is a 'Western' trait. As the character of Eddie in Lazaroo's *The World Waiting To Be Made* demonstrates, the designation of gayness or lesbianism as examples of Western corruption exists as a form of denying differences for sexual preferences in society. For example, in an experimental project by a group of students at the University of California, Berkeley, interview subject Eric, who is gay, states, "I didn't want to come out in English because I didn't want them to associate my sexuality with being 'American'" ("Grinding Tofu" 6).[18] Similarly, Ayres's documentary about gay Asian-Australians, *China Dolls*, emphasises the easy refusal of Asian-Australians to accept different sexual preferences within their own community by using the (corrupting) 'Westernisation' process as the reason behind homosexuality. Andrew Kaw expresses the confusion for younger men coming out or feeling different when he says that he attributed his feeling of 'difference' to his being Chinese-Australian and, therefore, an outsider already (Ayres, *China Dolls*). His additional confusion about sexual orientation became just another layer to add to his already chaotic emotions.

In Ayres's documentary, images of an Asian man applying make-up and gradually covering his entire face with white paint intersperse continually with the interviews. At the end, however, the man wipes off all of the make-up and his face is clean. The subtitle appears — "Cleanse, Tone, Exorcise" — and the point about seeking to extinguish personal demons is demonstrated by the rest of the show and its interviews. The subtitles of the sections also follow this focus on the 'whitening' of GAMs when they feel they have to leave their Asian communities for openly gay ones. Throughout the documentary and through the interview questions, Ayres maps the racial lines along which the gay communities are often divided. The sections of the documentary, moving from "Forbidden Fruit", "Potato Queen", then to "Sticky Rice" and "Fruit Salad", imply a progression in (self-) acceptance and the radical potential of same-race relationships. As well, it hints at the changing attitudes of gay Asians from different generations.

Many of the interviewees self-identified as the lowest rung on the desirability ladder. Some were told that they were lucky to be gay in Australia, as there were only two steps — Caucasian and Asian — as opposed to the three steps in the United States: Caucasian, Black, then Asian (Ayres, "Undesirable" 114). The hierarchy of value within the gay community, and the colour bar that applied in aspects of gay cruising, is a significant part of the struggle for visibility in homosexual and other communities for Asian men. Ayres comments that he had "already developed a native understanding that the East was inferior to the West, the legacy of growing up in Australia in the 60s and 70s" ("Undesirable" 112). This internalised racism, then, gives rise to the phenomenon of the potato queen, a gay Asian man who prefers white partners only. Having gay iconic figures of desire as mostly blond, white, and middle-class, leaves images of gay Asian men only in the novelty category. In gay porn, Ayres asserts, Asian men represent examples of exotica, not masculinity (*China Dolls*). Richard Fung's perspective tallies with that of Ayres in his study of the power and politics of gay pornography. In finding that most of the white characters took Asian men and that it was never the Asian man penetrating a white man, Fung quotes Fanon on black men being eclipsed and *turned into* the penis, and then discusses Asian men's representation as "desexualized Zen asceticism" ("Looking" 183). He questions the allowances for homosexuality in a group that is symbolically without a penis. To address this desexualisation, Asian-Canadian Wayne Yung created the *Beyond Yellow Fever* chapbook for inclusion in the Pomelo Project's "Work of Pleasure" series. He prefaces the 23-page text with:

> Peter's white, HIV+, and eighteen years older than me. I'm Chinese, HIV-, and relatively inexperienced. I can only imagine the sex, drugs, and alcohol he knew before AIDS. It would be easy to let race, age, and antibodies divide us. It takes constant negotiation to find our common ground. We never pretend these issues don't matter (i).

Beyond Yellow Fever is a close study of Yung's relationship with his white partner. The dialogue text encapsulates the racist and judgmental attitudes within the gay community and is accompanied by explicit line drawings and polemical titles. The "Work of Pleasure" project involved varying forms of media, including music on cassette (Don Chow's *Ancestral Tracks*) and multi-printed single sheet (Laura Kang's *The Work of 'Asian Woman'*). The chapbook's "candid exploration of homoerotic desire in an interracial context" (Mathur, Review 2) was not palatable for corporate sponsors, and the sexually detailed line drawings of naked male bodies probably shifted perceptions of whether the publication was one that would favourably reflect corporate aims. The Asia Pacific Foundation refused to be acknowledged as a supporter of this series by The Pomelo Project after the chapbook was sighted.

Yung's use of italicised commentaries work with the dialogue and summary to offer the reader a layered experience of how a personal relationship functions (or founders) when overdetermined by others', or one's own internalised, expectations. The chapbook's conversational structure emphasises the day-to-day negotiations for Peter and Wayne, about age, race, HIV discrimination, and public declarations. One part of their dialogue focuses on Peter's realisation that his reluctance to show affection publicly was linked to being "afraid that someone will think [he's] a rice queen or a chicken hawk" (12). Appearing with the title, "Asians are oversexed" is the summary:

> Rice Queen: a white fag who prefers Asians.
> Potato Queen: an Asian fag who prefers whites.
> Sticky Rice: an Asian fag who prefers Asians.
> Normal: a white fag who prefers whites (10).

Yung emphasises the hypocrisy of judging only interracial or coloured relationships as situations requiring categorisation. The centre of white/white relationships remains unquestioned, whereas white/Asian, white/black, or Asian/black become "uncommon desires" (16). Raymond Wei-Cheng Chu argues, however, that "not to represent such relationships as racially complicated at all can be judged only as uninformed romance or as escapist fantasy" (230). The apparent power disparities between white men and those from racial minorities transfer to relationships and their dynamics. Yung himself comments that "denying [his] racial preference was like denying [his] sexual preference" (18), a statement that lends the subtitle of 'the quintessential enemy within' a twist. His up-front admission of being unable to find other Asian men attractive stems from his difficulties with unsettling the negative connotations of 'Asianness'. He states, "I'm tired of convincing white boys that Asians are sexy. It's hard enough to convince myself I'm sexy" (20). The insidious racial hierarchy of desire engenders a self-hate that persists even though Yung is aware of the reasons behind it. As a whole, *Beyond Yellow Fever*'s close study of a single relationship provides no singular lesson of acceptance or contentment. Ashok Mathur applauds the appearance of a work like Yung's and comments that it "is of cutting-edge importance to literature in Canada today" and "explod[es] falsehoods about Asian gay sexuality" (Review 1). Although Yung certainly exposes many of the myths pertaining to mixed-race relationships and the effects of internalised racism, the chapbook perhaps does not explode falsehoods as much as reveal his complicity with these myths.

Numbers of publications for Asian-Canadian writing about queer issues are relatively low, and representation is complicated by the fact that many authors are subsumed in 'North American' or 'Asia Pacific American' compilations.[19] Yung's *Beyond Yellow Fever* is a beginning for altered literary versions of gay Asian representation in Canada. It is certainly one of the first that specifically focuses on issues of interracial male relationships and living with an HIV-positive partner.

Conclusion

The texts discussed in this chapter exemplify the complex task of eroding and re-forming versions of 'masculinity' by moving away from only answering to white versions of masculinity. Whereas *Pomeroy's* characters actively re-form connotations of masculine identities and question the strengths of Australian affiliations, Leong's photographs trade more on their juxtaposition of accepted Australian imagery with Other elements. They coalesce in several bodies the possibilities for representing Asian-Australian men. Their work undertakes Luke's challenge for diasporic men to occupy the "relatively open place, a gap, a space within which to reconstruct Asian masculinity" (34). I would temper Luke's contention about this "open" space, however, in as much as he compares it to the iconically cluttered white man's stage without acknowledging the power disparity between the two levels of representation. The significance of the texts examined in this chapter lies not only in their authors' creation of alternative or complex masculinities but also in their modes of circulation through publication. Re-creations have limited effect if they are not dispersed among various audiences, particularly audiences for whom the material is socially and culturally challenging.

Fulfilling this role in the Canadian context is Watada's work in *Daruma Days*, which offers aspects of masculine representation within the internment camps of the Second World War. It offers insight into the difficulties of adjusting from the relative stability of family and community for Japanese communities in Canada to the uprooted and vilified existence of the internment camps. The invalidation of family bonds and civic rights meant the compromise of family and community authority, completely shifting the terms of relations for men and women within Japanese-Canadian groups. The narrative of Toshiro and the *ofuro* epitomise these conflicted and denied roles, most particularly embodied in his small, poignant victory. In the same way, *Jade Peony* interrogates the community/family relations of Liang and Jung, focusing on various fraught times for the Chinese population in Vancouver: the remnants of the bachelor-men population, like Wong Suk, from the days of head tax restrictions, and participants in (masculine) nation-building activities such as enlisting in the Second World War. Watada's and Choy's works offer important cross-sections of diasporic men and interrogate their generational, gender influences, as well as focusing on class considerations within their communities. The silence hanging over Jung's story after Frank leaves for war lingers and raises questions of what is considered an 'appropriate' Chinatown narrative. The GAM seems to represent a potent threat on many levels and is not made overt in Choy's text. Accompanying the recent spate of publications and a higher profile for diasporic queer studies are new modes and, perhaps, 'rules' of representation. With a page in his *Beyond Yellow Fever* chapbook titled 'Not just a gwm in a yellow skin', Yung protests what he perceives as the prescriptiveness of recent representations: "I'm sick of these new 'positive' images of Asian men. Now we're so empowered that no one can fuck us up the ass anymore. We're supposed to be so strong, smart, and together. It drives me crazy" (3). As argued earlier, it is not a matter of only having better, stronger representations but a proliferation that shares the task of representing various types of diasporic Asian men and their masculinity. Yung's lament highlights the fact that the goal of new and recovered representations should not be to dictate, but to keep pushing at the boundaries of accepted depictions.

The works examined in this chapter extend and challenge existing depictions of Asian masculinities and their ability to be read simultaneously as diasporic Australian or Canadian. The erosion of Western national representations of the masculine, and the dismantling of ascribed identities for diasporic men in the texts I examine serve to diversify the categories of inclusion for diasporic masculinities. The representations of Asian men through more complex, nuanced characters and images enables, indeed perhaps forces, their necessary mobilisation in changing national and community discourses.

The multiplication of possible images of who is included in constructions of Australian or Canadian masculinity, and what Chinese or Japanese masculinities can mean, work towards establishing new modes of identification as well as eroding discriminatory stereotypes. This chapter offered an examination of a sampling of the work circulated thus far. Given the early stages of diasporic Asian studies as disciplines in both Australia and Canada, this is an area with many more avenues to explore and plenty more to be said. In conjunction with national moments such as war and internment in particular, this recasting of diasporic Asian men in literature and other contexts ensconces them in the national imaginary while interrogating existing versions of it.

Emerging Extravagance in Diasporic Asian Women's Writing

Attractive straight white male/middle-aged business executive looking for that special little/China Doll, preferably short, petite and obedient. Object:/ to fulfil typical fantasies of the stereotype of Oriental ladies/anxious to marry a Canadian in order to get out of Hong Kong or/the Philippines and willing to do anything to pamper and please/her man. Photo required.

(C. Allyson Lee, "Recipe" 335)

While literature by and about hyphenated Asian masculinities is only now garnering serious theoretical attention, Asian diasporic women's writing has developed into a recognisable body of work. More specifically, it is *Chinese* women's stories that have become the most associated with 'Asian women's literature'. Characterised by authors such as Jung Chang, Amy Tan, and Maxine Hong Kingston, the most visible works are those written by Asian-Americans and distributed, in the main, by multinational publishers. The gradual development of Asian women's writing in Canada and Australia, then, is partially eclipsed by the overwhelming amount of Asian-American publication and criticism, particularly along a feminist axis. Because of this, most recognition of hyphenated Asian women's writing as a body of literature comes with the price of easy and often inaccurate generic categorisations. The assumption that Asian women's stories are necessarily 'confessional' narratives, often in the form of autobiography (albeit 'disguised') is a stereotype that persists. This stereotype is encouraged by the strongly promoted Chinese revolution stories which are marketed as seemingly international texts, not grounded at all in nationally contextualised literary or social structures. The prevalence of these publications indicates a market demand for them, but to shift from reading Asian women's texts only in the autobiographical genre, or simply retelling stories, allows them to realise the oppositional elements found in literature of "Necessity" and "Extravagance" (Wong, Sau-Ling, *Reading* 13). Sau-ling Wong posits these abstractions as rhetorical opposites: Necessity figures as "contained, survival-driven and conservation-minded" whereas Extravagance connotes "freedom, excess, emotional expressiveness, and autotelism" (13). For Asian-Canadian and Asian-Australian literature, I would configure Necessity as more apparent in recoveries of social and political history, boosting representation from writers of Asian descent on the literary scene and instigating community awareness and activism. Particularly for Asian women's literature, having Extravagance as the dominant note configures a style of literature that often shifts perceptions of Asian identities and gender roles, playing with expectation and reversing voyeuristic reading practices. The two facets must, Wong argues, always accompany one another in theoretical readings of texts. This dual function bears emphasising for Asian women's texts because of the one-dimensional reading strategies often used to examine their work.

Discussing 'Extravagance' in literature is challenging for literary analyses of Asian-Canadian and Asian-Australian writing. It provides usefully overlapping discourses outside the understood and stereotyped educative purposes to which multicultural literature is often put. In the relatively new discipline of diasporic Asian feminist literary studies, many critical issues remain unaddressed, particularly those examining texts and their contexts in detail. This chapter focuses on 'Extravagant' possibilities for Asian women's writing in negotiating and re-forming categories of Asian-Canadian or Asian-Australian women's writing. A brief discussion about existing texts of 'Necessity' is followed by an examination of mythical subversion and transformative sexualities in Canadian Larissa Lai's *When Fox Is a Thousand* and the modulations of assimilation in Australian Hsu-Ming Teo's *Love and Vertigo*. The multi-layered address found in both novels engages with a radical concept of possible 'audiences' for Asian-Australian and Asian-Canadian women's literatures. The value of texts with the ability to dialogue with their own communities lies in their capacity for constituting these women as individuals within, and without, the rest of society. The representations that 'hail' their own community readers are not necessarily any less confronting for their audiences, and they are certainly less simplistic than some texts that are seemingly marketed only towards audiences hungry for exoticised tales.[1] Working towards a more complex form of identity politics validates a wider range of Asian women's subjectivities and their placements in the larger fields of women's, national, and diasporic literatures.

Although texts with more 'Extravagant' styles are now appearing, they are still outnumbered by the historical recovery or preservation projects (projects emphasised by 'Necessity') that constitute many of the earlier novels and non-fiction works by Australian and Canadian Asian women. In Australia, these works still have many gaps in historical knowledge to fill, their presence hopefully combating the persistent Anglicisation and 'masculinisation' of that history. Ingrained patriarchal attitudes across genders also threaten the recovery and re-establishment of women's roles in Canadian or Australian histories. A good example of this self-policing mechanism in Australia is offered in Diana Giese's book of interviews with Chinese-Australians, *Astronauts, Lost Souls, and Dragons.* This book is part of an ongoing oral history project about Chinese communities in Australia and how they negotiated two centuries of legislated and covert racism. As discussed elsewhere in this book, the contributions that women might have made to establishing these dynasties, and the rituals and pressures of the domestic sphere, remain suppressed and dismissed. To be fair, Giese does gesture to this as a symptom of the generation from which the interviewee belongs. The absence of other perspectives from that era, however, renders Kwong Chee's as the sole representative of attitudes towards women in the pioneer communities. Apparently, this attitude is one of discarding women's experiences as less than worthy of recording, let alone appreciating, compared with men's achievements in the public sphere of community work and business. Magdalene Ang-Lygate states that for immigrant women "the condition of marriage or family kinship is often a crucially important component of their identities because it had significant implications on their national status and subsequent legal rights" (378). Perhaps because of this, the Chinese women in Australian history are left on the periphery of records about community-building and achievement. As mentioned earlier, very few publications are directly concerned with Chinese-Australian women's history. Primary papers are available and research projects are in progress, but there is, as yet, very little published in this area. Similarly, in Canada, publications concerning the role of Asian women in building pioneer communities are also rare. *Jin Guo: Voices of Chinese Canadian Women* (Chinese Canadian National Council, 1992) is perhaps one of the most recognised examples of this type of project.[2] The continual historicisation of Asian women's presences in Australia and Canada emerge alongside diversification of literature and other creative arts. This double movement contributes to the depth and inclusiveness of representations for women as Asian-Australians and Asian-Canadians, members of various communities, and national citizens.

Considering the overdetermination of many Asian women's stories, C. Allyson Lee's epigraph for this chapter is exemplary of the mode that many writers adopt in their work. Because they understand the difficult, complicitous ways in which Western discourses about the 'Asian Woman' continue to interpellate them, they know that these are the conditions of the society into which their writing is published. This dual perspective and heightened awareness of possible receptions often lend contemporary Asian women's literature a knowingness regarding cultural pigeon-holes and assumptions about sexuality and personality. The publication of works that contribute new styles and content to Asian women's literature succeed in broadening the area and diluting the influence of the confessional narratives that have become so popularly dominant. In particular, the emphasis in this chapter on contextualising the texts, nationally and communally, serves to address the oft-levelled charge of universalising Asian women's experiences across countries and cultural groups. That said, Asian women's literature from 'Western' sites do have many aspects in common, especially in representing experiences of racialisation and patriarchal structures within and outside of their communities. These similarities work well towards coalition politics for Asian-Australian and Asian-Canadian literary profiles and anti-racist projects. Kwame Appiah and Henry Gates argue, "[a] literary historian might very well characterize the eighties as the period when race, class, and gender became the holy trinity of literary criticism. . . . In the 1990s, however, 'race', 'class', and 'gender' threaten to become the regnant clichés of our critical discourse" (1). They declare that the influence of race/class/gender considerations is disintegrating from overuse. More precisely, I would argue, it is the *unthinking* use of these terms that render them banal. These considerations are always necessary in theoretical literary work, alongside an equal concentration on stylistic and formal aspects. Avtar Brah specifies that these applications are part of the process of developing critique: "mantras are designed for repetition precisely because each repetitive act is expected to construct new meanings. Mantric enunciation is an act of transformation, not ossification" (14). Thus, the 'mantra' of race/class/gender allows the previously elided conditions of Asian women's literary production and issues of subjectivity to be brought to the fore and constructively interrogated.

The contextualisation of social-literary sites and the communities which surround hyphenated Asian women's texts remain underinvestigated areas. The layers of community apparent in any invocation of 'Asian-Australianness' or 'Asian-Canadianness' reveal the complexity of who is included in the category. Its open-endedness reflects the changing constitution of diasporic Asian women's literature: Whereas writers of Chinese or Japanese descent have dominated publication in the past few decades, there is an ever-increasing number of works by authors of Korean, Vietnamese, and Filipino descent.

Increasing also are the numbers of publications by and about Asian-Canadian and Asian-Australian women writers, all of which contribute to the establishment of a basis from which to theorise further the consequences of feminist and postmodern perspectives on national literatures. These works function in several ways: They establish Asian-Canadian and Asian-Australian literatures as areas of study and activism, they multiply versions of women's fiction and identities, and they continue to contribute to transforming discourses about Canadian and Australian literature. As Makeda Silvera comments in the "Foreword" of *The Other Woman: Women of Colour in Contemporary Canadian Literature*, "[t]he voices in [this book] speak not necessarily in unison but to and of a common interest" (x). Considering the white, middle-class agenda that represented 'Western Feminism' for decades (some would say it still does), the ambivalence directed at the concept of women's 'solidarity' across cultures and class is understandable though, as Silvera has stated, these moments of cohesion do not have to denote homogenisation. Rather, their active discussion and dissension with each other while being able to mobilise effectively as political groups becomes Kobena Mercer's version of 'solidarity' (68). Mercer speaks specifically about the emergence or recovery of black, women's, and gay movements in post-Thatcherite London, but his discussion of the political power negotiations for minority groups in the 'new right' environment is pertinent for Asian-Canadian and Asian-Australian concerns. This was particularly true of the late 1990s in Canada and Australia, where there was significant renewed political conservatism and a desire for a fallacious purer past, uncluttered by the messiness of identity politics and community negotiations. This defensive posture makes scapegoats of any group that does not suit the criteria of who is "'manly, true and white'" (Spence in Leach, 72), and thus 'a politics of blame' emerges. This form of simplifying and deflecting issues affects literary concerns as well as those of politics and economics. Especially in contemporary Australia, broadly attacking individuals, cultural icons, or texts as 'un-Australian' remains prevalent and deliberately ill-defined.

In comparison with Canada, Asian-Australian women's literature is 'nascent' in similar ways to the state of Asian-Canadian literature almost a decade ago. The issue is complicated by the cross-theorising between Asian-American, Asian-Canadian, and Asian-Australian literature and the fluidity of the 'diasporic' category into which these authors are sometimes placed. Further, a schism exists between the focused attention in academia on identity politics, including the articulation of racial minority politics within national frames, and the rate of Asian-Australian authors publishing texts. This gap speaks, partially, to a failure in dialogue between academic and mainstream discourses. Issues that have been thoroughly discussed in academia may not make it into other forms of media beyond the narrow range of academic publications. The emergence of authors and the gradual publication of new novels is, in some ways, not keeping up with the amount of interest manifested in it as a literary and theoretical category. This lack of dissemination in the wider public sphere is an institutional dilemma quite common in all fields but, for developing fields like Asian-Australian literature, the consequences of the disparity are more perplexing. It is difficult to keep an area growing when texts for study are slow to circulate or theoretical studies focus on a limited number of works.

Critical work in hyphenated Asian women's writing is necessarily interdisciplinary and has many crossovers with women's studies, multicultural literature, and race theory. Because of this splitting across areas, the invocation of any one category into which this type of literature could belong is difficult and probably undesirable. That said, however, strategic deployment of 'Asian-Australian' or 'Asian-Canadian' literary categories are useful for concentrating research in this area and building up a body of critical literature which addresses more specifically conditions of Asianness for women in Australia and Canada. These categories can become "instrument[s] for political mobilization under chosen circumstances" (Wong, Sau-ling, *Reading* 6), allowing examinations of gender, race, and class, as well as performing a critique on frames of knowledge regarding societal politics and culture. The expressions of Asian women's identities in literature upon which this chapter focuses develop a closer analysis of the representation of women's agency and power in social and family relationships. Lai says that she writes to redress the "absences and omissions" in our histories, "to do with things like women who rebel, women who love women, women who do not belong to the élite classes" ("Ritz Chow Interviews" 1). The contemporary works by Teo and Lai discussed here encapsulate these aspects in differing ways, offering portrayals of Asian women and their sexualities as they seek to reconcile their past and present 'homes'.

The enduring creation of an 'immigrant writer' category for Asian-

Australian and Asian-Canadian authors has become more and more difficult to sustain with such diverse communities of artists from different generations. While some still depend on and freeze this moment of arrival to justify profiles on 'Chinese' writers, Asian women authors are writing increasingly out of the similar social and cultural moments as other contemporary Australian or Canadian writers.[3] Arguably, persistent differences and emphases exist in the ways Asian women writers and their narratives engage with issues like sexism and racism on several levels, often involving a mix of internalised racism/sexism, community pressures, and examinations of national belonging.

Assimilation and the National Body

In this section, I examine the trope of assimilation, notions of cultural sacrifice, and the ways in which critics have positioned and discussed Hsu Ming Teo's novel *Love and Vertigo*. Assimilate means "to take in, fit into, or become similar". I want to mobilise this term and examine its manifestations in Teo's novel, particularly for the female protagonist and the rest of her family, as well as to examine the mechanisms accompanying the compulsion to assimilate in contemporary Australian society.

Teo's narrative uses a complex play of notions of acculturation and rejection, on personal, societal, and cultural levels. The representation of cultural assimilation in some fiction as a process only to be condemned contrasts with the valorisation of such integration in national policy up till today, perhaps even more so today than a decade ago. I am not talking here of the indigenous situation in which 'assimilation' was a forced, government-sanctioned process of dispersal and removal. I am referring to assimilation as the postwar strategy for building cohesion for Australia in the face of increasingly diverse communities, mainly from Europe. This policy of assimilation evolved into multiculturalism in the early to mid-1980s but, as many have argued, this form of multiculturalism was only a slightly progressive tweaking of the assimilationist imperative.

Certain aspects of hybridity and difference are valorised under the auspices of multiculturalism, but they are usually the ones that have little impact on gaining political or social status. In a 1999 report by the National Multicultural Advisory Council called "Australian Multiculturalism for a New Century: Towards Inclusiveness", one of the conclusions was: "The Council recommends that any communication strategy highlights the positive and mutually supportive relationship between Australian culture and Australian multiculturalism."While spending many pages extolling the cohesive virtues of multiculturalism as a policy and sometime reality, the Committee ends up with a statement which creates separate categories for 'Australian culture' and 'Australian multiculturalism'. This division typifies the additive model of multiculturalism in which those who are seen to benefit directly from multiculturalism — that is, the 'ethnics' — exist outside an already defined Australian society. Assimilation as the only laudable path for immigrants is confirmed by Prime Minister John Howard at the launch of the previously mentioned report. He states that "the debt that we owe to the successive waves of migrants *who have embraced the Australian way* is incalculable" ("Address"; emphasis added). Ghassan Hage characterises this supposed shift from assimilation to multiculturalism as moving from "'ethnophobia to ethnophilia'" (*White Nation* 236) and emphasises the power-play apparent in both policies when 'ethnics' are "people one can make decisions *about*: objects to be governed" (*White Nation* 17). Hage's argument challenges the lament of cultural loss staved off by multiculturalism. I would ask more specifically: Who categorises what is 'lost', what 'value' did it have in the first place, and to whom is the 'loss' detrimental? Given the gendered nature of cultural maintenance, examining the ways in which this 'loss' affects Teo's characters adds a layer to understanding Asian-Australian literary representations of family. Most often, these representations are understood through their capacity for dysfunction, as Teo's and Simone Lazaroo's novels demonstrate.

Some representations of the acculturation dynamic, especially for racial minority groups, configure it only as a cultural trade — if you gain, you must lose — flattening the complexity of achieving cultural literacy and adaptation. Walter Benn Michaels states that "[r]ace transforms people who learn to do what we do into the thieves of our culture and people who teach us to do what they do into the destroyers of our culture; it makes assimilation into a kind of betrayal and the refusal to assimilate into a form of heroism" (685). When we consider the multiple sites of being for individuals and communities of Asian descent, the Australian/not-Australian binary fails to capture the interconnectedness of communities, their heritage cultures, and their current political positions. Particularly in Australia's present state of jingoistic fervour for border protection and punishing asylum-seekers, the government's demarcation of Australian and not-Australian has become increasingly extreme and arbitrary. Parts of Australia that are territorially 'Australian' are not-Australian if one is trying to seek refugee status. The government has carved the nation so that some areas are more 'Australian' than others.

Through the 1970s, the political trend may have been a gradual move towards multiculturalism as a containment strategy, but the reality for non-white migrants was very much one of fitting in and being seen to be non-disruptive members of Australian society. As Sneja Gunew has described it: "the host wants only the food and only the mute or stammering bodies cut off from their words and histories" ("Against" 41). Elsewhere, Gunew elaborates this notion of limited acceptance by stating that:

> [t]he mark of sanity and cultural assimilation is that the body of the undesirable alter ego is consumed and transmuted into speech. As part of the process, the foreign and visibly different aspects of the body of the narrator are screened or camouflaged through her ability, finally, to project the familiar language of the dominant culture ("Melting Pot" 152).

Given Gunew's observation, examining Teo's novel also means examining the Vogel award–winning author herself as part of the 'cultural exchange'. The constraint on 'multicultural' writers to perform only within certain frames of understanding often leads to a form of compromised cultural participation. This highlights the need for careful consideration of how these literatures travel as part of the larger body of Australian cultural production.

Teo's *Love and Vertigo* won the 1999 *Australian*/Vogel Award for best unpublished manuscript. Published in 2000, the book comes three years after what Suvendrini Perera and Joseph Pugliese call the "re-licensing of racism in Australia" (1). This re-licensing, attributable to One Nation influence and Coalition complicity, targeted "those racialised groups least conducive, corporeally and culturally, to the process of assimilation, and therefore least likely to be re-cycled into Anglo-Australians" (2). In cultural histories, assimilation is a term which has taken on only negative connotations. It most often signifies loss of homeland cultures and languages, compromise of self, and 'selling out' to dominant cultural mores. Teo herself has made the observation that her assimilative upbringing, and the cultural capital accrued because of it, is what allows her the ease to occupy a variety of employment and social spaces (Chinatownsydney.com 2). She says that "her father's attitude had given her a 'voice and enough cultural ground to communicate with a wide society'" (Moran 5). Presumably, the opportunity to write books such as *Love and Vertigo* is also a symptom of ensuing privilege.

The novel divulges the process of assimilation, detailing its motivations and consequences. Newly published Asian–Australian novels, particularly those by women, are most often compared to Amy Tan and Jung Chang. Teo is no exception and reviewers, although in the main positive, also deposit her novel constantly in the categories of immigrant tales and confessionals and yet highlight Teo's clarification that it is not autobiography. Descriptions of *Love and Vertigo* include Thuy On's comment that it "plays happily with the game of unhappy families" (1) and Louis Nowra stating that the narrator has "a darkly comic vision of life where everyone is a mixture of greed, passion, hope and practical betrayals" (2). Leonie Lamont's article in the *Sydney Morning Herald* announced Teo as the winner of the *Australian*/Vogel Award. Within it, Ivor Indyk comments on works by writers of "migrant background". He states: "Either they are going to be hollow, in a sense because they are between cultures and draw upon neither, or they are going to be rich because they draw on both, and I think this novel is the latter case" (Lamont 3). Indyk's positive representation of the multiple histories upon which Teo can draw contrasts with Nowra's complaint that "the first half of the novel is such a delight that it comes as a disappointment when the family migrates to Australia" (3). Although being in the main complimentary, Nowra's review points out the mundane and 'colourless' nature of the Tay's experiences once they are in Australia, implying that there are 'enough' of these 'migrant' tales already. He goes on to clarify his disappointment by pointing out that Grace is not as "colourful" as her family back home, and that the sections set in Australia lack "exuberant charm" (3). In a similar type of protest, Rebekah Scott says "it is a pity that [narrator] Grace sounds more like an articulate authorial voice and not a hesitant young immigrant with a smattering of 'Singlish' patois" (5). A hunger for the exotic and the 'authentic' is bluntly exposed in Scott's assessment of the novel. She invites readers to 'sample' the wares of *Love and Vertigo,* a book she describes as possessing "the pungent spiciness of an Asian supermarket" (5). Teo has stated that she is actively rewriting the exotic (Chinatownsydney.com 2). She also flags class as of more critical concern than race or ethnicity, identifying herself as a "a middle-class woman" rather than Chinese or Asian (2). Through most of the reviews and other write-ups, much mention is made of Teo's youth, intelligence (she has a doctorate in history) and attractiveness.[4] Alongside the expectation and desire both Nowra and Scott seem to have for sensational colourful tales from an Asian-Australian author, their reaction to the less exciting setting of suburban Burwood in Australia indicates an impatience with the familiar and an easy dismissal of 'migrant' narratives having 'been done'.

The Tay family in *Love and Vertigo* moved to Australia from Malaysia in the 1970s, not long after the White Australia policy was officially dismantled and not quite into the heyday of a reinvented multicultural nation. The novel examines the power relationships in the family and is narrated by Grace, the only daughter. The father, Jonah, seeks the betterment of his family through establishment in Australia, and his wife Pandora demands the move to distance them from the heavy influence of her somewhat stereotypical dragon-lady mother-in-law, Madame Tay. Grace's parents' relationship — ambivalent and unenthusiastic from an early stage — disintegrates further in Australia, so much so that her mother eventually commits suicide.

For Grace and her brother Sonny, the accelerated deterioration of their parents' ability to communicate with each other and their children leaves them as the prime cultural translators. They are in charge of managing their own schooling and the way their family interacts with surrounding communities. Brian Castro describes his coping strategy when he first migrated from Hong Kong as an experience in projection: "Having come to Australia in the early sixties when assimilation and integration were the big things, and going to boarding school and having no people here in Australia, you have to masquerade, you have to impersonate" ("Interview with Ramona Koval" 8). The children realised that making their lives easier meant assimilating 'Australian ways', masquerading Australianness as quickly as possible, and working on Westernising their families:

> We grew to hate the sound of our voices, and those of our parents. They loved all things British, but they couldn't speak English. Their accents, their syntax and their vocabulary mirrored in language our cultural difference and our social leprosy before the age of multiculturalism (178).

Attempts to find acceptance and affirmation in the Australian schoolyard are as much about bringing proof to their parents of their viability as 'Australians' as it is about making life tolerable for themselves.

Pandora's inability to cope with the loneliness of Australia accelerates her decline and the 'bad' days she spent staring vacantly into the suburban streets of Burwood. On the bad days, her fear of the people outside and of new social interactions is a lesson in the isolation and stunted existence faced by women who are housebound and language restricted. Her children learned to downgrade their sometimes violent experiences of 'assimilation' in the schoolyard, sparing their mother the details because they know she cannot provide support and would panic at her inability to engage on their behalf. While Pandora could vicariously see them learning a new lifestyle, she remained trapped in the stalled domestic sphere.

Jonah, on the other hand, was rabidly assimilationist in outlook, and Grace goes so far as to describe her father as a racist and misanthrope: "His politics were conservative and his pleasure lay in complaining: he was the Chinese Bruce Ruxton" (181). Linking her father to an outspoken and consistently xenophobic Australian figure — the former president of the RSL[5] no less — Teo juxtaposes migrant with anti-migrant, demonstrating the discriminatory impetus in both. Jonah, dubbed 'The Patriarch' by Grace, wants his children to assimilate on several contradictory levels. He tries to make them take on his controlling, traditional 'Chinese' values while wanting them to be doing well in the new country, which means assimilating into the Australian socio-cultural body. Jonah sees himself as actively building a new life in Australia, and his wife's inability to cope or 'progress' frustrates him.

Both parents waited for Australian success to be theirs, through the progress of their children. This deferred gratification can, according to Sau-ling Wong, become a form of cannibalism when migrant parents are living lives of assimilation through their offspring. Grace explains how "immigration is an act of sacrifice on the part of your parents that you can never atone for" (196). Figuratively, Jonah and Pandora want to consume their children, to incorporate their experiences and thereby gain validation of their choice to emigrate. Wong states that Westernised children can be configured as sources of nourishment for the parents, acting as sacrifices to their parents' appetites for a 'better life' (*Reading* 37). Considering again the 'additive' model of multiculturalism in Australia, one could say the nourishment of the Australian cultural body depends on incorporation of its new migrants.

Part of the children's assimilation into Australian society was the internalisation of discriminatory attitudes, whereby they learnt precisely why they were unacceptable and had to change. The irony of this moment in the assimilation process is that, at the point of realising they had to change to fit in, they also started to recognise that 'fitting in' could never be fully achieved. Teo uses Sonny's predicament as a clear contradiction of the 'either/ or' model of belonging. His displacement from various social groups is much closer to 'neither/nor'. Sonny was bullied by 'white' classmates, so he withdrew to the relative safety of generic ethnicism with Greek and Lebanese students. When more Chinese started attending the school, he threw his lot in with them but found that he was an outsider, linguistically and culturally

— as Grace observes, "Chinese culture was foreign to him" (179). After this, he retreated into an obsession with jazz and, later, reification of African–American culture. Sonny's attempts to identify with another racial minority group signify, on some levels, a recognition of the limits of the assimilation rhetoric. Sonny identified that 'Asians' had an asymptotic relationship with true 'Australianness' and could never be properly 'assimilated' into idealised white Australian society because of their racially marked bodies. Grace still wanted to "bleach [herself] into 'Advanced Australian Fairness'" (183).

The overarching sentiment in *Love and Vertigo* is one of loss and failed expectations. The family persists in rejecting each other's needs, finding destructive ways to curtail their loneliness and neglect. Teo focuses especially on Pandora in the novel, and although the emphasis in the Tay family relationships is on Pandora's emotional opacity, her character is perhaps the most exposed to the reader. She performs 'good wifehood' through recreating Singaporean meals for Jonah and has episodes of obsessive housecleaning and shopping. The issue of his violence against her is never brought to the fore but exists as an indicator of familial instability set against the children's attempts to be 'normal Australian'. Pandora's avid search for meaning and connection in life culminated in an affair with the local church pastor. She left Jonah and thought the relationship with Rodney was one in which, finally, someone would choose her above others. This hope also failed, and the hypocrisy of the church liaison forced her slide into deeper depression and her final act of suicide. Although reviewers have compared the story to the 'confessional' ones of Amy Tan, Teo's narrative does not indulge in matrilineal discourses in the same way. One of the toughest and most ambivalent reconciliations in the novel is at the end, between Grace and her father. Teo portrays Jonah as similarly trapped and ruled by his generation's mores and his gender. Grace's acceptance of her responsibility for her father is not coupled with understanding or revelations about her mother or their relationship. It is a confused and makeshift response to a situation over which she feels she has little control: "there will never be a reconciliation with those we have lost. But maybe this is all I can do, maybe this is all we can ever do: to make up to the living our debt to the dead" (287).

It is ironic that Pandora commits suicide at 'home' — meaning Singapore — indicating that she was not a migrant who 'lost' everything in the process of migration but a person who realises that she never had enough in the first place and never would in the life she and Jonah had made. In the chapter titled "The Spite of Life", she and her children take vicious delight in ousting

Jonah's mother, Madame Tay, when she comes to stay. The actions are revenge for the older woman's bad treatment of Pandora in Singapore, and the power Pandora feels from having assimilated basic information about her locale and the English language enables her to subject her mother-in-law to emotional blackmail and humiliation. Pandora's limited integration into 'Australian' life allows her to harass and threaten her mother-in-law, harnessing the knowledge of another culture against her: "Gradually, [Pandora] realised that the power relationship had changed. In Sydney, she was on her home turf and Madame Tay was the alien. All the advantage was on her side" (207–8). The breaking of Madame Tay only served to exacerbate Pandora's feelings of hopelessness, having wielded the empty negativity of her newfound power. Her mother-in-law's subsequent death on her return to Singapore charged her and her children with guilt at their cruelty.

After Pandora's suicide, the wake held in Singapore makes room for a homecoming moment of sorts. However, Teo resists the lure of having the homecoming as a resolution or phase of reminiscing. In fact, she uses it as a point of permanent fracture for Sonny and his mother's extended family, and for renewed estrangement from his father. Grace also takes leave of Singapore with fewer family ties and a sense of finality. She says, "Although at last I've learned to love my mother's homeland, this time I won't be coming back" (280). On one level, the assimilation of Grace and Sonny into Australia is 'successful' — they certainly do not perceive of Singapore or Malaysia as their homeland, and they go 'home' to Australia. On other levels, however, it is obvious that the dysfunction in the family has ruined chances of finding any sense of 'home'. Penelope Davie describes the family as "emotionally homeless" with "no refuge from themselves or from the world around them" (1). The children's failure to meet Jonah's expectations leave him a man starved of assimilative fodder and with limited avenues for emotional recovery.

Teo does not offer us a success story. The return home for the funeral is also a knowing deflection of the enhanced ethnicity and cultural fulfilment cliché. Singapore is never configured in the novel as an unmarked, utopian, or nostalgic site. In fact, Teo's narrative provides little emphasis on homeland at all. Grace's ambivalence about belonging, be it in Singapore or Australia, leads her to assimilate many cultural faces and to feel at home with none of them. *Love and Vertigo* leaves us with Grace's ambivalent and reluctant resolution with her father.

Liam Davison chooses to read the Tay family's self-destruction as a symptom of the fact that they are "[r]emoved from the potentially enriching aspects of their Chinese heritage" (R13). I would argue that the unit was doomed precisely because of this form of 'Chinese heritage', one which fostered Madame Tay's bullying, Jonah's split loyalties and guilt, Pandora's resentment and isolation, and the effect of all this on the next generation. Although the move to Australia and the associated pressures of assimilation could be seen as catalysts for the family's breakdown, they were by no means the cause. Teo's novel teases apart the complications inherent in cultural change and acculturation for the Tays but, moreover, it emphasises the gender and generational nuances for Jonah and Pandora. In crucial and destructive ways, they saw themselves as already spent on arrival in Australia, failed transplants in the new country hoping for renewal and vindication through their children.

Foxing Myths of Identity and Belonging

In Canadian literary culture, the emphasis on narratives of 'recovery' or writing into history is more prevalent than in Australia. As well as the Japanese-Canadian internment period, a number of texts offer versions of Chinese-Canadian literary cultural history, concentrating on writing Asian-Canadian lives into historical Canadian sites. These works include Judy Fong Bates's *China Dog and Other Tales from a Chinese Laundry* (1997), a collection of short stories that detail the beginnings of community-building for isolated Chinese families in rural Canadian towns. Many of the narratives are from the perspectives of mothers or daughters, concentrating on intergenerational shifts and community expectations. In many ways, the establishment-of-community sentiments found in Bates's collection of laundry stories is similar to those in Wah's café tales in *Diamond Grill*, though the latter is stylistically more adventurous and significantly more politically engaged. Bates's use of overlapping characters also resonates with Watada's *Daruma Days*, which uses recurring figures in the linked short stories. Both *China Dog* and *Daruma Days* contain narratives that map, by necessity somewhat erratically, the development of racial minority group identities, the pressures on individuals to conform to perceived cultural authenticities, and elements of biography in the linearity of the stories. Bates and Watada reclaim community and literary spaces for Asian-Canadians, a process of 'colouring-in' that works to extend social and cultural validation to racial minority groups.

In contrast, Lai's novel is more overtly interested in stylistic experimentation and subversive textual playfulness. It is a deliberate literary intervention that fills gaps and, in Lai's own words, to "contact things that had been forgotten" ("Ritz Chow Interviews" 1). The novel incorporates three main voices: the Fox, the ninth-century poetess Yu Hsuan-Chi, and the contemporary character of Artemis who lives in Vancouver. The graphic symbols in the book denote each voice and lend the text a theatrical feel, visibly shifting narrative perspectives. The system of signposting accelerates by the end of the novel, as characters' perspectives start overlapping and the storylines converge. This overrunning signifies the breakdown between the characters and the collapsing, and then separation, of the Fox with her human targets.

Themes of transplantation and assimilation are prominent in *Fox*. It concentrates on the social clashes brought about by the actions of the circle of friends and their infighting, 'in-loving', and the effects of the Fox spirit's predations and transformations. The novel contrasts how Art manages to be 'Chinese-Canadian' in the sense that she seems to negotiate actively both sides of the hyphen, and Mercy's failure to juggle her Chinese and Canadian identities. Mercy loses herself in grappling with her father's questionable ethics in the workplace, because of her Christian faith and her belief in the inheritance of family honour.

Throughout the novel, the US–Canada border exists as an analogy for the characters' increasingly ambivalent reconstructions of personal identity and their abilities to cross socio-cultural boundaries. In the first part of the novel, we meet Art and Mercy coming home to Vancouver after visiting the Museum of History in Seattle. At the border checkpoint, Mercy lies for them about not declaring anything, even though Art has purchased an ivory keepsake. When Mercy mutters that she does not like lying, Art dismisses it with "[c]ome on. That was just the border. That doesn't count." (10) Years later, Art meets Mercy on a bus after Mercy has reinvented herself as Ming. They are both on a bus going 'home' to Canada from the US. Ming has transformed from grown-out perms and worrying over family duty to buzz-cut hair, tattoos, and a tough, confrontational attitude. In Ming, we are challenged with the uneasy transference in becoming an activist and more politically confrontational (a form of rejecting clichéd Asian 'Model Minority' behaviour) and, in this instance, at the expense of community and her own family. Deborah Wills argues that Ming's deliberately 'androgynous' guise and ensuing death is similar to the murder of Diane's gay brother (6). They become two outsider figures erased from paradigms of 'community' and exposing the fissures caused by homophobia, conservatism, and radicalism within Asian-Canada. In crossing the US-Canada border, itself a site of enduring cultural tensions, Art and Mercy's ease of national transferral speaks to their already foreign identities in each of these countries. Their alienness as racial-minority Canadians confuses categorisations as 'citizens' of either Canada or the United States. Arif Dirlik describes this process as one in which "[n]ew diasporas have relocated the Self there and Other here, and consequently borders and boundaries have been confounded" ("Postcolonial Aura" 352). The progression from a relatively innocuous lie at the beginning of the novel to the fraught, unpredictable situation of the border search in the latter part of the book marks the movement for the characters from casual identity-switching to the real political and cultural consequences of this fluidity. Transgressing physical or political borders becomes a less dangerous activity than that of crossing the borders of the self. Ming's androgynisation, her radical transformation from her younger self, leads to tragedy when she is mistaken for a gay boy cruising in Stanley Park and is murdered.

Though the novel is peppered with changing character perspectives and a range of narrative time zones, it is set for the most part in 1989. The book is peopled with Asian-Canadians like flamboyant artist-photographer Eden, university liberal arts students like Artemis and Mercy, and their sometime-friend Diane. The 'taken-for-grantedness' of evoking Asian-Canadian community and friendship disturbs the more typical story of coping with being an outsider, or in-between, in Canadian society. This is not to say that this aspect is absent, and Karlyn Koh argues that "the impetus of the novel is indeed one of in-betweenness — but one which erodes the stability of the terms rather than being trapped between them" (Interview). Lai herself comments that: "[Artemis] navigates the strange social world that many first generation children navigate, negotiating friendship and desire through all the complicated screens of race and class and gender and sexuality" ("Stories" 4). In the novel, these screens are further complicated by Lai's doubling of characters within the text, a style which deliberately exploits the doppelganger figure and its connotations. This effect is most apparent in the characters of Artemis and Diane, whose names echo each other even as they represent opposing perspectives and elided histories. The ease with which the characters negotiate their sexualities also adds to the open-ended possibilities of the novel.

Artemis/Art is a character with whom Lai produces an effective style of self-conscious cultural engagement. Art is adopted by Anglo-Canadian parents who decide to keep the name her birth parents gave her, a name which alludes to "a generation of immigrant children whose parents loved the idea of the Enlightenment and thought they would find it blooming in the full heat of its rational fragrance right here in North America" (10). It becomes symbolic of "an aesthetic, like fortune cookies, or spaghetti noodles in hot dog soup" (11). These references to hybrid, created foods signify that Lai's version of 'Chinese-Canadian' is not one of seamless transplantation from 'homeland' to Canada, but one of process and 'bricolage'. Moreover, Art's cultural 'lack' becomes her rallying point when her friend, Diane, is worrying about the dismissal of an unknown past. Art feels compelled to answer with "I am no less who I am for where I've ended up" (97). This example of speaking against the prescription of an ethnic history, significantly coming from one of 'her own', emphasises Art's deliberate distancing from false creations of community.

The most striking aspect of Lai's novel is her manipulation of traditional Chinese folktales, or what I would read as their 'feminisation'. This offers her novel's characters a chance to speak about and against exclusionary times and more constrained roles. Again in her new novel, *Salt Fish Girl*, Lai chooses to engage with, and reconstruct, traditional tales. She states that her "strategy in recent years has been to make a project of constructing a consciously artificial history for myself and others like me — a history with women identified women of Chinese descent living in the West at its centre" ("Political Animals" 149). The figure of the fox spirit is one that haunts Chinese legends: a spirit that hungers for the life/energy of young (usually male) scholars. These foxes "have the power to change into women", and "in this form they can seduce and manipulate, teach moral lessons or expose political hypocrisies" (Press Gang webpage). Significantly, Lai's Fox is bisexual, as are Art and Diane, and her 'hauntings' involve a process of spiralling, socially and sexually, closer to her targets. According to the novel, through the centuries, there is a repeated scene where a (literal) coupling between the Poetess and the Fox takes place because they are reincarnations of girl spirits who were promised to one another before either was born. The continual pairing is presented as a Chinese fable. To alter the dynamic from male-female to female-female lends the pairings further subversive connotations. The purpose of a fox demon's predations on young scholars is usually to distract and devour them morally and spiritually. In making the prey female, and considering the queer overtones of most of the Fox's adventures, this incisive feminine rewrite of a misogynistic tale offers an ironic and adventurous critical journey away from certain types of tradition and the unquestioned authority of 'master' texts.

Lai reinvents the story of the Poetess from the information she manages to find: fragments in Chinese history books and short entries in encyclopaedias of traditional tales. In the West, the experience of reading dynastic myths or historical tales in English is a highly mediated process, as Lai explains:

> since English is my only language, I have access into histories such as this only through White or Westernized sinologists, themselves interpreting records left behind by a very specific class of privileged intellectual male Chinese scholars. . . . But then, if all the truths that I can find are already ideologically determined, what harm is there in producing another, true to my own quirky sense of the world, one that takes into consideration the long path of colonialism, migration and Westernization that has brought me to own particular circumstances — circumstances which allow me to access my own history only in this way! ("Stories" 4)

In Lai's novel, the Poetess is no longer vilified for her promiscuity, and so the moral impetus for the sanctioned versions of her life is lost. Accusations of 'selling out' and disrespect are sometimes levelled at authors who manipulate ancestral stories and legends, the most notorious example of this being the much-cited arguments between Chin and Kingston. Lai chooses to make new stories and characters, because otherwise "we run the danger of creating a battery of new stereotypes made all the more potent by the sanction bestowed by 'authenticity'" ("Ritz Chow Interviews" 1). Within these re-created tales, an affinity with women is a recurring aspect of the Fox's hauntings. In many parts of the novel, she enacts feminist sensibilities, setting out to 'save' women from their menfolk or sporting with those who exist on the fringes of towns and away from the protection offered by population or traditional male/female relationships. The Fox figure flickers through the novel "as a creature of darkness, death, germination and sexuality" (Lai, "Political Animals" 151). These tales, dispensed in the narrative rhythm of fables, often end with twists. For example, in the first story, the Fox moves in next to a rich, powerful man who ignores his First Wife. The Fox and the Wife conspire as the relationship between the husband and his new concubine grows. Ostensibly to recover the First Wife's 'place' in the household, the Fox clothes her in rich robes and offers her dainty embroidered shoes, "taught her how kisses come not from the mouth but from a well deep below the earth" (5), until the wife captivates the husband once more — and then the wife and the concubine run away together. The other foxes blame "the evil influence of the West, where personal whims come before family pride and reputation" (5) — a satirical reference to the sentiment often expressed against queer Asians, that they are only homosexual because of Western corruption. The Fox groups with Art and her friends because they all seem to have rejected family bonds and are setting out to differentiate themselves from the ones who criticise them.

Lai's conscious decision to move away from telling a more conventional immigrant tale erodes the established 'Western/Other' dichotomy in the novel by making the equation reflect a juxtaposition of Fox and Human. The Fox's habit for choosing women's bodies, and especially haunting lone scholars, makes her an outcast among her own kind. Her fascination with humans was considered odd and pointless, even shameful:

> [the other foxes] do see themselves in me; that recognition is precisely what terrifies them, what causes them to hurry back to their mates and cubs, their animal carcasses and shadow dwellings as though to say, "See, here are the things that make us civilized, here are the things that make us *not like her*" (16–7).

The desire to live vicariously with a human body takes further what is submerged in imperial discourse regarding interactions or association with Native Others. The more Fox dallies with humans, the less acceptable she is as a fox among her own kind. Her role-play in the human world is thought to threaten the integrity of the traditional fox world, forcing the other foxes to seek solace in, and emphasise the significance of, the activities that 'make [them] not like her'.

The analogies for reading the Fox's appropriative behaviours include taking on the corporeality of the Human Other and playing at being human while remaining ever 'fox-like'. Gail Ching-Liang Low considers the issue of whether, for colonial subjects, "the primary attraction of the cross-cultural dress is the promise of 'transgressive' pleasure without the penalties of actual change" (93). The Fox takes further the complicated notion of cross-cultural dress as she actually *embodies* humanity for various spans of time while being able to abandon it. In this way, she moves completely within the human world but is not bound by it.

When she moves to Canada, the Fox is faced with densely populated Vancouver and resorts to a different type of 'target' from was her wont in China: someone who may not be physically isolated, but who is in many ways emotionally and socially alone. Art is an example of someone whose 'family' is a constant "absence" (Goto, Review 18). The vain search for a true genealogy is exemplified by the Fox posing as Art's 'real' mother. She courts Art with behaviours and foods that she thinks reflects what Art would want of a mother. The falsity of the Fox's parental claim corresponds to an equally false and futile search for any untainted, 'real' Chineseness.

Alongside the destabilising of accepted community and cultural definitions, the female characters also 'fake' maleness in the novel, and the instances of cross-dressing and gender confusion mix within the narrative. At one point, Art dresses up as a man to frequent a gay bar with Eden (98– 102). Her final look is one of boyishness, which Eden assures her is acceptable because "Oriental boys are very slender" (99). The Fox also poses as a man, trading on her "lean, squarish jaw and plain dark robes" and "obscenely masculine feet" (104) until she is discovered by the prostitute with whom she is dallying. The prostitute turns out to be a transvestite, and the 'happily ever after' of that particular evening is rich with irony. Unlike other narratives in which the moment of being found out in a sexual disguise equates with some form of penalty, none of the gender transgressions in *Fox* is punished. The varying sexualities of many of the characters, however, are not gestures to a utopian sexual 'fluidity'. Indeed, the criss-crossed loyalties and desires complicate the friends' relationships to such an extent that, in the end, their social ties fade and, it is implied, disintegrate after Ming's death. The doubling of the book's characters allows for what Wills describes as "an intense and immediate intimacy" but also, she states, "for betrayal and substitution, for theft and destruction" (5). The ambiguity of the characters and their doubles matches the destabilising impetus of the novel. Networks of associations and contradictions within the text confuse and expose allocations of identity, making their contingencies as apparent as their restrictions.

Leaving behind more straightforward and traditional immigrant narratives of juxtaposing homeland and new society, works like those of Lai and her contemporary, Hiromi Goto, form fresh renditions of Canadian identities through their use of Canadian social and cultural space. For Lai, the sites are located in the city, whereas Goto's *Chorus of Mushrooms* takes place in a small regional town. With its female empowerment and "conscious corruption" (Lai, "Corrupted" 6) of traditional tales, Lai's deployment of Chinese stories matches Goto's appropriation of Japanese creation and other folktales in *Chorus* and *Kappa Child*. In these instances, the main characters appear in contemporary times while the flashbacks, historical and mythical, present re-created versions of the classics using feminist perspectives. This process of rewriting history and legend does more than just set the record straight, because both Goto and Lai use contemporary settings for the majority of their novels. Siting the narratives in modern-day Canada, they imbue the versions of the past with reflected significance for society and individuals in contemporary Canada. The characters in Lai's novel evolve through bodily change and manipulation, what Wills asserts is "a tremendously heady sense of denying fixed boundaries: the body can be elusive, and illusive, can move freely between and within disguises, can wilfully assume plural roles, can invoke masquerade as a way of investigating the possibilities of alternative subjectivities" (3). As argued previously, however, this boundary-crossing for the human characters that have a stake in the outcomes of the relationships is neither simplistic nor unfettered. Muriel/ Murasaki reclaims the 'Japanese' part of her lineage in Goto's *Chorus* whereas Artemis and her friends affirm, among other things, the ambivalent 'Canadianness' of their Chinese identities. In reworking and eroding these often essentialist labels, Lai and Goto map more complex literary versions of Asian-Canadianness and femininity. Through the intricate and playful knowingness of their work, they hail Asian-Canadians as audiences for their work in ways, which, perhaps, Asian-Australian writers working from within a nation with only a 'nascent' engagement with racial minority literature cannot.

Conclusion

Through their manipulation of expected stories, *Fox* and *Love and Vertigo* extend and tease out the possibilities of literary representations for Asian women's identities and experiences. In addition to textual levels of intervention, the authors under examination are active and vocal about identity issues, race politics, and the burden of stereotypes for racial minority artists. Lai and Teo are, presumably, influenced also by their critical research backgrounds and their stated awareness of class issues when it comes to representation and community. With Lai's *Fox*, Press Gang's alternative agenda for publication serves well the aim of allowing Asian-Canadian women to write for *each other* as well as for the general public.

This capacity to include Asian women's communities as readers of texts denotes a shift away from works that only serve to sensationalise or confess, towards narratives in which Asian women can constitute themselves as involved, authoritative subjects. Teo's novel, published by Allen and Unwin as a consequence of winning the *Australian/*Vogel literary prize, confronts the assumption that many readers will label (and dismiss) it as yet another 'migrant tale'. Teo parries this simplistic categorisation by insisting on the universality of the themes about which she writes (Lamont 3). Transforming existing forms of exclusion and racism in the literary cultures of Canada and Australia requires diversification and dissemination of diasporic Asian texts. Well aware of the predilection of major publishing houses and sectors of the general reading public for exotic, sensational tales, Lai argues that:

> unless a wide range of work from marginalized communities, including those narratives that don't easily fit within a dominant sense of history and/or national identity, is widely promoted and read, the equation of our bodies and our very being solely with histories of violence and exclusion ensures our continued marginalization within mainstream culture, sanctioned by the voices of 'our own', unwittingly co-opted by the editorial power of capital ("Corrupted" 2).

Given the current climate of incorporation and narrowing of publishers' author lists in both Canada and Australia, opportunities for publication for different narratives from Asian women and new authors in general may be scarce. That said, however, I would suggest that there is an emerging trend for hyphenated Asian texts to 'travel', precisely because of heightened interest in diasporic communities in other countries. Particularly for Asian women's texts, this opportunity is double-edged — what is it that the texts are thought to represent and what level of decontextualisation occurs when, say, an Asian-Canadian text turns up in a Taiwanese or Singaporean bookstore? Many Asian women's novels become defined by their historical nature, participating as many of them do in reclaiming space in communities and national memories. Lisa Lowe emphasises, however, that these "[f]orms of individual and collective narratives are not merely representations disconnected from 'real' political life; nor are these expressions 'transparent' records of histories of struggle. Rather these forms . . . are crucial media that connect subjects to social relations" (156). As Lowe and others have noted,[6] it is not enough to have books published. The modes of marketing, consumption, and pedagogy of the text are crucial to understanding the ways in which the 'mantra' of race, class, and gender develop.

The novels by Teo and Lai examined in this chapter are examples of alternative, resistant narratives that operate strongly on irony and (often dark) humour. Mixing up Wong's terms, I would argue that writings and critiques such as these are a 'necessary extravagance' in establishing alternative reading strategies and a broader vision of what constitutes diasporic Asian women's literature in Australia and Canada. Further, their cultural currency in contexts other than that in which they are written signals a shift in audience and text mobility. Although this holds true for most diasporic Asian texts, particularly those originating in Western nations, the ways in which these women's narratives are qualified and become transnational cultural commodities bears monitoring.

Conclusion

These are the gates and you can either kick them open or walk through in silence. Same dif.

(Fred Wah, *Diamond Grill* 164)

It is crucial at this point in the growth of diasporic Asian literatures and their criticism to emphasise the Australian and Canadian contexts in which particular works operate. This act of demarcation is a deliberate resistance to the threats posed by the continual development and dominance of Asian-American studies, as well as the danger of buying into myths of 'diasporic community'. While it is undeniable that Asian-American studies and its objectives affect the study of diasporic Asian writing elsewhere, it is equally important to maintain caution about homogenising international contexts. Fears of engulfment or generalisation have been realised with the inclusion of Asian-Canadians as 'American' authors, and the broad categorisation and marketing of many Asian women's texts without particular siting of the works or their authors. This book has argued for complex consideration of the politics and permissions in self-representations of Asian subjectivities in Australia and Canada, particularly addressing facets of nation, community, and the gendered self. In doing so, *Banana Bending* delineates the multiple and layered effects of these factors on individuals, groups, and how they negotiate their creative and socio-political living spaces.

The analysis of the Australian national context emphasises the points at which the government has neglected to activate anti–racist strategies to accompany the nation's multicultural realities. Australia's historical trajectory is not encouraging for changes in societal practices, as it consistently fails to recognise *and address* the roots of inequity. Examples of this include the deferred efforts for reconciliation with the Aboriginal communities of Australia, as well as the neglected, mostly unknown, historical incidents of Japanese-Australian internment, head tax, and other regulations enacted on Chinese peoples in Australia. Considering the political state of post-Hansonite, John Howard-led Australia — one in which race and politics have become more than ever inextricably tied — the awareness of racialisation and exclusionary processes would seem to promise a more active engagement with these issues. A result of the fraught period of One Nation's rise is the politicisation of Asian communities in Australia. The formation of the Unity Party is just one example of Asian-Australians choosing the political track to vocalise to the government their concerns about Australian society and its policies. Even without the agitation provided by the One Nation Party, this type of civic participation and cultural confrontation can only accelerate once it has been established. This momentum depends on continued growth in Asian-Australian community activism and participation in the public spheres of government policy and the arts. Their confidence in challenging existing structures of discrimination or exclusion signifies the ability to conceive of themselves and their communities as very much a part of Australia and, therefore, with the same levels of citizenship and civic rights. Contrary to some attempts to portray ethnic constituents as 'innocent pawns' for major party recruitment, Gianni Zappala argues that 'ethnic' constituents/groups are quite specific, and strategic, about why they are interested in joining a party or election campaign (70–2). In realising the need for assertive establishment of their citizenship and active repudiation and recreation of representations, many Asian-Australians have undertaken roles in arenas of politics, community management, literature, and other artistic fields.

The building of intercommunity coalitions is important for lobbying impetus as well as creating different (Asian-)Australian spaces. Moreover, the inability or reluctance to work with other racial minority groups for common political causes reinforces the stereotype of anti-racist politics being self-serving or 'ghettoised'. Enduring issues include the politics of 'divide and conquer' endemic to identity politics, maintenance of gender divisions, manifestations of homophobia in ethnic communities, and effects of internalised racism on individuals and communities. Forging more links with other racial minority groups drives future prospects for social change to combat precisely these forms of division and racialisation. Ella Shohat and

Robert Stam claim this cohesion is "what neoconservatives . . . find threatening about the more radical forms of multiculturalism", that is "the intellectual and political regrouping by which different 'minorities' become a majority seeking to move beyond being 'tolerated' to forming active intercommunal coalitions" (299–300). In Australia, the next step for Asian communities after establishing a profile and their politicisation involves broadening the focus of anti-racist work to dismantle discrimination and exclusion for all people of colour, not just their own groups. Lack of certainty and confidence in voicing their own grievances maintains the difficult relationship between ethnic communities and Aboriginal peoples.

Although the Asian communities in Australia have yet to make significant overtures to Aboriginal groups in forming coalitions against racism in Australia and in Australian social structures, this neglect is not a one-way street. Addressing this point, Sneja Gunew argues that:

> [t]here have been certain kinds of alliances between the old colonizers and Aboriginal peoples, and that has now come out in rather dreadful ways in relation to the continuing battles around what is termed Asian immigration. You have spokespeople from the Aboriginal communities who are combining with the right wing in denouncing Asian immigration. Partly that is because of those earlier histories — there are alliances amongst the oppressed and the oppressor that unite against the new groups, particularly Asians from South-East Asia ("Postcolonialism/Multiculturalism" 212).

She adds that the concerns that Aboriginal activists have expressed are "understandable and substantiated fears that discussion of multiculturalism can distract attention from the issue of land rights" ("Multicultural Multiplicities" 455). For a movement of Asian-Australian activism and critical politics to advance constructively, and for Australian institutions to engage constructively with issues of racialisation, one of the most pressing projects is the formation of coalition affiliations between Asian-Australian groups and other racial minority communities in Australia as well as similar groups in other countries. Until racial judgements and resulting inequities are exposed, interrogated, and perhaps even solved, Asian-Australian studies, and multicultural work in general, risks remaining more reactive than original. This is not to say that work currently in circulation is not challenging, but I would emphasise the importance of leading the agenda and not only being subject to it.

In contrast, Canada as a nation has a longer history of, and seemingly more effective processes for, engaging with racial minority concerns. One of the most significant is the recognition and redress of the wartime injustice meted out to Japanese-Canadian citizens, and the official government apologies to Native Canadian groups. The significance of official Redress in 1988 accompanied the validation of racial-minority citizens as Canadians and, as such, able to claim for injustice and to demand equal opportunity. Being able to constitute themselves as 'Canadian' in the eyes of the law fuels the ability to conceive of their own communities and their activities as part of nation-building and, in turn, nation-splitting. An essential part of empowering communities and individuals of Asian descent is the discovery and exploitation of avenues of challenge for status quo representations and processes.

Although the Canadian government has acknowledged some past wrongs, the task of eroding or dismantling the racist and exclusionary structures of society remains ongoing. Black Canadian writer and activist Dionne Brand observes that "[n]otions of access, representation, inclusion, exclusion, equity, etc., are all ways of saying 'race' in this country. . . So it's made comfortable to talk covertly about race in this country without saying that we live in a deeply racialized and racist culture which represses the life possibilities of people of colour" (in Monika Gagnon, "Building" 116). Groups of Asian-Canadian literary and political activists who are agitating precisely to expose the racialised culture of Canada have taken up Brand's point. The mobilisation of anti-racist organisations, especially in focusing on racism in the creative arts, testifies to the impetus for changes in existing representations of Canadian culture. Gunew contends that, in contrast to Australia, "in Canada there appear to have been more frequent alliances among indigenous and ethnic groups, which have been united especially by the fact that both are targets of racism by virtue of their status as 'visible minorities'" ("Multicultural Multiplicities" 455). Lucy R. Lippard adds that:

> tentative coalitions forged between the various so-called minority cultural communities are not only providing a respite from the confrontational aspect of white/other relationships, but are providing tremendous emotional support and a broader, kinder buffer zone within which to ally and act (in Wah, "Half-Bred" 2).

As others have argued, changes to systems of power and representation, dismantling and exposés of the "sanctioning filter[s]" (Gagnon, *Other Conundrums* 24) of government funding, are ongoing processes that require vigilance. The coalitions between racial minority artists and indigenous Canadians, such as the now defunct artist-run group Minquon Panchayat, signal a step away from the destructive politics of infighting. Maryka Omatsu attributes the initiatives between Asian-Canadians and Native Canadians to a deliberate solidarity in the face of common discriminations. She describes the formation of the Japanese Canadian–Native Task Force, however, as motivated by impulses beyond contingent politics: "Japanese Canadians feel bonds of kinship with the people of the First Nations, perhaps because at base we come from the same racial stock and there's a sense that together we've shared a history of discrimination in North America" (175). The vastly different histories of Native Canadians and Asian-Canadians, I would argue, invalidate this kind of comparison. The reason is that the particular colonial oppressions and legacies of Canada's indigenous groups are situations for which Asian-Canadians can express sympathy and some forms of solidarity but cannot claim to share. In saying this, I am not advocating a hierarchy of victimage; rather, I want to iterate the strategic quality of coalitions and their potential for contingent but powerful effects.

Even with the level of attention Asian-Canadian authors have had in the past few years, making inroads into Canadian literary discussions, being in the early stages of the discipline means that there is still much in process. The aims of *Asianadian*, a now defunct journal founded in the 1970s and run by an activist group of Asian-Canadians were:

1. To find new dignity and pride in being Asian in Canada.
2. To promote an understanding between Asian Canadians and other Canadians.
3. To speak out against those conditions, individuals, and institutions perpetuating racism in Canada.
4. To stand up against distortions of our history in Canada, stereotypes, economic exploitations, and the general tendency towards injustice and inequality practised on minority groups.
5. To provide a forum for Asian Canadian writers, artists, musicians, etc.
6. To promote unity by bridging the gap between Asians with roots in Canada and recent immigrants. (Journal Cover)

All of these aims are still valid, and the fact that none has been made obsolete indicates the slowness of real changes in social relations between dominant Anglo-Europeans and increasingly proactive racial minority communities.

For Asian-Canadian activists and scholars, the influence of Asian-American studies remains strong. Its proximity means that Asian-Canadian studies continually treads a fine line between critical inspiration and following theoretical trends. The recent crises in Asian-American studies offers a few lessons for disciplines which are only just establishing themselves and emphasising their independence from the umbrella categories of multicultural and Canadian (or Australian). Various State Governors' conservative pushes for 'equality' in educational institutions, particularly in California, had seen the abolition of affirmative-action quotas at some universities. This led to a reduction in the enrolment numbers of African-American and Hispanic-American students, but an increase for Asian-Americans (Kenneth Lee 1). Affirmative action appeared after the fight against the inequalities of judging *only* on merit-based entry exams had already taken place. Two-thirds of Asian-Americans support the arguments against quotas in California — Kenneth Lee asserts that "Asians say they have more in common with whites than with blacks or Latinos" (1). Lee's statement corresponds with Palumbo-Liu's contention that Asian-Americans are the "frontline forces of the white bourgeoisie" ("Los Angeles" 371). These perspectives indicate the inadequacy of self-serving anti-racism; that is, maintaining enthusiasm for the measures only when there is a direct gain for one's own community.

For the survival of ethnic studies in American universities, long-time activist and Asian-American academic Ling-Chi Wang proposed the idea of merging with the smaller but extremely broad-ranging stream of American studies. American studies has met this proposal with little enthusiasm, fearing that their areas of study will be overtaken by the ethnic studies areas. Ironically, the potential abolition of ethnic-identified schools of study meant that taking this drastic step into American studies might have been their only chance to survive. Although Australia and Canada have not implemented the same measures of affirmative action as the United States, the dynamics of the situation are equally applicable. To gain recognition and validation for, say, Asian-Australians is only ever a partial and deceptive gesture if equal autonomy and efficacy is not afforded Aboriginal or Torres Strait Islander Australians. The processes of racism are the same; they may only differ in the intensity of their application.

Writing Asian-Australian and Asian-Canadian narratives into the historical and creative spaces of each nation broadens definitions of who belongs in those societies. These groups need to see themselves as part of the national, as contributors and transformers, creators and deconstructors. Many Asian-Canadians and Asian-Australians echo 'Model Minority' traits in their attempts to assimilate and not call attention to themselves or their communities. As the discussion of Kogawa's and Sakamoto's texts confirm,

Japanese-Canadians felt themselves somehow to blame for their predicament in the Second World War internment camps. The Redress movement proved that the government of the time acted unjustly and in abrogation of their citizenship rights, apportioning blame away from the communities themselves. Japanese-Australians who were interned in the same period, however, have yet to publicise or discuss their cases. Yuriko Nagata indicated that, during her research for *Unwanted Aliens*, some interviewees refused to talk about the war years, because they were ashamed of what had happened to their communities ("Chrysanthemum"). Until these groups in Australia have the confidence to deliberate openly about these issues, they remain trapped in self-effacement and without the full quota of their civic entitlements. The dissemination of Asian community participation in Australia's and Canada's defining national moments — such as fighting in the wars, rebuilding after national floods, and pioneering the growth of small towns — recreate figurations of who 'rightly' belongs and instil a grounded sense of how these communities have developed. Whether they are oral history-/documentary-style publications such as those by Diana Giese, or the hybrid biotext and photobiographic forms of Fred Wah and William Yang, they succeed in 'colouring' in national narratives and literatures and, therefore, composing Asian groups as whole citizens within Canada and Australia.

Asian-Canadian and Asian-Australian authors rework representations and modulations of what 'community' can mean, for all its contradictory facets of restriction, encouragement, judgement, and nurturing. Asian communities are taking more control over the representation of their group identities, creative possibilities, and achieving social change at legislative levels through various group coalitions and conditional affiliations. The ethnicity tag, and the contemporary racialised overtones which accompany it, can be refitted and employed for reasons other than 'ghettoisation'. A like-minded writing community, such as the Asian-Canadian Writers' Workshop (ACWW), facilitates the work and publication of a growing group of Asian-Canadian authors. The political lobbying and knowledge power derived from such arrangements enables the staging of a wider range of artistic and literary events, more streamlined funding applications, and a higher chance of success in these projects. Moreover, when discussing the increase in Asian-Canadian publications, Hiromi Goto states: "I would specify that there is a recent growth not in Asian-Canadian creativity, but in the distribution of Asian-Canadian works" (Interview 3). Her attribution of successes to increased attention, and not increasing numbers of writers or amount of writing, supports the argument that the contemporary coalitions and cannier negotiations with Canadian literary funding bodies by Asian-Canadians gains results.

The situation in Australia, however, is not as conducive to racial minority coalitions. The rapid rise and fall of Pauline Hanson's One Nation Party and its racist election rhetoric boosted the politicisation of Asian-Australians. Leigh Dale argues that "[c]rucial to [One Nation's] rhetoric is the appropriation by various speakers of majority status, usually termed 'the mainstream', a trope that derives particular force and legitimacy when it is framed in terms of the national and specifically of protecting the national interest" ("Mainstreaming" 9). Dale's contention about the trope of the mainstream gaining importance when framed nationally fixes precisely on the reason why this book locates Asian-Australians in Australian history while also insisting on community activism and the forming of coalitions to induce specific changes. Although Asian-Australians have been involved previously in politics and various public roles, the momentum for lobbying government or other institutions has not yet been apparent.

The range of publications in this book demonstrates the possibilities and progressive initiatives of alternative or smaller presses, as well as the willingness of some larger publishers to support Asian-Canadian literature that engages with challenging issues for Canadian society (an example of the latter being Sakamoto's first novel). These instances of wider and more steady dissemination of Asian-Canadian literature mesh with community-oriented projects, festivals, and writing groups. The outcome is an Asian-Canadian literary scene that sustains itself through public profile and 'grass-roots' support of authors, established and new. Another aspect on which Canada and Australia differ quite significantly is the way in which the potential reading audience for Asian-Australian texts is, at the moment, quite narrowly defined as a majority 'white' one, whereas Asian-Canadian work can justify the effort of launching novels at specific Asian community functions or festivals. The readings of Simone Lazaroo and Hiromi Goto manifest the complicated positionings and possible strategies within the constraints of different community discriminations and exclusions. Both novels interrogate any clear-cut definitions of community and ethnicity while still presenting narratives with culturally specific myths, in-jokes, and anxieties. These discussions advance beyond merely rejecting ascriptions of ethnicity (though this is a significant aspect) to connecting new renditions of Asian families, individuals, and their connections in society. Similarly, as the chapters on gender demonstrate, alternate visions of Asian-Australian and Asian-

Canadian masculinities and new directions for diasporic Asian women's literature require a multi-pronged approach which includes further historical establishment and 'writing-in' narratives alongside rhetorically adventurous and more textually playful literatures. Richard Fung emphasises the point that "[w]hatever formal strategies [Asian artists] choose, we need to situate and question ourselves as *subjects*. Not how we are seen but how *we* see. We must center our work on our own problems, desires and foibles" ("Multiculturalism" 19). The ability to frame themselves in society gives Asian-Australian and Asian-Canadian writers the power to create fresh depictions of themselves as subjects *and*, I would add, as readers. This latter point is important to ensure that narratives can be read in frames other than those of reactiveness or the expectation to inform or educate. An example of this is Gordon Brent Ingram's declaration that Paul Wong's video, *Blending Milk and Water*, is "the stuff of new Canadian mythology" (18). Ingram warns against classifying it *only* as a gay or AIDS film, while also emphasising its radical view on the sexual displacement of gay Asians in Canada.

For Asian-Australian gay and lesbian studies, the momentum is only just beginning. The ability for gay and lesbian texts to cross cultural and national borders to site examinations within 'queer' frames may dilute the particularities of Asian-Canadian or Asian-Australian queer studies. As I have argued consistently, however, coalitions are as necessary as specification and context.

After making themselves visible, literally and politically, on various levels of representation, Asian writers in Australia and Canada must persist in interrogating the continual casting of racial minority citizens as 'out of the ordinary'. Many authors engage in this project by locating Asians in national histories and other hegemonic narratives. In this context, Australian cultural studies scholar Ghassan Hage playfully recasts the question of whether multiculturalism is 'good for the nation' by asking whether Whites are still good for Australia and whether they need help escaping their ghettoes for the "multicultural mainstream" (*White Nation* 247). Hage's satire urges the development of the ability to think of Other communities and individuals as part of the decision-making and society-building structures of Australia and Canada. Until Asian-Australian and Asian-Canadian literatures can be read not only for their cultural specificities but also for their ability to more broadly represent 'Australianness' and 'Canadianness', they remain within the confines of 'old-style' multicultural literature.

The core issues of defining Asian-Australians or Asian-Canadians and what 'Asianness' in these contexts might mean in literary and other representations must be coupled with interrogations of citizenship and belonging in formations of national literatures. It is this overarching, yet closely engaged, perspective that progresses these areas of study beyond merely binaristic or oppositional models. The difference in size of Asian populations creates very specific differences in political and creative momentum for artists of Asian descent in Canada and Australia. While these factors will still dictate community ability to build momentum and initiate larger changes, the interrelationship of Asian-Australian, Asian-Canadian, and Asian-American studies provides powerful encouragement to sustain and improve levels of literary and political representation. A proliferation of Lisa Lowe's 'alternative social practices' is not an instance of supplementing or degrading the existing national literatures but of rebuilding definitions of what national literatures are for. Especially in Australia, authors of Asian descent (with the exception of Brian Castro) are hardly established and, as yet, without a literary history directly addressing their work.

For both Asian-Canadian and Asian-Australian bodies of literature, this book initiates part of this specific and disregarded history. In doing so, I hope "it expands our field of vision without being expansionist; it includes without consuming; it appreciates without appropriating; and it seeks to temper politics with ethics" (Mae G. Henderson 26). In many ways, this study is a starting point, one that establishes a basis from which to discuss these new disciplines, their attendant histories, and their complex interactions with existing versions of reading and representation. The processes of writing, publishing, and reading literature are imbued with a certain set of power relations that are central to changing the status quo. Avtar Brah concludes *Cartographies of Diaspora* by emphasising the importance of asking about:

> what patterns of equity or inequality are inscribed; what modes of domination or subordination are facilitated; what forms of pleasure are produced; what fantasies, desires, ambivalence and contradictions are sanctioned . . . what types of political subject positions are generated by the operations of given configurations of power (248).

Researchers in Asian-Canadian and Asian-Australian literary studies need to confront these issues and consider how the politics of production mesh with reading and/or funding strategies for creative artists. A larger project, heralded by this book, is the examination of diasporic Asian literary studies, whether such a creature exists, and the implications of such a 'globalised' field of inquiry.[1]

Increasingly, the study of diasporic and other racial minority literatures is less about straightforward reclaiming a voice or asserting identity and more to do with charting the constantly shifting processes of 'identity politics'. Smaro Kamboureli advises critics and artists to view "comfortable positions with suspicion" and posits the goal as being "mastery of discomfort, a mastery that would involve shuttling between centre and margin while displacing both" (*Scandalous* 130). Although population plays a significant part in the momentum and profile of critical and artistic activities, essential aspects of nurturing a dynamic community culture include drawing on strategic coalitions, establishing mentor structures, and the ability to exercise full cultural citizenship through confrontation, re-creation, and validation. Asian-Australian and Asian-Canadian literary studies have moved on from questioning their own presence to become forceful areas that pose broad, incisive questions about national cultures, conditional 'solidarity', and the transformative possibilities of individual creativity.

Notes

Introduction

1   'Banana bender' is a colloquial term for someone from Queensland, Australia, where I am based.

2   See the "Banana Blog" ('blog' is slang for 'web-log', a form of online diary) at http://drivel.ca/banana/index.html.

3   Stratton and Ang continue with these details, emphasising some of the mechanics at work in official multiculturalism:

> [I]n the US, the politicisation of multiculturalism has been largely from the bottom up, its stances advanced by minority groups (African Americans, Hispanic Americans, Native Americans, Asian-Americans and so on) who regard themselves as excluded from the American mainstream (and for whom the multicultural idea, *pace* Schlesinger, acts as an affirmation of that exclusion), while in Australia multiculturalism is a centre piece of official government policy, that is, a top-bottom political strategy implemented by those in power precisely to improve the inclusion of ethnic minorities within national Australian culture (126–7).

4   See Katharyne Mitchell, "Fast Capital, Modernity, 'Race', and the Monster House."

5   Significant new publications bringing together the important work of Asian-Canadian cultural theorists include Monika Kin Gagnon's *Other Conundrums: Race, Culture, and Canadian Art* (2000) and Richard Fung's *Like Mangoes in July: The Works of Richard Fung* (2002). The appearance of these books indicates, to some degree, the interest and currency of these topics.

6   Opponents of Asian immigration and some right-wing politicians always emphasise the overwhelming and villainous presence of Asian-Australians. This tactic often involves inflating the population of Asians in Australia (approximately 7 per cent of the overall Australian population in 1998) to magnify the threat.

7   See the special issue of *Overland*, "New World Borders".

8   See the dissertations of Alan Lawson (1987) and Margery Fee (1981), both of which establish the history of 'Canadian literary studies' as a discipline.

Chapter 1

1   Some of the most significant developments in recent years are the ramifications of the Mabo ruling, a judgment that conceded for the first time that Aboriginal Australians were the original owners of the land. For more information see Michael Bachelard's *The Great Land Grab* (1997) and Peter Butt, Robert Eagleson, and Patricia Lane's *Mabo, Wik, and Native Title* (2001).

2   See special issue of *Overland* (164 [2001]) and Peter Mares' *Borderlines: Australia's Treatment of Refugees and Asylum Seekers* (2001).

3   Suvendrini Perera and Joseph Pugliese argue, still, that the situation has not altered that much: "[t]he current re-racialisation of Australian identity targets in particular indigenous groups who must be re-situated, structurally, at the bottom of the ethnic scale. That is, it targets those racialised groups least conducive, corporeally and culturally, to the process of assimilation, and therefore least likely to be re-cycled into Anglo-Australians" ("Racial" 2).

4   See Ellie Vasta and Stephen Castle's *The Teeth Are Smiling: The Persistence of Racism in Multicultural Australia* (1996), which engages principally with issues of racialisation in the Australian context. Also, see the John Docker and Gerhard Fischer collection of essays, *Race, Colour, and Identity in Australia and New Zealand* (2000).

5   Texts about Japanese-Australians in general are scarce, and the publication of Keiko Tamura's *Michi's Memories: The Story of a Japanese War Bride* (2001) is significant because of this dearth.

6   These include Gerhard Fischer's *Enemy Aliens: Internment and the Homefront Experience in Australia 1914–1920* (1989) about German-Australians in the First World War, Barbara Winter's *Stalag Australia: German Prisoners of War in Australia* (1986), and Bill Bunbury's *Rabbits and Spaghetti: Captives and Comrades, Australians, Italians and the War 1939–1945* (1995) detailing the experiences of Italo-Australians during the Second World War. There are several books about the 'Cowra breakout', but these works speak more of the fear of 'contamination' from within than of the political and social conditions for Japanese-Australians.

7   In February 1999, a visit and seminar by Japanese-Canadian academic and Redress activist Roy Miki forged new links between Canadian and Australian Japanese communities. The smaller Australian communities lack the momentum necessary for instigating legal protests so, Nagata hoped, the seminars would attract interest and bring these issues to general public and academic attention.

8   Part of the Japanese-Canadian redress funds went towards anti-racist imperatives

and the creation of the Canadian Race Relations Foundation, an institution that has not been without controversy over the ways in which money has been spent.

9   At the national Federation of Ethnic Community Councils Association (FECCA) conference in November 1998, the prime minister's intentions to privatise translation and language services were greeted with criticism and derision. Members of the community councils viewed it as yet another indication of the Howard government's failure to support the needs of different communities in Australia.

10 The amorphous asset of being a true Australian is a card played by former Senator Bill O'Chee when he accuses One Nation's Heather Hill of being 'not Australian enough' for a Senate seat. O'Chee, an Australian of Chinese descent, is a figure who is caught between pacifying the conservative rural segments of the National Party and directly confronting One Nation about racist policies and xenophobic comments.

11 Kalantzis and Cope end, however, on a note of economic rationalism which sits uncomfortably in a piece that hoped to widen conceptualisations of culture and art: "[a]s we form increasingly significant trading and cultural relationships in the [Asia], these will have to be packaged in the openness of multiculturalism. . . . we might then be able to sell this multiculturalism to Asian countries as a *cultural technology*" (33, emphasis added).

12 Consider the statement by one of the Asian Diaspora Day (23 August 1997, University of Queensland) participants who tried to rally a Japanese workmate to take part in anti-racist protests. The Japanese friend replied that the Japanese did not consider themselves 'Asian' and therefore were not the target of Hanson's rhetoric.

13 Politicians who spoke at the FECCA conference include: Prime Minister John Howard, then Opposition Leader Kim Beazley, the Premier of Queensland Peter Beattie, the Federal Immigration Minister Phillip Ruddock, and the Democrats' Immigration spokesperson (and new party leader from 2002) Andrew Bartlett.

14 See *Ethnicity, Class and Gender in Australia* (Bottomley and de Lepervanche), *Intersexions: Gender/Class/Culture/Ethnicity* (Bottomley, de Lepervanche, and Martin), *Mistaken Identity: Multiculturalism and the Demise of Nationalism in Australia* (Castles et al).

15 These authors are: Yasmine Gooneratne, Ninh Nguyen, Ding Xiaoqi, Subhash Jaireth, Le Hang, Ouyang Yu, and Leslie C. Zhao. All of their work for *Influence* is new.

16 For books on the Demidenko/Darville events, see Reimer, as well as Jost, Totaro, and Tyshing.

17 Allen and Unwin, who publish Vogel award-winning manuscripts, now check their authors' bona fides and require the writers to sign a statutory declaration.

See also Kateryna Olijnyk Longley's article on these issues, "Fabricating Otherness."

18   This exposing of 'inauthentic' Aboriginality extends to authors such as Wanda Koolmatrie, Bobbi Sykes, and Sally Morgan.

19   Recent publications in the area of Asian-Australian literary and cultural studies include Shen Yuanfang's *Dragonseed in the Antipodes: Chinese-Australian Autobiographies* (2001), Ien Ang et al.'s *Alter/Asians: Asian-Australian Identities in Art, Media and Popular Culture* (2000), and Helen Gilbert, Tseen Khoo, and Jacqueline Lo's *Diaspora: Negotiating Asian-Australia* (2000).

20   A number of historical and oral history works examine the engagement with Asian communities and their movements in Australia's history, engaging with the process of rewriting 'Australia' through history. These include the popular historical work of Eric Rolls' *Sojourners* (1993) and *Citizens* (1996), and David Walker's *Anxious Nation* (1999). Several sociological and demographic studies detail community concentrations and/or other types of statistical data. This includes publications such as James Coughlan and Deborah McNamara's *Asians in Australia: Patterns of Migration and Settlement* (1997). Still others have focused on particular ethnic/cultural groups such as Mandy Thomas' *Dreams in the Shadows: Vietnamese-Australian Lives in Transition* (1999), and Nancy Viviani's *The Indochinese in Australia, 1975–1995: Burnt Boats to Barbecues* (1996).

21   See Neil Gotanda's article, "Multiculturalism and Racial Stratification", about the contrasting representational spaces occupied by Korean-American and African-American communities.

22   'Model Minority' is often used to describe Asian communities in Western nations because of the stereotype of their non-confrontational attitudes and quiet success in business. It also becomes a restrictive ascription when applied by the communities to themselves. See Henry Yu's *Thinking Orientals: Migration, Contact, and Exoticism in Modern America* (2001) and Robert G. Lee's *Orientals: Asian Americans in Popular Culture* (1999).

Chapter 2

1   Reform became the Canadian Alliance party in 2000. Manning was voted out as leader in favour of Stockwell Day. This book locates the Canadian Reform party as complementary to the Australian One Nation party, marking a concurrent resurgence of conservative politics in both nations in the mid-late 1990s. References to this party, then, are to Reform and Preston Manning rather than its current incarnation of Canadian Alliance (and Stephen Harper).

2   The motives of the Canadian Club in Hong Kong included trying to change the representation of Asian investment in Vancouver (and Canada in general) from only a negative one, and "they did not want Canada to be tarred with

the same racist image that was being applied to Australia at that time [1988–89]" (Mitchell, "The Hong Kong Immigrant" 306).

3 Ong and Nonini argue that "diasporic populations can introduce new or revive older forms of oppression into a nation-state" (*Ungrounded* 326) but also champion "the need to develop a new utopian imaginary that combines the experiences of displacement, travel, and disorientation, which many Chinese transnationalists have successfully negotiated, with an emergent sense of social justice" (330). As well as her universalisation of what might constitute 'social justice', I would question what it means for Chinese transnationals to "successfully negotiate" displacement and disorientation. The multi-targetted forms of racism encountered in the West must surely also have effects.

4 The commission was headed by Henry Bird and awarded Japanese-Canadians $1.2 million for *material* losses during the internment period. There was no acknowledgement of the abrogation of their human rights or of the continuing effects that this uprooting caused the communities (Kobayashi, "Japanese-Canadian Redress" 3).

5 See the Head Tax Redress movement's webpage http://www.asian.ca/redress/.

6 See Miki "Asiancy", Goellnicht "A Long Labour", and Beauregard "What Is at Stake".

7 See Miki's chapter "Sliding the Scale of Elision" in *Broken Entries*.

8 The success for NeWest Press was Goto's *A Chorus of Mushrooms* (1994), which won the Commonwealth Writers Prize for Best First Book in the Caribbean and Canada Region 1995, was co-winner of the Canada-Japan Book Award 1995, and won the Grant MacEwan College Book 2000–01. Larissa Lai's *When Fox Is a Thousand* (1995), published by Press Gang, was short-listed for the Chapters/Books in Canada First Novel Award.

9 The following publications have special issues focused on Asian-Canadian, diasporic Asian, or 'ethnic' literatures: *Essays on Canadian Writing* (57 [1995] "Writing Ethnicity"; 75 [2002] "Race"), *Canadian Literature* (140 [1994] "East Asian-Canadian Connections"; 163 [1999] "Asian Canadian Writing"), *West Coast Line* (13–4 [1994] "Colour: An Issue"; 30.3 [1996–97] "Transporting the Emporium: Hong Kong Art and Writing through the Ends of Time"), *Prairie Fire* (21.4 [2001] "Race Poetry, Eh?").

Chapter 3

1 See Ouyang Yu's article, "Will Words Not Hurt Them?" for examples of enduring "verbal violence to Chinese in Australian literature" (103).

2 See Walker's *Anxious Nation*, particularly Chapter Seven, "Pacific Visitors".

3 For examples of continuing discourses of disease surrounding 'Asians' in Australia, see Khoo, "Who" 18. A detailed examination of the rhetoric of disease and

infection and the ways in which it was deployed in colonial Australia can be found in Jo Robertson's PhD dissertation, "In a State of Corruption: Dreaded Disease and the Body Politic" (1999).

4   This programme involved 'bringing home' United States servicemen's scattered progeny, conceived during their tours of duty in Vietnam. Their status as citizens of the United States is constantly in question through intricate and often contradictory criteria (having to prove themselves the children of fathers who often did not even give their real names to their sex partners) even though, ostensibly, the policy of welcoming them 'home' is straightforward.

5   See Neilson's article "Threshold Procedures: 'Boat People' in South Florida and Western Australia."

6   See Guy Beauregard, "After *Obasan*: Kogawa Criticism and Its Futures."

7   See Ueki's discussion of the stone bread and its analogies with Biblical manna, emphasising the Christian symbolism in the text and the forms of 'love' eventually discovered in the novel. Sau-ling Wong includes the sections "The Case of the Stone Bread" and "Stone Bread: An Intratextual Reading" (19–29) in the first chapter of her book, *Reading Asian-American Literature*.

8   Mason Harris draws a rather generalised line between responses to internment and generational placement for Japanese-Canadians, attributing various reactions to whether they are *issei, nisei,* or *sansei.* Although this model of criticism remains problematic because of its inherent generalisations, it is usefully used when Harris focuses on recollections and their effects: "[f]or Emily remembering means re-establishing the facts of history; for Naomi, it forces the reliving of a damaged development" (44).

9   The name of the hill is most likely an allusion to Mackenzie King, the prime minister of Canada in the period of Japanese-Canadian internment.

10   See Roy Miki's "Unclassified Subjects: Question Marking 'Japanese Canadian' Identity" in *Broken Entries.*

11   This is Sneja Gunew's term in her article discussing obligation and immigrant 'gratitude', "Against Multiculturalism". She uses the analogy of the 'host/parasite-guest' throughout a whole section, playing on notions of invitation, etiquette, and who has control of the party.

12   The majority male population of these Australian and Canadian Chinatowns was often disillusioned by the lack of opportunity for, and discrimination against, them once they were in these countries. The prices for bringing in family or a bride became so prohibitive that many never married and eked out lonely lives in Chinatown rooming houses, becoming a generation of 'old uncles' to the children of families that prospered after exclusionary laws were lifted.

13   Timothy Tsu, writing about Chinatowns in Kobe, Japan, states:

> The Chinatowns were . . . the victim of a vicious cycle that prevented them from physical and social upgrading. Over the decades, not a few Chinese had become economically successful. Most of them chose to move their homes out into the

suburbs. By moving they were after not just a more salubrious living environment, but also the social status of the suburban Westerners and upper-class Japanese. The wealth generated by the Chinatowns thus made little impact on their physical conditions (3).

14 See the CHAF site at http://www.chaf.lib.latrobe.edu.au/.

15 See Denise Chong's *The Concubine's Children*, Wayson Choy's *Jade Peony* and *Paper Shadows*, Sky Lee's *Disappearing Moon Café*, and Judy Fong Bates's *China Dog* for fictional/autobiographical depictions of Chinatown.

16 *Survival and Celebration* details the lives of Chinese-Australian women from colonial to contemporary Australia. It tells of the intensely discriminatory environment in many Australian towns and cities and, more specifically, it includes white Australian women's lives and the difficulties of living with a Chinese partner in strongly racially divided social spheres.

Also, see *Banquet: Ten Courses to Harmony* (1999) by Annette Shun Wah and Greg Aitken. The book is a popular overview of the evolution and influence of Chinese food and restaurants in Australia. It includes oral histories from restaurant families outlining their experiences and those of their predecessors. Partial recollections of women's roles and positions within these outlets can be gleaned.

17 See Kate Bagnall's doctoral dissertation, "Golden Shadows on a White Land: The Real and Imagined Lives of Chinese Men, White Women and Their Children in Colonial Australia".

18 Referring to the odd circumstance of a government intervening in field workers' sex lives, Evans points out that:

> it is a measure of the racist nature of colonial society that any European prostitute found "cohabiting with Chinese" or ministering to the "carnal lust of niggers" was logically defined as being "of the very lowest class." The Queensland Government was thus prepared to countenance, in towns adjacent to areas where large aggregations of "coloured" male labourers were indentured upon sugar plantations or pearling luggers, the importation of a controlled number of Japanese females to serve as "suitable outlets for their sexual passion" (13).

19 There was also an instance when one of Zhou's line drawings of an Aboriginal group was deemed "caricature", and Zhou argued against this categorisation with its implication of 'making fun' of his subject matter.

20 Consider the current Australian debates around authenticity and validation epitomised by the Leon Carmen/Wanda Koolmatrie hoax, Eddie Burrup, Archie Weller, and the accusations from his own family against Mudrooroo.

21 See Brewster, *Literary Formations* 16–7.

22 In an article which purportedly seeks to interrogate the manner in which One Nation and Pauline Hanson mobilise racial stereotypes and how these might be acceptable in 'Inalan' politics, Mudrooroo deploys numerous unquestioned clichés of his own about Vietnamese communities, and Asians in general ("Perils

of Pauline"). Although he might have been attempting to depose 'popular' myths about the Vietnamese in Inala, what results is a listing of what 'is said', or 'is thought' of Vietnamese-Australians by the equally collapsed category of 'Inalans'.

23 Another case which galvanised black and Asian groups was that of Korean mother and shopkeeper, Soon Ja Du's shooting of a teenage black girl, Latasha Harlins. The case exposed many of the issues involved in "'minority-minority' conflict" (Gotanda 238).

24 Scholars such as Regina Ganter, Peta Stephenson, Guy Ramsay, and Ann McGrath have written on Chinese/Aboriginal issues and relations. A publication from the 2000 colloquium held in Canberra, "Lost in the Whitewash: Aboriginal-Chinese Encounters from Federation to Reconciliation", is forthcoming from the Centre for the Study of the Chinese Southern Diaspora (ANU).

25 Yang's narrative about far North Queensland ranges through Mourilyan, Cairns, Cooktown, Dimbulah, and Innisfail, and includes Brisbane as part of the journey 'north' from his usual base in Sydney.

26 Wah was closely involved in the establishment of TISH, a highly influential literary group founded in 1961 by writers dedicated to "a poetry of spoken idiom written in lines determined by oral rhythms" (Davey 790).

27 In contrast, Neil Bissoondath argues against multiculturalism as being too much about cosseting minorities and emphasising difference to promote intranational divisions. He titles his anti-multiculturalism book, *Selling Illusions*.

28 Similarly, Yang writes of discovering his Chineseness only after a name-calling incident in the playground when he is six (64–5). After retelling the incident to his mother and brother, he is admonished with "[a]nd you'd better get used to it."

29 Yang's other shows include *The Face of Buddha*, *China Diary*, *The North, Blood Links* and most recently *Shadows* in 2002; several versions of these shows, as with *Sadness*, were performed at various major international theatre festivals.

30 Johnston's article on Eric Michaels' autobiography, *Unbecoming: An AIDS Diary*, examines the discourses surrounding HIV/AIDS representation, disease, and national identity. The cover of *Unbecoming* shows Michaels, covered in the distinctive patches of Kaposi's Sarcoma, "tongue fully extended challenging the gaze of the camera" ("Unbecoming" 66).

31 The long-running dislike between the families meant that Yang's mother did not want him to see his Aunty Kath and admonished him not to believe anything she said (31). This recalls, once again, Wah's Acknowledgements in which he feels compelled to include a declaration of his intention not to hurt anyone and to cloak his 'biotext' as "faking it".

32 Several prominent Chinese-Australian members of the Liberal Party broke away after the perceived ineffectiveness of the Coalition in addressing and denouncing the racist rhetoric apparent in One Nation's policies. They formed the Unity Party, a party that has the promotion and maintenance of multicultural ideals at the centre of its policy platform.

Chapter 4

1   See Joan Walsh's e-article, "As American as Ethnic Studies."

2   For example, see the work of Canadians Dionne Brand, Richard Fung, Monika Kin Gagnon, Ashok Mathur, and M. Nourbese Philip for perspectives on racialisation in the creative arts; and for Asian-Australian arts criticism, see Dean Chan, Melissa Chiu, Sneja Gunew, Jacqueline Lo, and Suvendrini Perera.

3   Referring to the partial shift to the postmodern lack of fixity or, in some instances, the ability to explicate a subjective position, Debra P. Amory comments:

> Doesn't it seem funny that at the very point when women and people of color are ready to sit down at the bargaining table with the white boys, that the table disappears? That is, suddenly there are no grounds for claims to truth and knowledge anymore and here we are, standing in the conference room making all sorts of claims to knowledge and truth but suddenly without a table upon which to put our papers and coffee cups, let alone to bang our fists (in Shohat and Stam 345).

4   First-time ethnic authors are often funded by government grants. After one publication, they are in better positions to negotiate contracts with more established presses. In Canada, some presses are awarded government funds to publish multicultural writers or studies. In Australia, this happens to a lesser degree, as the current Howard government is phasing out support for (what they deem superfluous) 'multicultural' projects.

5   'Preston Terre Blanche' refers to a melding of Preston Manning, former leader of the Reform Party in Canada, and Eugene Terre Blanche, a South African right-wing extremist. The Reform Party ran on a platform of conservative rhetoric, harkening to days before politics were supposedly dominated by minority groups. The Seven Deadly Disclaimers which encourage and perpetuate racism are denial, diversion, silence, defensiveness/anger, minimizing, discounting, and tokenising.

6   The One Nation cultural policy, unveiled in the federal election campaign in 1997, basically abolished funding for the arts because the arts were not 'necessary'.

7   The connotations of naming Muriel after the woman who is considered the first novelist ever (she wrote *Genji Monogatari* [Rimer 36–7]) entwines with the activities encouraged by Goto's novel: reading for one's own sense of the world, making the story one's own, and knowing that to have the power of storytelling means that one can have the power to effect change.

8   In many incidents in the book, these stereotypes are applied to Muriel. One of the most incisive instances is Valentine's Day during school when, every year, she received multiple copies of the same card with "the press-out Oriental-type girl in some sort of pseudo-kimono with wooden sandals on backwards" (62).

9   See Ien Ang, "On Not Speaking Chinese", and Allen Chun, "Fuck Chineseness".

10 See Maria Ng's "Chop Suey Writing". Ng seems to take exception to the use of Chinese terms and expressions which may not necessarily be understood by non-Chinese readers (or even certain other groups of Chinese readers) and chooses to interpret these linguistic interventions only as new forms of exoticising Chinese culture (181).

11 His name connotes both a brand of industrial cleaner and a household deodoriser.

12 *Puberty Blues* started as a novel by Gabrielle Carey and Kathy Lette. It went on to become a film by Bruce Beresford in 1981. The novel is about the coming-of-age of two Australian teenage girls in an urban coastal setting. It uses the beach as a site of conflict, desire, and performance.

13 Some of this concern was oblique, in that the narrator fell into shoplifting expeditions for acceptance and to be a 'cool girl', but also because her father cut off her pocket money.

Chapter 5

1   A handful of masculinity-focused publications have appeared recently, including David Eng's *Racial Castration* (2001), the collection by Eng and Alice Hom *Q&A: Queer in Asian America* (1998), and Jachinson Chan's *Chinese American Masculinities* (2001). Chinese-Canadian Song Cho's collection *Rice: Explorations into Gay Asian Culture + Politics* (1998) covers similar social territory to Eng and Hom's *Q&A* but provides much-needed Canadian perspectives to break up the US hegemony in diasporic queer studies.

2   Outside the North American context, there are few books that focus on diasporic masculinities. Exceptions include sections of Kam Louie's *Theorising Chinese Masculinity* (2002), a publication that addresses classical and modern Chinese texts as well as diasporic intertextualities such as the Hollywood Bruce Lee/Jackie Chan/Chow Yun Fat phenomenon. In Australia, the work of filmmaker Tony Ayres and photographer William Yang introduces discussions of representing Chinese-Australian masculinity and desire, specifically from queer perspectives.

3   See Michael Leach regarding the racial antagonism of socialist and union groups in turn-of-the-century Australia, and K. Victor Ujimoto for Canadian perspectives. Ujimoto, in particular, engages with Peter Li and B. Singh Bolaria's argument that "racism is not an outcome of cultural misunderstanding, but rather 'a deliberate ideology designed to justify the unjust treatment of the subordinate group for the purpose of exploiting its labour power'" ("Studies of Ethnic Identities" 224).

4   Ling states that the term 'Model Minority' "distinguished Asian Americans from

blacks, Hispanics, and Native Americans during the political ferment of the 1960s because the latter's back-talking militancy is typically viewed as a sign of male potency" (315).

5   Spivak argues that the process of entry to "civil society is a form of gendered admittance with permission "negotiated on the bodies of women" (9).

6   Chin has published many novels (e.g., *The Chinaman Pacific & Frisco R. R. Co.* and *Gunga Din Highway*) and short stories. He was on the editorial committee for the pioneering *Aiiieeeee!! An Anthology of Asian-American Writers.* Kingston wrote what are arguably the most studied and influential novels in Asian-American literary history, *The Woman Warrior* and its companion work, *China Men.*

7   A chapbook is a small book or pamphlet formerly sold by chapmen (merchants, traders, peddlers or hawkers of an itinerant nature) containing popular tales, treatises, ballads, or nursery rhymes.

8   "Digger" is slang for an Australian soldier.

9   Aside from his own head superimposed on recognisable white bodies to connote a level of incongruity, Leong has also reversed this by merging Princess Diana's head over the body of a "woman in exotic costume" (Cover of Perera 1995).

10   For specific examination of the politics of comedy, see Wagg.

11   ANZAC is the acronym for Australian and New Zealand Army Corps and has become a common term in Australian popular discourse. Most often, usage of 'ANZAC' bundles national pride in bravery against the odds with an element of anti-authoritarianism and assertion of Australian individuality.

12   See Nagata, *Unwanted Aliens.*

13   Teruyo Ueki lists the Morii gang as one of several "disturbing elements" in Kogawa's depiction of the Japanese-Canadian community, stressing that "a close-range view of this small community, of course, reveals that it is not a uniform entity" (6).

14   Kitagawa and Miki collaborated in assembling *Letters to Wes*, a collection of communications between Muriel and Wes during their internment, which emphasised the activist role that Muriel undertook. Omatsu wrote *Bittersweet passage: Redress and the Japanese Canadian experience,* which further documented the conditions and process of redress with historical background about the internment procedures. 'Internment literature' includes many collections of photographs and interviews with internees, as well as *O-Bon in Chimunesu: A community remembered* by Catherine Lang, which focused on the return of some inmates to their old site of incarceration at Lemon Creek.

15   When the *daruma* doll is bought, it does not have its eyes. The owner makes a wish and draws in one of the eyes, and when that wish is fulfilled, the owner must draw in the other eye to complete the face.

16   In the short stories, Watada relates incidents of vindictive bashings of rivals and "price gouging" at local camp grocery stores ('Kangaroo Court'). The latter

habit finally drove the community to oust the "village leader", or *soncho*, Isamu Sasaki.

17   Christopher Lee writes specifically about the third section by Sek-Lung in "Engaging Chineseness in Wayson Choy's *The Jade Peony*". Sek-Lung's narrative encompasses the Chinese-Canadian/Japanese-Canadian tensions in Vancouver during the Second World War.

18   This seems to be a recurring trope when ethnic groups seek to consolidate against 'Western' ideals. Kobena Mercer details the mobilisation of the Haringey Black Pressure group in London against gays in their midst, declaring that "homosexuality is something that has been introduced into our culture by Europeans: it is an unnatural set of acts that tend toward genocide" (45–6).

19   See Andy Quan's books *Slant* (2001) and *Calendar Boy* (2001). Quan's work has featured in several anthologies, many 'North American' and some 'international'.

Chapter 6

1   See Khoo, "Selling Sexotica."

2   Also see the exhibition titled "But Women Did Come: 150 Years of Chinese Women in North America", a project of The Global Gathering Place (a joint initiative of the Multicultural History Society of Ontario and the Centre for Instructional Technology Development at the University of Toronto at Scarborough): http://citd.scar.utoronto.ca/ggp/Exhibits/Chinese_Women/index.html.

3   See Anna King Murdoch's article outlining "the China Syndrome" in which 'Asian-Australian' writers come to mean only mainland Chinese authors who stayed on or emigrated after the Tiananmen Square incident and Southeast Asian immigrants who are forever configured as examples of their 'homeland'.

4   For examples, see reviews by James Hall, Leonie Lamont, and Murray Waldren.

5   The RSL (Returned and Services League of Australia) is an advocacy and assistance group for Australia's war veterans and their dependents. Ruxton retired in 2002, after twenty-three years as RSL President. He is notorious as an outspoken homophobe, xenophobe, and monarchist.

6   See Chandra Talpade Mohanty, "Cartographies of Struggle".

Conclusion

1   See *Culture, Identity, Commodity: Diasporic Chinese Literatures in English* (Ed. Kam Louie and Tseen Khoo), forthcoming.

Bibliography

Altman, Dennis. "(Homo)Sexual Identities, Queer Theory, and Politics." Stokes 105–14.

Anderson, Benedict. *Imagined Communities: Reflections on the Origin and Spread of Nationalism*. London: Verso, 1991.

Anderson, Kay J. "Otherness, Culture and Capital: 'Chinatown's' Transformation Under Australian Multiculturalism." *Multiculturalism, Difference and Postmodernism*. Ed. Gordon L. Clark, Dean Forbes, and Roderick Francis. Melbourne: Longman Cheshire, 1993. 68–89.

Anderson, Kay J. *Vancouver's Chinatown: Racial Discourse in Canada, 1875–1980*. Montreal: McGill-Queen's University Press, 1991.

Andreoni, Helen. "Multicultural Artworkers: Sacrifical Anodes?" *Artlink* 11.1–2 (1991): 8–10.

Ang, Ien. "The Curse of the Smile: Ambivalence and the 'Asian' Woman in Australian Multiculturalism." *Feminist Review* 52 (1996): 36–49.

———. "Migrations of Chineseness." *SPAN* 34–35 (1992–93): 3–15.

———. "On Not Speaking Chinese: Postmodern Ethnicity and the Politics of Diaspora." *New Formations* 24 (1994): 1–18.

———. *On Not Speaking Chinese: Living between Asia and the West*. London and New York: Routledge, 2001.

Ang, Ien, et al. *Alter/Asians: Asian-Australian Identities in Art, Media and Popular Culture*. Sydney: Pluto Press, 2000.

Ang-Lygate, Magdalene. "Everywhere To Go but Home: On (re) (dis) (un) location." *Journal of Gender Studies* 5.3 (1996): 375–88.

Appiah, Kwame Anthony, and Henry Louis Gates. "Editors' Introduction: Multiplying Identities." *Identities*. Ed. Appiah and Gates. Chicago and London: University of Chicago Press, 1995. 1–6.

Araeen, Rasheed. "Cultural Identity: Whose Problem?" *Third Text* 18 (1992): 3–5.

Ayres, Tony. *Short Stories: China Dolls*. ABC, 1997.

————. "Undesirable Aliens." *HQ* March/April 1998: 110–15.

Bachelard, Michael. *The Great Land Grab: What Every Australian Should Know About Wik, Mabo and the Ten-Point Plan.* South Melbourne: Hyland House, 1997.

Bagnall, Kate. "Golden Shadows on a White Land: The Real and Imagined Lives of Chinese Men, White Women and Their Children in Colonial Australia." PhD thesis, University of Sydney, forthcoming.

Baker, Candida. "Maximum Exposure." *The Australian Magazine* 31 January–1 February 1998: 16–23.

Bates, Judy Fong. *China Dog and Other Tales from a Chinese Laundry.* Toronto: Sister Vision, 1997.

Beauregard, Guy. "After *Obasan*: Kogawa Criticism and its Futures." *Studies in Canadian Literature* 26.2 (2001): 5–22.

————. "Hiromi Goto's *Chorus of Mushrooms* and the Politics of Writing Diaspora." *West Coast Line* 29.3 (1995–96): 47–62.

————. "Rattling a Noisy Hyphen: Review of Fred Wah's *Diamond Grill*." *Canadian Literature* 156 (1998): 171–2.

————. "Unsettled, Unsettling: Review of Kerri Sakamoto's *The Electrical Field*." *Canadian Literature* 163 (1999): 191–3.

————. "What Is at Stake in Comparative Analyses of Asian Canadian and Asian American Literary Studies?" *Essays on Canadian Writing* 75 (2002): 217–39.

Bissoondath, Neil. *Selling Illusions: The Cult of Multiculturalism in Canada.* Toronto: Penguin, 1994.

Boehmer, Elleke. *Colonial and Postcolonial Literature.* Oxford and New York: Oxford University Press, 1995.

Bolaria, B. Singh, and Peter Li. "Race and Racism." *Racial Oppression in Canada.* Ed. Bolaria and Li. 2nd ed. Toronto: Garamond, 1988. 13–25.

Boreland, Marian. "Either/Or: Multiculturalism and Biculturalism." *SPAN* 36.1 (1993): 174–81.

Bottomley, Gillian. *From Another Place: Migration and the Politics of Culture.* Cambridge: Cambridge University Press, 1992.

————. "Identification: Ethnicity, Gender and Culture." *Journal of Intercultural Studies* 18.1 (1997): 41–8.

Bottomley, Gillian and Marie de Lepervanche. *Ethnicity, Class and Gender in Australia.* Sydney: Allen and Unwin, 1984.

Bottomley, Gillian, Marie de Lepervanche, and Jeannie Martin, ed. *Intersexions: Gender/Class/Culture/Ethnicity.* Sydney: Allen and Unwin, 1991.

Brah, Avtar. *Cartographies of Diaspora: Contesting Identities.* London and New York: Routledge, 1996.

Brennan, Geoffrey. "The Baby Trade: The Political Economy of Inter-Country Adoption." *Multicultural Citizens: The Philosophy and Politics of Identity.* St Leonards: Centre of Independent Studies, 1993. 159–73.

Brewster, Anne. *Literary Formations: Post-colonialism, Nationalism, Globalism.* Carlton

South: Melbourne University Press, 1995.

Broinowski, Alison. *The Yellow Lady: Australian Impressions of Asia*. 2nd ed. Melbourne: Oxford University Press, 1996.

Brydon, Diana. "Discovering 'Ethnicity': Joy Kogawa's *Obasan* and Mena Abdullah's *Time of the Peacock*." *Australian/Canadian Literatures in English: Comparative Perspectives*. Ed. Russell McDougall and Gillian Whitlock. Melbourne: Methuen, 1987. 94–110.

Bunbury, Bill. *Rabbits and Spaghetti: Captives and Comrades, Australians, Italians, and the War 1939–1945*. Fremantle, WA: Fremantle Arts Centre Press, 1995.

Bulbeck, Chilla. *Re-Orienting Western Feminisms: Women's Diversity in a Postcolonial World*. Cambridge: Cambridge University Press, 1998.

Butt, Peter, Robert Eagleson, Patricia Lane. *Mabo, Wik & Native Title*. 4th ed. Leichhardt, NSW: Federation Press, 2001.

Carey, Gabrielle, and Kathy Lette. *Puberty Blues*. Carlton, VIC: McPhee Gribble, 1979.

Carpenter, Carole. "Folklore as a Tool of Multiculturalism." *Twenty Years of Multiculturalism: Successes and Failures*. Ed. Stella Hryniuk. Winnipeg, MN: St John's College, 1992. 149–60.

Castles, Stephen. "The Racisms of Globalisation." *The Teeth Are Smiling: The Persistence of Racism in Multicultural Australia*. Ed. Ellie Vasta and Stephen Castles. St Leonards: Allen and Unwin, 1996. 17–45.

Castles, Stephen, et al. *Mistaken Identity: Multiculturalism and the Demise of Nationalism in Australia*. 2nd ed. Sydney: Pluto Press, 1990.

Castro, Brian. "Interview with Ramona Koval." *Australian Book Review* May 1997: 8–10.

————. *Pomeroy*. North Sydney: Allen and Unwin, 1990.

————. *Writing Asia and Auto/biography: Two Lectures*. Canberra: School of English, ADFA, 1995.

Chan, Jachinson. *Chinese American Masculinities: From Fu Manchu to Bruce Lee*. New York and London: Routledge, 2001.

Chao, Lien. "Anthologizing the Collective: The Epic Struggles To Establish Chinese Canadian Literature in English." *Essays on Canadian Writing* 57 (1995): 145–70.

————. *Beyond Silence: Chinese Canadian Literature in English*. Toronto: TSAR, 1997.

————. "Constituting Minority Canadian Women and our Sub-Cultures: Female Characters in Selected Chinese Canadian Literature." *The Other Woman: Women of Colour in Contemporary Canadian Literature*. Ed. Makeda Silvera. Toronto: Sister Vision, 1995. 333–54.

Chicago Cultural Studies Group. "Critical Multiculturalism." *Critical Inquiry* 19 (1992): 530–55.

Chin, Frank. *The Chinaman Pacific and Frisco R. R. Co: Short Stories*. Minneapolis, MN: Coffee House Press, 1988.

————. *Gunga Din Highway*. Minneapolis. MN: Coffee House Press, 1994.

————. "West Meets East: A Conversation with Frank Chin by Robert Murray Davis." *Amerasia Journal* 24.1 (1998): 87–103.

Chin, Frank, et al, ed. *Aiiieeeee!: An Anthology of Asian-American Writers.* Washington, DC: Howard University Press, 1974.

Chinatownsydney.com. "The 'Right' Australia." 1999. Webpage. <http://www.chinatownsydney.com/afocus.cfm?id=144>, 18 July 2001.

Chinese Canadian National Council. *Jin Guo: Voices of Chinese Canadian Women.* Toronto, ON: Women's Press, 1992.

Ching, Yau. "Can I Have MSG, an Egg Roll To Suck on and Asian American Media on the Side?" *Fuse* 20.1 (1997): 27–34.

Cho, Lily. "Rereading Chinese Head Tax Racism: Redress, Stereotype, and Anti-Racist Critical Practice." *Essays on Canadian Writing* 75 (2002): 62–84.

————. "Serving Chinese and Canadian Food: Chinese Restaurant Counterculture and the Time of the Menu." Draft Chapter Two, PhD in progress, "*On Eating Chinese: Diaspora Politics and the Chinese Restaurant.*" University of Alberta, Canada.

Cho, Song, ed. *Rice: Explorations into Gay Asian Culture + Politics.* Toronto, ON: Queer Press, 1998.

Chong, Denise. *The Concubine's Children.* Toronto, ON: Penguin, 1995.

Chow, Rey. "The Politics of Admittance: Female Sexual Agency, Miscegenation and the Formation of Community in Frantz Fanon." *UTS Review* 1.1 (1995): 5–29.

————. "Women in the Holocene: Ethnicity, Fantasy, and the Film *The Joy Luck Club.*" *Feminisms and Pedagogies of Everyday Life.* Ed. Carmen Luke. Albany, NY: University of New York Press, 1996. 204–21.

————. *Writing Diaspora: Tactics of Intervention in Contemporary Cultural Studies.* Bloomington, IN: Indiana University Press, 1993.

Choy, Wayson. *The Jade Peony.* Vancouver and Toronto: Douglas and McIntyre, 1995.

————. *Paper Shadows: A Chinatown Childhood.* Toronto, ON: Penguin, 1999.

"A Chrysanthemum by Any Other Name: Ethnicity and Identity of Japanese in Queensland." Informal seminars, University of Queensland, 25 July 1998.

Chu, Wei-Cheng Raymond. "Some Ethnic Gays Are Coming Home; or, the Trouble with Interraciality." *Textual Practice* 11.2 (1997): 219–35.

Chun, Allan. "Fuck Chineseness: On the Ambiguities of Ethnicity as Culture as Identity." *Boundary 2* 23.2 (1996): 111–38.

Clark, Gordon L., Dean Forbes and Roderick Francis, eds. *Multiculturalism, Difference and Postmodernism.* Melbourne: Longman Cheshire, 1993.

Cochrane, Peter. "Voices of the Past in Anglo Primal Scream." *The Australian* 10 October 1996: 11.

Cook, Ramsay. *Canada, Quebec and the Uses of Nationalism.* 2nd ed. Toronto, ON: McClelland and Stewart, 1995.

Cornell, Michiyo. "Living in Asian America: An Asian American Lesbian's Address before the Washington Monument (1979)." Leong, *Asian American Sexualities* 83–4.

Coronil, Fernando. "Can Postcoloniality Be Decolonized? Imperial Banality and Postcolonial Power." *Public Culture* 5 (1992): 89–108.

Coughlan, James E., and Deborah J. McNamara. *Asians in Australia: Patterns of Migration and Settlement.* Melbourne: Macmillan Education, 1997.

Dale, Leigh. "Mainstreaming Australia." *Journal of Australian Studies* 53 (1997): 9–19.

Darville, Helen. *The Hand that Signed the Paper.* 3rd ed. St Leonards, NSW: Allen and Unwin, 1995.

Davey, Frank. "TISH." *Oxford Companion to Canadian Literature.* Ed. William Toye. Toronto and Oxford: Oxford University Press, 1983. 790–1.

Davidson, Arnold. *Writing against the Silence: Joy Kogawa's Obasan.* Toronto, ON: ECW Press, 1993.

Davie, Penelope. "Exceptional First Novel: *Love and Vertigo* by Hsu-Ming Teo." 9 August 2000. Online book review. <http://www.dotlit.qut.edu.au/reviews/vertigo.html>

Davis, Angela Y. "Gender, Class, and Multiculturalism: Rethinking 'Race' Relations." *Mapping Multiculturalism.* Ed. Avery F. Gordon and Christopher Newfield. Minneapolis, MN: University of Minnesota Press, 1996. 40–8.

Davison, Liam. "Three Generations of Pain." *The Weekend Australian* 22 July 2000: R13.

Deer, Glenn. "Interview with Wayson Choy." *Canadian Literature* 163 (1999): 34–44.

Department of Canadian Heritage. *Guide to the Funding Application Form.* Government of Canada. 1997.

Department of Immigration and Multicultural Affairs (DIMA) "Abolition of 'White Australia' Policy." Prepared by the Public Affairs Section, DIMA, Canberra, December 1996. Downloaded 1 July 1997. <http://www.immi.gov.au/facts/info9.htm>

Devadas, Vijayandran. "(Pre)Serving Home: 'Little India' and the Indian Singaporean." *Critical Arts* 10.2 (1996): 67–90.

Deves, Michael. "Brian Castro: Hybridity, Identity, Reality." *Land and Identity: Proceeding of the Nineteenth Annual Conference 1997, ASAL.* Ed. Jennifer McDonell and Michael Deves. Canberra: ASAL, 1998. 220–5.

Dirlik, Arif. "Asians on the Rim: Transnational Capital and Local Community in the Making of Contemporary Asian America." *Amerasia Journal* 22.3 (1996): 1–24.

———. "The Postcolonial Aura: Third World Criticism in the Age of Global Capitalism." *Critical Inquiry* 20 (1994): 328–56.

"Diversity, Writing, and Social Critique: An Interactive Forum." Day conference. University of British Columbia, Vancouver, BC, Canada, 25 April 1998.

Dixon, Robert. *Writing the Colonial Adventure: Race, Gender and Nation in Anglo-Australian Popular Fiction, 1875–1914.* Cambridge: Cambridge University Press, 1995.

Docker, John. "Post Nationalism." *Arena* February–March 1994: 40–1.

———. "Rethinking Postcolonialism and Multiculturalism in the *fin de siècle.*" *Cultural Studies* 9.3 (1995): 409–26.

Docker, John, and Gerhard Fischer, eds. *Race, Colour and Identity in Australia and New Zealand.* Sydney: University of New South Wales Press, 2000.

Dunn, John, and Judy Ellis. "Paul Hogan." *Life* July 1988: 17–8. Downloaded from IAC Database. 27 October 1998.

Dyson, Michael Eric. "Essentialism and the Complexities of Racial Identity." *Multiculturalism: A Reader.* Ed. David Theo Goldberg. Cambridge, MA: Basil Blackwell, 1994. 218–29.

Eng, David. *Racial Castration: Managing Masculinity in Asian America (Perverse Modernities).* Durham, NC: Duke University Press, 2001.

Eng, David, and Alice Hom, eds. *Q & A: Queer in Asian America.* Philadelphia, PA: Temple University Press, 1998.

Evans, Raymond. "'Soiled Doves': Prostitution and Society in Colonial Queensland — An Overview." *Hecate* 1.2 (1975): 6–24.

Faulk, Tina. "A Different Perspective: Ethnic Chinese Photographer Taps His Background and Sexual Orientation to Chronicle Sydney Life." *Far Eastern Economic Review* 3 March 1994: 62.

Fee, Margery. "English-Canadian Literary Criticism, 1890–1950: Defining and Establishing a National Literature." PhD Dissertation, University of Toronto, 1981.

Feng, Peter. "Redefining Asian American Masculinity: Steven Okazaki's *American Sons.*" *Cineaste* 22.3 (1996): 27–9. Downloaded IAC Database. 27 October 1998.

Fischer, Gerhard. *Enemy Aliens: Internment and the Homefront Experience in Australia, 1914–1920.* St Lucia, QLD: University of Queensland Press, 1989.

Fish, Stanley. "Boutique Multiculturalism, or Why Liberals Are Incapable of Thinking about Hate Speech." *Critical Inquiry* 23.2 (1997): 378–95.

Frankenberg, Ruth. *White Women, Race Matters: The Social Construction of Whiteness.* London: Routledge, 1993.

Frow, John. *Marxism and Literary History.* London: Blackwell, 1986.

Frow, John, and Meaghan Morris. *Australian Cultural Studies.* St Leonards: Allen and Unwin, 1993.

Fulford, Robert. "George Orwell, Call Your Office." *Globe and Mail* 30 March 1994: n.p.

Fung, Richard. "Conference Calls: Race as Special Event." *Take One* 5 (1994): 38.

———. "Looking for My Penis: The Eroticized Asian in Gay Video Porn." Leong, 181–98.

———. "Multiculturalism Reconsidered." *Yellow Peril: Reconsidered.* Ed. Paul Wong. Vancouver, BC: On Edge on the Cutting Edge, 1990. 17–9.

Fuss, Diana. "Interior Colonies: Frantz Fanon and the Politics of Identification." *Diacritics* 24.2–3 (1994): 20–42.

Gagnon, Jean. "Paradox in Paul Wong's Work." *On Becoming a Man*. Paul Wong. Ottawa: National Gallery of Canada, 1995. 12–9.

Gagnon, Monika Kin. "Building Blocks: Recent Anti-Racist Initiatives in the Arts." *Ghosts in the Machine: Women and Cultural Policy in Canada and Australia*. Ed. Alison Beale and Annette Van den Bosch. Toronto, ON: Garamond Press, 1998. 115–30.

———. *Other Conundrums: Race, Culture, and Canadian Art*. Vancouver and Kamloops, BC: Arsenal Pulp Press, Artspeak Gallery, and Kamloops Art Gallery, 2000.

———. "Story within a Story": Review of Hiromi Goto's *Chorus of Mushrooms*. *Kinesis* November 1994: 17.

Gee, Kenda. Interview with Tseen Khoo. 17 December 1998.

Gerster, Robin. Review of *Sadness* by William Yang. *Australian Book Review* December 1996–January 1997: 24.

Gertsakis, Elizabeth. "An Inconstant Politics: Thinking about the Traditional and the Contemporary." Gunew and Rizvi 35–53.

Giese, Diana. *Astronauts, Lost Souls, and Dragons: Voices of Today's Chinese Australians in Conversation with Diana Giese*. St Lucia, QLD: University of Queensland Press, 1997.

———. *Beyond Chinatown: Changing Perspectives of the Top End Chinese Experience*. Canberra: National Library of Australia, 1995.

Gilbert, Helen, Tseen Khoo, and Jacqueline Lo. *Diaspora: Negotiating Asian-Australia*. St Lucia, QLD: University of Queensland Press, 2000.

Goellnicht, Donald C. "A Long Labour: The Protracted Birth of Asian Canadian Literature." *Essays on Canadian Writing* 72 (2000): 1–41.

Goldberg, Barry. "Historical Reflections on Transnationalism, Race, and the American Immigrant Saga." *Towards a Transnational Perspective on Migration: Race, Class, Ethnicity, and Nationalism Reconsidered*. Ed. Nina Glick Schiller, Linda Basch, and Cristina Blanc-Szanton. New York: New York Academy of Sciences, 1992. 201–15.

Gotanda, Neil. "Multiculturalism and Racial Stratification." *Mapping Multiculturalism*. Ed. Avery F. Gordon and Christopher Newfield. Minneapolis: University of Minnesota Press, 1996. 238–52.

Goto, Hiromi. "The Body Politic." *West Coast Line* 13–4 (1994): 218–21.

———. *Chorus of Mushrooms*. Edmonton: NeWest Press, 1994.

———. Interview with Tseen Khoo. January 1998.

———. *The Kappa Child*. Calgary, AB: Red Deer Press, 2001.

———. Review of *When Fox Is a Thousand* by Larissa Lai. *Bulletin* [Japanese-Canadian newsletter] March 1996: 18.

———. "Tales from the Breast." *Ms* September–October 1996: 86–90.

———. *The Water of Possibility*. Toronto, ON: Coteau, 2001.

Gottlieb, Erika. "The Riddle of Concentric Worlds in *Obasan*." *Canadian Literature* 109 (1986): 34–53.

Gourevitch, Philip. "The Boat People." *Granta* 50 (1995): 13–59.

Govier, Katherine. "Beyond *Obasan* toward Forgiveness: Review of Kerri Sakamoto's *The Electrical Field*." *Globe and Mail* 23 May 1998: D18, D10.

"Grinding Tofu: Eric." Interview from an Internet project on Asian lesbianism and gayness. Downloaded 29 January 1998. <http://www.geocities.com/Tokyo/Towers/4289/eric.html>

Gunew, Sneja. "Against Multiculturalism: Rhetorical Images." *Multiculturalism, Difference and Postmodernism.* Ed. Gordon L. Clark, Dean Forbes, and Roderick Francis. Melbourne: Longman Cheshire, 1993. 38–53.

———. "Culture, Gender and the Author-Function: 'Wongar's' *Walg*." *Australian Cultural Studies.* Ed. John Frow and Meaghan Morris. St Leonards: Allen and Unwin, 1993. 3–14.

———. "Ethnicity and Excellence in the Arts." *Artlink* 11.1–2 (1991): 4–6.

———. *Framing Marginality.* Carlton, VIC: Melbourne University Press, 1994.

———. "The Melting Pot of Assimilation: Cannibalizing the Multicultural Body." *Transnational Asia Pacific: Gender, Culture, and the Public Sphere.* Ed. Shirley Geok-lin Lim, and Wimal Dissanayake. Urbana and Chicago, IL: University of Illinois Press, 1999. 145–58.

———. "Multicultural Multiplicities: US, Canada, Australia." *Meanjin* 52.3 (1993): 447–61.

———. "Performing Ethnicity: The Demidenko Show and its Gratifying Pathologies." *Australian Feminist Studies* 11.23 (1996): 53–63.

———. "Postcolonialism/Multiculturalism — Australia 1993: An Interview with Sneja Gunew." *Postcolonial Discourse and Changing Cultural Contexts: Theory and Criticism.* Ed. Gita Rajan and Radhika Mohanram. Westport, CT: Greenwood, 1995. 205–17.

Gunew, Sneja, and Kateryna Longley. *Striking Chords: Multicultural Literary Interpretations.* Sydney: Allen and Unwin, 1992.

Gunew, Sneja, and Fazal Rizvi. *Culture, Difference, and the Arts.* St Leonards, NSW: Allen and Unwin, 1994.

Gunn, J. S. "In Search of Ocker and the Missing Link." *Quadrant* January–February 1982: 92–5.

Gunn, Janet. *Autobiography: Towards a Poetics of Experience.* Philadelphia: University of Pennsylvania Press, 1982.

Hage, Ghassan. "Locating Multiculturalism's Other: A Critique of Practical Tolerance." *New Formations* 24 (1994): 19–34.

———. *White Nation: Fantasies of White Supremacy in a Multicultural Society.* Sydney: Pluto Press, 1998.

Hall, James. "Vertigo Takes Author to Dizzy Heights." Book review. *Australian* 29 September 1999: Local 1.

Hannerz, Ulf. "Borders." *International Social Science Journal* 49.4 (1997): 537–48. Downloaded from IAC Database. 14 December 1998.

Harris, Mason. "Broken Generations in *Obasan*: Inner Conflict and the Destruction of Community." *Canadian Literature* 127 (1990): 41–57.

Hattori, Tomo. "The Location of Origins: The Eaton Sisters and Nationalist Imagination." Paper given at the 15th Annual Meeting of the Association for Asian American Studies, Honolulu, Hawaii. 23–28 June 1998.

Henderson, Mae G. "Introduction: Borders, Boundaries, and Frame(works)." *Borders, Boundaries, and Frames: Essays in Cultural Criticism and Cultural Studies*. Ed. Mae G. Henderson. New York and London: Routledge, 1995. 1–30.

Hongo, Garrett. "Introduction." *Under Western Eyes: Personal Essays from Asian America*. New York: Doubleday, 1995. 1–33.

Horne, Donald. "Introduction." *Redefining Australians: Immigration, Citizenship, and National Identity*. Ann-Mari Jordens. Sydney: Hale and Iremonger, 1995. i–xii.

Howard, John. "Address at the Launch of the National Multicultural Advisory Council Report '*Australian Multiculturalism for a New Century: Towards Inclusiveness*'." 1999. Webpage transcript. <http://www.pm.gov.au/ news/ speeches/1999/MulticulturalAdvisoryCouncil.htm.> 24 September 2002.

Hunter, Lynette. *Outsider Notes: Feminist Approaches to Nation State Ideology, Writers/ Readers, and Publishing*. Vancouver, BC: Talon Books, 1996.

Hutcheon, Linda, and Marian Richmond, eds. *Other Solitudes: Canadian Multicultural Fictions*. Toronto, ON: Oxford University Press, 1990.

Ingram, Gordon Brent. "Sex Migrants: Paul Wong's Video Geographies of Erotic and Cultural Displacement in Pacific Canada." *Fuse* 20.1 (1997): 17–26.

Ismail, Jamila. "From *scared texts*." *Many-Mouthed Birds*. Ed. Bennett Lee and Jim Wong-Chu. Vancouver, BC: Douglas and McIntyre, 1991. 124–35.

Ito, Roy. *We Went to War: The Story of the Japanese Canadians Who Served during the First and Second World Wars*. Etobicoke, ON: S-20 and Nisei Veterans' Association, 1992.

Iwama, Marilyn. Review of *Chorus of Mushrooms* by Hiromi Goto. *Bulletin* [Japanese-Canadian newsletter] March 1996: 17–8.

Jacobson, Lisa. "The Ocker in Australian Drama." *Meanjin* 49.1 (1990): 137–47.

Jamrozik, Adam, Cathy Boland and Robert Urquhart. *Social Change and Cultural Transformation in Australia*. Cambridge: Cambridge University Press, 1995.

Johnston, Anna. "The 'Memoirs of Many in One': Post-Colonial Autobiography in Settler Cultures." MA Dissertation, University of Queensland, 1995.

———. "U-nbecoming Post-Colonial Narratives: Eric Michaels' *Unbecoming: An AIDS Diary*." *Southern Review* 32.1 (1999): 60–71.

Johnstone, Craig. "Broken Dream." *Courier-Mail* 25 January 1997: 29.

Jordens, Ann-Mari. *Redefining Australians: Immigration, Citizenship, and National Identity*. Sydney: Hale and Iremonger, 1995.

Jost, John, Gianna Totaro, and Christine Tyshing, ed. *The Demidenko File*. Ringwood, VIC: Penguin, 1996.

Jupp, James. "Australian Culture: Multicultural, Aboriginal or Just Plain Australian?" *Artlink* 11.1–2 (1991): 11–3.

Kalantzis, Mary and Bill Cope. "Vocabularies of Excellence: Rewording Multicultural Arts Policy." Gunew and Rizvi 13–34.

Kamboureli, Smaro. "Canadian Ethnic Anthologies: Representations of Ethnicity." *Ariel* 25.4 (1994): 11–52.

———. *Scandalous Bodies: Diasporic Literatures in English Canada.* Don Mills, ON: Oxford University Press, 2000.

———. "The Technology of Ethnicity: Canadian Multiculturalism and the Language of Law." *Multicultural States: Rethinking Difference and Identity.* Ed. David Bennett. New York and London: Routledge, 1998. 208–22.

Kaplan, Gisela. *The Meagre Harvest: The Australian Women's Movement 1950s–1990s.* St Leonards: Allen and Unwin, 1996.

Keefer, Janice Kulyk. "For or Against Multiculturalism: Could the Demidenko Scandal Have Happened in Canada?" Address to the Sydney Institute, June 1996.

Keefer, Janice Kulyk. "Multiculturalism and the Millennium." Paper given at ACSANZ Conference, Hobart, Australia. 1–7 July 1996.

Khoo, Tseen. "Selling Sexotica: Oriental Grunge and Suburbia in Lillian Ng's *Swallowing Clouds.*" *Diaspora: Negotiating Asian-Australia.* Ed. Helen Gilbert, Tseen Khoo, and Jacqueline Lo. Brisbane: University of Queensland Press, 2000. 164–72.

———. "Someone Else's Zoo: Asian-Australian Women's Writing." *Current Tensions: Proceedings of the 18th Annual Conference.* Association for the Study of Australian Literature. Brisbane, 6–11 July 1996. 23–9.

———. "Who Are We Talking about? Asian-Australian Women Writers: An Overview." *Hecate* 22.2 (1996): 11–30.

Kim, Elaine H. "Beyond Railroads and Internment: Comments on the Past, Present, and Future of Asian-American Studies." Okihiro et al. 11–20.

Kingston, Maxine Hong. *China Men.* New York: Ballantine, 1981.

———. *The Woman Warrior: Memoirs of a Girlhood among Ghosts.* New York: Vintage, 1976.

Kitagawa, Muriel, and Roy Miki, eds. *Letters to Wes and Other Writings on Japanese-Canadians 1941–1948.* Vancouver, BC: Talon Books, 1985.

Kobayashi, Audrey. "The Japanese-Canadian Redress Settlement and its Implications for 'Race Relations.'" *Canadian Ethnic Studies* 24.1 (1992): 1–19.

Kogawa, Joy. "The Heart-of-the-Matter Questions": An Interview with Karlyn Koh. *The Other Woman: Women of Colour in Contemporary Canadian Literature.* Ed. Makeda Silvera. Toronto, ON: Sister Vision, 1995. 19–41.

———. Interview by Magdalene Redekop with Joy Kogawa. *Other Solitudes: Canadian Multicultural Fictions.* Ed. Linda Hutcheon and Marian Richmond. Toronto, ON: Oxford University Press, 1990. 94–101.

———. *Itsuka.* Toronto, ON: Viking, 1992.

————. *Obasan*. Markham, ON: Penguin, 1981.

Koh, Karlyn. Interview with Tseen Khoo. 4 May 1998.

Krishnaswamy, Revathi. "Mythologies of Migrancy: Postcolonialism, Postmodernism and the Politics of (Dis)location." *Ariel* 26.1 (1995): 125–46.

Lai, Larissa. "Corrupted Lineage: Narrative in the Gaps of History." 2000. Webpage. <http://www.ucalgary.ca/~lalai/lineage.htm> Downloaded 25 September 2002.

————. "Political Animals and the Body of History." *Canadian Literature* 163 (1999): 145–54.

————. "Ritz Chow Interviews Larissa Lai on Email (February)." 2002. Webpage. <http://www.ucalgary.ca/~lalai/chowlai.htm> Downloaded 25 September 2002.

————. "Stories within Stories: In Conversation with Larissa Lai." Interview by Karlyn Koh. *Rice Paper* 2.3 (1996): 3–5, 16.

————. *When Fox Is a Thousand*. Vancouver, BC: Press Gang, 1995.

Lake, Marilyn. "'Stirring Tales': Australian Feminism and National Identity, 1900–40." Stokes 78–91.

Lamont, Leonie. "Young Writer Reveals Universal Family." *Sydney Morning Herald* 29 September 1999: 3.

Lang, Catherine. *O-Bon in Chimunesu: A Community Remembered*. Vancouver, BC: Arsenal Pulp Press, 1996.

Langer, Beryl. "Hard-boiled and Soft-boiled: Masculinity and Nation in Canadian and Australian Crime Fiction." *Meridian* 15.2 (1996): 237–55.

Lawson, Alan. "Postcolonial Theory and the 'Settler' Subject." *Essays on Canadian Writing* 56 (1995): 20–36.

————. "The Recognition of National Literatures: The Canadian and Australian Examples." PhD Dissertation, University of Queensland, 1987.

Lazaroo, Simone. *The World Waiting To Be Made*. Fremantle: Fremantle Arts Centre Press, 1994.

Le, Hung. *The Yellow Peril from Sin City*. Ringwood: Penguin, 1997.

Leach, Michael. "'Manly, True and White': Masculine Identity and Australian Socialism." Stokes 63–77.

Lee, Bennett, and Jim Wong-Chu. *Many-Mouthed Birds: Contemporary Writing by Chinese Canadians*. Vancouver and Toronto: Douglas and McIntyre, 1991.

Lee, C. Allyson. "Recipe." *The Very Inside: An Anthology of Writing by Asian and Pacific Islander Lesbian and Bisexual Women*. Ed. Sharon Lim-Hing. Toronto, ON: Sister Vision, 1994. 333–9.

Lee, Christopher. "Engaging Chineseness in Wayson Choy's *The Jade Peony*." *Canadian Literature* 163 (1999): 18–33.

Lee, Kenneth. "Angry Yellow Men: Exploiting Asian Discontent." *The New Republic* 9 September 1996: 11. Downloaded from IAC Database. October 1997.

Lee, Robert G. *Orientals: Asian Americans in Popular Culture*. Philadelphia, PA: Temple University Press, 1999.

Lee, Sky. *Disappearing Moon Cafe*. Seattle, WA: Seal Press, 1990.

————. " 'Writing Thru Race' Response." *Rice Paper* 1.3 (1995): 8.

Leong, Hou. "An Australian." *Asian and Pacific Inscriptions: Identities, Ethnicities, Nationalities.* Ed. Suvendrini Perera. Bundoora, VIC: School of English, La Trobe University, 1995. 111–20.

Leong, Russell. "Home Bodies and the Body Politic." *Asian American Sexualities* 3–18.

————. "Lived Theory: Notes on the Run." *Amerasia Journal* 21.1-2 (1995): v–x.

————. "Transnationalism, Media and Migration." *Amerasia Journal* 22.3 (1996): iii–vi.

Leong, Russell, ed. *Asian American Sexualities: Dimensions of the Gay and Lesbian Experience.* New York: Routledge, 1996.

Levy, Bronwen. "Third Time Lucky, or After the Wash-Up." *Imago* 7.3 (1995): 108–17.

Lim-Hing, Sharon, ed. *The Very Inside: An Anthology of Writing by Asian and Pacific Islander Lesbian and Bisexual Women.* Toronto, ON: Sister Vision, 1994.

Ling, Jinqi. "Identity Crisis and Gender Politics: Reappropriating Asian American Masculinity." *An Interethnic Companion to Asian American Literature.* Ed. King-Kok Cheung. Cambridge: Cambridge University Press, 1997. 312–37.

Litson, Jo. "A Witness to his Times." *Australian* 7 August 1998: 16.

Loh, Morag, and Christine Ramsay. *Survival and Celebration: An Insight into the Lives of Chinese Immigrant Women, European Women Married to Chinese and Their Female Children in Australia from 1856–1986.* Melbourne: Morag Loh and Christine Ramsay, 1986.

Loh, Morag, and Judith Winternitz. *Dinky-Di: The Contributions of Chinese Immigrants and Australians Chinese Descent to Australia's Defence Forces and War Efforts 1899–1988.* Canberra: AGPS, 1989.

Longley, Kateryna O. "Fabricating Otherness: Demidenko and Exoticism." *Westerly* 42.1 (1997): 27–45.

Lorde, Audre. *The Audre Lorde Compendium: Essays, Speeches and Journals.* London: Pandora, 1996.

Louie, Kam. *Theorising Chinese Masculinity: Society and Gender in China.* Cambridge: Cambridge University Press, 2002.

Louie, Kam, and Tseen Khoo, eds. *Culture, Identity, Commodity: Diasporic Chinese Literatures in English.* Hong Kong: Hong Kong University Press, forthcoming.

Loukakis, Angelo. "Homeless Again." *Outrider* 3.2 (1986): 103–10.

Low, Gail Ching-Liang. "White Skins/Black Masks: The Pleasures and Politics of Imperialism." *New Formations* 9 (1989): 83–103.

Lowe, Lisa. *Immigrant Acts: On Asian American Cultural Politics.* Durham and London: Duke University Press, 1996.

Luke, Allan. "Representing and Reconstructing Asian Masculinities: This Is Not a Movie Review." *Social Alternatives* 16.3 (1997): 32–4.

Ma, Sheng-Mei. *Immigrant Subjectivities in Asian American and Asian Diaspora Literatures.* Albany, NY: State University of New York Press, 1998.

Maclear, Kyo. "Plots of Land." *This Magazine* November–December 1996: 32–5.

Magnusson, A. Lynne. "Language and Longing in Joy Kogawa's *Obasan*." *Canadian Literature* 116 (1988).

Malak, Amin. "From Margin to Main: Minority Discourse and 'Third World' Fiction Writers in Canada." *From Commonwealth to Post-Colonial*. Ed. Anna Rutherford. Sydney: Dangaroo, 1992. 44–52.

Mares, Peter. *Borderline: Australia's Treatment of Refugees and Asylum Seekers*. Sydney: University of New South Wales Press, 2001.

Mathur, Ashok. Review of the Pomelo Project's "The Work of Pleasure" series. <http://www.ucalgary.ca/~amathur/pomelo.html>

McDonald, Kevin. "Identity Politics." *Arena* June–July 1994: 18–22.

McFarlane, Scott. "Covering *Obasan* and the Narrative of Internment." Okihiro et al. 401–11.

———. "The Haunt of Race: Canada's *Multiculturalism Act*, the Politics of Incorporation, and Writing Thru Race." *Fuse* 18.3 (1995): 18–31.

McGoogan, Ken. "Calgary Novelist Wins Top Award." *Calgary Herald* 12 July 1995: B5, 1.

McLaren, Peter. "White Terror and Oppositional Agency: Towards a Critical Multiculturalism." *Multiculturalism: A Reader*. Ed. David Theo Goldberg. Cambridge, MA: Basil Blackwell, 1994. 45–74.

Mercer, Kobena. "Welcome to the Jungle: Identity and Diversity in Postmodern Politics." *Identity: Community, Culture, Difference*. Ed. Jonathan Rutherford. London: Lawrence and Wishart, 1990. 43–71.

Michaels, Walter Benn. "Race into Culture: A Critical Genealogy of Cultural Identity." *Critical Inquiry* 18 (1992): 655–85.

Miki, Roy. "Asiancy: Making Space for Asian-Canadian Writing." Okihiro et al. 135–51.

Miki, Roy. *Broken Entries: Race, Subjectivity, Writing*. Toronto, ON: Mercury Press, 1998.

Mishra, Vijay. "The Diasporic Imaginary." University of California, Santa Cruz, 1994.

———. "New Lamps for Old: Diasporas Migrancy Border." *Interrogating Post-Colonialism: Theory, Text and Context*. Ed. Harish Trivedi and Meenakshi Mukherjee. Rashtrapati, Shimla: Indian Institute of Advanced Study, 1996. 67–85.

———. "Postmodern Racism." *Meanjin* 55.2 (1996): 346–57.

———, ed. *SPAN* 34–5 (1993).

Mitchell, Katharyne. "Fast Capital, Modernity, 'Race', and the Monster House." *Burning Down the House: Recycling Domesticity*. Ed. R.M. George. New York: Westview Press, 1998. 187–212.

———. "The Hong Kong Immigrant and the Urban Landscape: Shaping the Transnational Cosmopolitan in the Era of Pacific Rim Capital." *Asia/Pacific as Space of Cultural Production*. Ed. Rob Wilson and Arif Dirlik. Durham and London: Duke University Press, 1995. 284–310.

Mitchell, Tony. "Wogs Still Out of Work: Australian Television Comedy as Colonial Discourse." *Australasian Drama Studies* 20 (1992): 119–33.

Mohanty, Chandra Talpade. "Cartographies of Struggle." *Third World Women and the Politics of Feminism*. Ed. Mohanty, Ann Russo, and Lourdes Torres. Bloomington, IN: Indiana University Press, 1991. 1–47.

Moran, Jennifer. "Diverse Voices Unite at Inaugural Forum." *The Canberra Times* 29 August 2001, sec. A: 5.

Morrissey, Michael. "'Migrantness', Culture and Ideology." *Ethnicity, Class and Gender in Australia*. Ed. Gillian Bottomley and Maria de Lepervanche. Sydney: Allen and Unwin, 1984. 72–81.

Mudrooroo. "The Perils of Pauline: Consensus and Dissent in Australian Politics." *Overland* 148 (1997): 3–7.

Murdoch, Anna King. "The China Syndrome." *The Age Extra* 21 March 1998: 6.

Nagata, Yuriko. "Illegal Entrants: Japanese Prostitutes in Australia 1890s–1945." "Transforming Cultures/Shifting Boundaries: Asian Diasporas and Identities in Australia and Beyond" conference, Brisbane. 30 November–2 December 2001.

———. *Unwanted Aliens: Japanese Internment in Australia*. St Lucia, QLD: University of Queensland Press, 1996.

National, Multicultural Advisory Committee. *Australian Multiculturalism for a New Century: Towards Inclusiveness*. 1999. Webpage. <http://www.immi.gov.au/multicultural/nmac/index.html.> 15 January 1998.

Neilson, Brett. "Threshold Procedures: 'Boat People' in South Florida and Western Australia." *Critical Arts* 10.2 (1996): 21–40.

Newman, Paul. "One Nation: Who's To Blame?" *Journal of Australian Studies* 57 (1998): 1–9.

Ng, Wing Chung. *The Chinese in Vancouver, 1945–1980*. Vancouver, BC: University of British Columbia Press, 1999.

Nowra, Louis. "A Tale of Two Singapores: Reviews of *Love and Vertigo* (Teo) and *the Australian Fiance* (Lazaroo)." *Sydney Morning Herald* 2000: <http://www.smh.com.au/news/0009/09/books/A27234-2000Aug25.html> Accessed 25 October 2001.

Okihiro, Gary, et al. *Privileging Positions: The Sites of Asian-American Studies*. Pullman, WA: Washington State University Press, 1995.

Omatsu, Maryka. *Bittersweet Passage: Redress and the Japanese Canadian Experience*. Toronto, ON: Between the Lines, 1992.

Omi, Michael, and Howard Winant. *Racial Formation in the United States*. New York: Routledge and Kegan Paul, 1986.

Ommundsen, Wenche. "Multiculturalism, Identity, Displacement: The Lives of Brian (Castro)." *From a Distance: Australian Writers and Cultural Displacement*. Ed. Ommundsen and Hazel Rowley. Geelong: Deakin University Press, 1996. 149–58.

On, Thuy. "Journeys of Love and Loss: Reviews of *Love and Vertigo* (Teo), *the Australian*

Fiance (Lazaroo), and *under the Same Sun* (Kissane)." *The Age* 2000: n.p. <http://www.theage.com.au/books/20000807/A54071-2000Aug6.html> Accessed 3 July 2001.

Onodera, Midi. "Dishing It Out and Taking It." *The Very Inside: An Anthology of Writing by Asian and Pacific Islander Lesbian and Bisexual Women.* Ed. Sharon Lim-Hing. Toronto, ON: Sister Vision, 1994. 141–54.

Ouyang, Yu. "An Interview with Brian Castro." *Bastard Moon: Essays on Chinese-Australian Writing.* Ed. Wenche Ommundsen. Melbourne: Otherland, 2001. 73–81.

———. "Will Words Not Hurt Them? Verbal Violence to the Chinese in Australian Literature." *Rubicon* 1.2 (1995): 103–19.

Overland. "Special Issue: New World Borders." 64 (2001).

Palumbo-Liu, David. "Los Angeles, Asians, and Perverse Ventriloquisms: On the Function of Asian America in the Recent American Imaginary." *Public Culture* 6 (1994): 365–81.

———. "Introduction." Ed. Palumbo-Liu. *The Ethnic Canon: Histories, Institutions, and interventions.* Minneapolis and London: University of Minnesota Press, 1995. 1–27.

Paquet, Gilles. "Political Philosophy of Multiculturalism." *Ethnicity and Culture in Canada: The Research Landscape.* Ed. J.W. Berry and J.A. Laponce. Toronto, ON: University of Toronto Press, 1994. 60–80.

Pasquarelli, John. "Seven Deadly Sins." *Bulletin* 3 June 1996: 17–8.

Perera, Suvendrini, ed. *Asian and Pacific Inscriptions: Identities, Ethnicities, Nationalities.* Bundoora, VIC: School of English, La Trobe University, 1995.

Perera, Suvendrini, and Joseph Pugliese. "'Racial Suicide': The Re-licensing of Racism in Australia." *Race and Class* 39.2 (1997): 1–19. Downloaded from IAC Database. 5 August 1998.

Pettman, Jan Jindy. "Race, Ethnicity and Gender in Australia." *Unsettling Settler Societies: Articulations of Gender, Race, Ethnicity, and Class.* Ed. Daiva Stasiulis and Nira Yuval-Davis. London: Sage, 1995. 65–94.

Powell, Diane. *Out West: Perceptions of Sydney's Western Suburbs.* St Leonards: Allen and Unwin, 1993.

Powell Street Revue and the Chinese Canadian Writers' Workshop. *Inalienable Rice: A Chinese and Japanese Anthology.* Vancouver, BC: Powell Street Revue and the Chinese Canadian Writers' Workshop, 1979.

Pybus, Cassandra. "Guest Editorial." *Australian Book Review* October 1996: 2.

Quan, Andy. *Calendar Boy.* Vancouver: New Star, 2001

———. *Slant.* Roberts Creek, BC: Nightwood, 2001.

Quan, Betty. Review of Goto's *Chorus of Mushrooms. Quill and Quire* 60.6 (1994): 45.

Quimby, Karen. "'This Is My Own, My Native Land': Constructions of Identity and Landscape in Joy Kogawa's *Obasan.*" *Cross-Addressing: Resistance Literature and Cultural Borders.* Ed. John C. Hawley. New York: SUNY Press, 1996. 257–73.

Radhakrishnan, R. *Diasporic Mediations: Between Home and Location*. Minneapolis and London: University of Minnesota Press, 1996.

Rengger, Patrick. "Goto's Chorus of Voices Converge in Her Fiction." *Globe and Mail Metro Edition* 2 January 1996: C1, C2.

Riemer, Andrew. *The Demidenko Debate*. St Leonards, NSW: Allen and Unwin, 1996.

Rimer, J. Thomas. "The Tale of Genji: Murasaki Shikibu/ *Genji monogatari.*" *A Reader's Guide to Japanese Literature: From the Eighth Century to the Present*. Tokyo and New York: Kodansha International, 1988. 36–40.

Rizvi, Fazal. "The Arts, Education, and the Politics of Multiculturalism." Gunew and Rizvi 54–68.

Robertson, Jo. "In a State of Corruption: Dreaded Disease and the Body Politic." PhD Dissertation, University of Queensland, 1999.

Rolls, Eric. *Citizens*. St Lucia, QLD: University of Queensland Press, 1996.

———. *Sojourners: Flowers and the Wide Sea*. St Lucia, QLD: University of Queensland Press, 1992.

Sakamoto, Kerri. *The Electrical Field*. Toronto, ON: Alfred A. Knopf, 1998.

———. "The Perfect Place: In a Writer's Personal Utopia, All Ethnic Distinctions Would Be Honored as the Same." *Time International* 1999: 54.

San Juan, E. "The Cult of Ethnicity and the Fetish of Pluralism." *Cultural Critique* 18 (1991): 215–29.

Sang, Ye. *The Year the Dragon Came*. St Lucia, QLD: University of Queensland Press, 1996.

Sasano, Mari. "'Words like Buckshot': Taking Aim at Notions of Nation in Hiromi Goto's *Chorus of Mushrooms.*" MA Project, University of Alberta, Canada, 1996.

Saul, Joanne. "Displacement and Self-Representation: Theorizing Contemporary Canadian Biotexts." *Biography* 24.1 (2001): 259–72. Downloaded from Infotrac Searchbank database 24 September 2002.

Savran, David. "The Sadomasochist in the Closet: White Masculinity and the Culture of Victimization." *Differences* 8.2 (1996): 127–52.

Schwenger, Peter, and John Whittier Treat. "America's Hiroshima, Hiroshima's America." *Asia/Pacific as Space of Cultural Production*. Ed. Rob Wilson and Arif Dirlik. Durham and London: Duke University Press, 1995. 324–44.

Scott, Rebekah. "Cruel and Carnal." *Courier Mail* 29 July 2000, sec. BAM: 5.

Selzer, Linda. "Race and Domesticity in *The Color Purple.*" *African American Review* 29.1 (1995): 67–82. Downloaded from Infotrac Searchbank Database, 27 October 1998.

Shen, Yuanfang. *Dragonseed in the Antipodes: Chinese-Australian Autobiographies*. Carlton South, VIC: Melbourne University Press, 2001.

Sheridan, Greg. "Our Northern Exposure." *Australian's Review of Books* April 1997: 13–5.

Shih, Shu-mei. "Globalization, Minoritization, and Ang Lee's Films." Paper given at the 15th Annual Meeting of the Association for Asian American Studies, Honolulu, HI. 23–28 June 1998.

Shohat, Ella, and Robert Stam. *Unthinking Eurocentrism: Multiculturalism and the Media.* London and New York: Routledge, 1994.

Shun Wah, Annette, and Greg Aitkin. *Banquet: Ten Courses to Harmony.* Moorebank, NSW: Doubleday, 1999.

Siemerling, Winfried. "Writing Ethnicity: Introduction." *Essays on Canadian Writing* 57 (1995): 1–32.

Silvera, Makeda. *The Other Woman: Women of Colour in Contemporary Canadian Literature.* Toronto, ON: Sister Vision, 1995.

Sinfield, Alan. "Diaspora and Hybridity: Queer Identities and the Ethnicity Model." *Textual Practice* 10.2 (1996): 271–93.

Skrzynecki, Peter. Introduction. *Influence: Australian Voices.* Ed. Skrzynecki. Sydney: Anchor, 1997. ix–xiii.

Soo, Jacalyn. Chinacity Interview with Denise Chong. Author of *The Concubine's Children.* Downloaded 10 November 1996. <http://www.alvin.org/acr/jsoo.htm>

Spivak, Gayatri. "Culture Alive." *Australian Feminist Law Journal* 5 (1995): 3–11.

Srivastava, Aruna, and Ashok Mathur. "Preston Terre Blanche, Snow White, and the Seven Deadly Disclaimers, or the Dos of Racism (a not so far off fairy tale)." *West Coast Line* 28.1–2 (1994): 7–14.

Stasiulis, Daiva, and Radha Jhappan. "The Fractious Politics of a Settler Society: Canada." *Unsettling Settler Societies: Articulations of Gender, Race, Ethnicity, and Class.* Ed. Stasiulis and Nira Yuval-Davis. London: Sage, 1995. 95–131.

Steketee, Mike. "Face of Our Future." *The Weekend Australian* 3–4 May 1997: 4.

Stokes, Geoffrey, ed. *The Politics of Identity in Australia.* Cambridge: Cambridge University Press, 1997.

Stratton, Jon, and Ien Ang. "Multicultural Imagined Communities: Cultural Difference and National Identity in Australia and the USA." *Continuum* 8.2 (1994): 124–58.

Swift, Richard. "Spitting in the Soup." *New Internationalist* March (1996): 20–2.

Takagi, Dana Y. "Maiden Voyage: Excursion into Sexuality and Identity Politics." Leong, *Asian American Sexualities* 21–35.

Tamura, Keiko. *Michi's Memories: The Story of a Japanese War Bride.* Canberra: Pandanus, 2001.

Tan, Joel, et al. "Communion: A Collaboration on AIDS." Leong, *Asian American Sexualities* 201–17.

Teo, Hsu-Ming. *Love and Vertigo.* St Leonards, NSW: Allen and Unwin, 2000.

Thomas, Mandy. *Dreams in the Shadows: Vietnamese-Australian Lives in Transition.* St Leonards: Allen and Unwin, 1999.

Trinh T. Minh-ha. *Woman, Native, Other: Writing Postcoloniality and Feminism.* Bloomington, IN: Indiana University Press, 1989.

Tsu, Timothy. "Chinatown as 'Gourmet Republic': Transformation of Chinese Ethnicity in Modern Japan." Paper presented at Culture and Citizenship Conference, Brisbane, Australia. 30 September–2 October 1996.

Tucker, Shirley. "Xenophobia? Please Explain: Review of Lachlan Strahan (*Australia's China*), Sang Ye and Linda Jaivin (*Year the Dragon Came*), Diana Giese (*Astronauts, Lost Souls, and Dragons*) and Yuriko Nagata (*Unwanted Aliens*)." *Overland* 148 (1997): 82–4.

Turbide, Diane, and John Bemrose. "New High-Wire Acts: First Novels Are Risky, but Several Debuts Soar." *Maclean's* 1 June 1998: 74–6.

Turner, Graeme. "'It Works for Me': British Cultural Studies, Australian Cultural Studies, Australian Film." *Cultural Studies*. Ed. Larry Grossberg, Cary Nelson, and Paula Treichler. London: Routledge, 1992. 640–53.

Ueki, Teruyo. "*Obasan*: Revelations in a Paradoxical Scheme." *MELUS* 18.4 (1993): 5–21. Downloaded from IAC Database. 14 September 1998.

Ujimoto, Victor K. "Racism, Discrimination and Internment: Japanese in Canada." *Racial Oppression in Canada*. Ed. B. Singh Bolaria and Peter Li. 2nd ed. Toronto, ON: Garamond, 1988. 127–60.

———. "Studies of Ethnic Identities and Race Relations." *Race and Ethnic Relations in Canada*. Ed. Peter S. Li. Toronto, ON: Oxford University Press, 1990. 209–30.

Ungerleider, Charles S. "Immigration, Multiculturalism, and Citizenship: The Development of the Canadian Social Justice Infrastructure." *Canadian Ethnic Studies* 24.3 (1992): 7–22.

Vasta, Ellie. "Dialectics of Domination: Racism and Multiculturalism." *The Teeth Are Smiling: The Persistence of Racism in Multicultural Australia*. Ed. Ellie Vasta and Stephen Castles. St Leonards: Allen and Unwin, 1996. 46–72.

Vasta, Ellie, and Stephen Castles, eds. *The Teeth Are Smiling: The Persistence of Racism in Multicultural Australia*. St Leonards: Allen and Unwin, 1996.

Viviani, Nancy. *The Indochinese in Australia, 1975–1995: From Burnt Boats to Barbecues*. Melbourne: Oxford University Press, 1996.

Wagg, Stephen, ed. *Because I Tell a Joke or Two: Comedy, Politics, and Social Difference*. London and New York: Routledge, 1998.

Wah, Fred. *Diamond Grill*. Edmonton, AB: NeWest, 1996.

———. *Faking It: Poetics and Hybridity, Critical Writing 1984–1999*. The Writer as Critic series. Ed. Smaro Kamboureli. Vol. VII. Edmonton, AB: NeWest Press, 2000.

———. "Half-Bred Poetics." *absinthe* 9.2 (1996): 60–5.

———. *Waiting for Saskatchewan*. Winnipeg, MN: Turnstone Press, 1985.

Waldren, Murray. "Sweet Word of Youth." 1999. Webpage. <http://members.ozemail.com.au/~waldrenm/young.html.> 3 July 2001.

Walker, David. *Anxious Nation: Australia and the Rise of Asia 1850–1939*. St Lucia, QLD: University of Queensland Press, 1999.

Walsh, Joan. "As American as Ethnic Studies." *Salon (Ivory Tower)* Downloaded 29 September 1998. <http://dir.salon.com/it/feature/1998/09/28feature.html>

Wang, Dorothy. "The Making of an 'Australian' Self in Simone Lazaroo's *The World Waiting To Be Made.*" *Diaspora: Negotiating Asian Australia.* Ed. Helen Gilbert, Tseen Khoo, and Jacqueline Lo. St Lucia, QLD: University of Queensland Press, 2000. 44–9.

Wat, Eric. "Preserving the Paradox: Stories from a *Gay-loh.*" Leong, *Asian American Sexualities* 71–80.

Watada, Terry. *Daruma Days: A Collection of Fictionalised Biography.* Vancouver, BC: Ronsdale, 1997.

———. "Interview with Kuan Foo." Downloaded 1 April 1998. <http://www.vcn.bc.ca/acww/html/body_interview.html>

———. Interview with Tseen Khoo. 5 May 1998.

What's so Funny? Sydney: Australian Broadcasting Corporation, 1993.

Whitaker, Charles. "Alice Walker: *Color Purple* Author Confronts Her Critics and Talks about Her Provocative New Book." *Ebony* May 1992: 86–9. Downloaded from IAC Database. 27 October 1998.

Williams, Mark. "Immigrants and Indigenes: Some Problems for Multiculturalism." Paper presented at the ACSANZ Conference, Hobart, Australia. 1–7 July 1996.

Wills, Deborah. "'But Do You Have To Write about It?': Transgression and Multiplicity in Larissa Lai's *When Fox Is a Thousand.*" Paper presented at Association of Canadian College and University Teachers (ACCUTE), Learned Societies Conference, Memorial University, St John's, NF. 1–4 June 1997.

Wilson, Rob, and Arif Dirlik. *Asia/Pacific as Space of Cultural Production.* Durham and London: Duke University Press, 1995.

Winter, Barbara. *Stalag Australia: German Prisoners of War in Australia.* North Ryde, NSW: Angus and Robertson, 1986.

Wong, Marjorie. *The Dragon and the Maple Leaf: Chinese Canadians in World War II.* London, ON: Pirie, 1994.

Wong, Paul. *On Becoming a Man.* Ottawa, ON: National Gallery of Canada, 1995.

Wong, Sau-ling (Cynthia). *Reading Asian American Literature: From Necessity to Extravagance.* Princeton, NJ: Princeton University Press, 1993.

———. "Subverting Desire: Reading the Body in the *1991 Asian Pacific Islander Men's Calendar.*" *Hitting Critical Mass* 1.1 (1993). Downloaded 30 January 2002. <http://socrates.berkeley.edu/~critmass/v1n1/wongprint.html>

Wong-Chu, Jim. "A Brief History of ACWW." *Rice Paper* 1.1 (1994): 1.

———. "How Feel I Do?" *Many-Mouthed Birds: Contemporary Writing by Chinese-Canadians.* Ed. Bennett Lee and Wong-Chu. Vancouver and Toronto: Douglas and McIntyre, 1991. 17.

"Writing Thru Race." Conference. Vancouver. 30 June–3 July 1994.

Yang, William. *Sadness.* St Leonards: Allen and Unwin, 1996.

Yee, Paul. Interview with Geoff Hancock. *Other Solitudes: Canadian Multicultural*

Fictions. Ed. Linda Hutcheon and Marian Richmond. Toronto, ON: Oxford University Press, 1990. 343–8.

Yi, Sun-Kyung. *Inside the Hermit Kingdom: A Journey through the Koreas.* Toronto, ON: Key Porter, 1997.

Young, Robert. *White Mythologies: Writing History and the West*. London and New York: Routledge, 1990.

Yung, Wayne. *Beyond Yellow Fever.* Vancouver, BC: Pomelo Project, 1996.

Zappala, Gianni. "The Phases of the Political Participation of Ethnic Minorities in Australian Politics." *Journal of Intercultural Studies* 20.1 (1999): 65–79.

Index